Barbarian Architecture

T0304417

Barbarian Architecture
Thorstein Veblen's Chicago

Joanna Merwood-Salisbury

THE MIT PRESS
Cambridge, Massachusetts . London, England

Introduction: The Book and the City

The economist Thorstein Veblen is something of a spectral presence in histories of the modern city and its architecture. Though his name appears frequently, his identity, biography, and milieu remain largely unfamiliar. Just as his most famous work, *The Theory of the Leisure Class: An Economic Study in the Evolution of Institutions*, haunts academic writing, Veblen himself remains enigmatic almost to the point of invisibility. Published in 1899, Veblen's book explores the role of aesthetics in urban life. It has been used for over a century to support and define not only the nascent modern disciplines of political economics and sociology but every imaginable concept of architectural modernity, even if such references are only fleetingly explained, never entirely graspable. No doubt, the reason for this simultaneous ubiquity and ambiguity is that the book itself is notoriously opaque, offering a ponderous mix of nineteenth-century scientific analysis and teasingly oblique social criticism. More often cited than read, *The Theory of the Leisure Class* is best known for the concept of "conspicuous consumption," the ostentatiously wasteful display of goods to demonstrate social superiority. A condemnation of the deep divide between capital and labor in Gilded Age America, this influential book is a crucial source for many disciplines including architecture and design. *The Theory of the Leisure Class* has retained its cultural currency: never out of print, it has been translated into many languages and reproduced in over five hundred editions. Loosely structured and repetitive, wrapped in many equivocating layers, it lends itself to varied interpretations. In this way, *The Theory of the Leisure Class* sits in the privileged category of classic texts that have become crucial references despite their fundamental obscurity.

Working late at night, Veblen drafted *The Theory of the Leisure Class* in a boarding house sandwiched between the emergent University of Chicago campus and the burned-out remains of the World's Columbian Exposition. The book was a product of the so-called social problem that consumed intellectuals, reformers, and civic leaders during the 1890s, one of the most turbulent periods in American history. Deeply troubled by the social consequences of the rapid growth of industry, the instability of financial markets, and extreme inequities in wages, social critics and academics began to publicly question the wisdom of laissez-faire governance and the benefits of unchecked capitalist expansion. While muckraking journalists like Henry Demarest Lloyd and novelists such as Theodore Dreiser and Upton Sinclair condemned the greed of oil barons and the intemperance of railway tycoons, Veblen took a different approach. *The Theory of the Leisure Class* was written as a contribution to academic debate over theories of wealth distribution. It confronted the paradox that rising industrial productivity had resulted in sustained benefit for only a few and not for the community at large. While intended for a narrow audience of economists, the book combined concepts drawn from contemporary anthropology, sociology, and psychology with provocative examples taken from everyday life in a style that ensured the book received a wide readership. Rather than focusing on wealthy and socially prominent men such as John D. Rockefeller, Marshall Field, George Pullman, or Philip Armour, Veblen's book outlined the long history, collective psychology, and institutionalized habits of an entire class, the descendants of a northern European race characterized by aggression and competitiveness. A junior faculty member in the Department of Political Economy at the University of Chicago, he had never written about economics in these terms before. His approach attracted notice and opened a new and original perspective on the labor-capital divide. Depending on the reader, the result may be seen as earnest scientific endeavor, strident iconoclasm, or sly satire.

Today, *The Theory of the Leisure Class* is primarily understood as a work of sociology. A pioneering study of consumption, it supports a novel theory of the way that goods are valued in modern society, an area of study just beginning to emerge in the late nineteenth century.[1] Drawing a fundamental distinction between the symbolic and practical function of everyday objects, Veblen argued that from an early period, such objects were created not only to satisfy basic needs but also to communicate affiliation within a social group. The genesis of this idea lay in an essay he published in *Popular Science Monthly* in 1894, "The Economic Theory of Woman's Dress." The topic was hardly original: Veblen was probably inspired by his academic colleagues to use women's dress as an illustration of his economic theory. Influenced by his anthropologist colleague and friend Frederick Starr, Veblen argued that, dating back to the earliest modes of adornment (jewelry, tattooing, and scarification), the purpose of clothing has been not comfort and modesty but the exhibition of social rank. In "civilized" societies, the impulse is the same, although women of Veblen's time preferred silk dresses, sealskin wraps, and hats adorned with ostrich plumes and elaborate artificial flowers. In other words, women's dress continues to hold an essentially honorific function: it is a form of code, a material language embedded with meaning. The more stylish, ornate, and constrictive her clothing, the more prominent a woman's position within the privileged class.

While Veblen's presentation of these ideas was not new, his theory was unusual in the prominence he gave to the concept of waste, the expenditure of time and money necessary to establish one's reputability in the eyes of others. According to his theory, the law of conspicuous waste shapes the "canons of taste" and thus directs all aesthetic production. What is simple and inexpensive is deemed unworthy: in spending money on extravagances, he concluded, people are attempting to live up to the standards of decency of the society in which they live. As the sociologist Norbert Elias noted, conspicuous consumption, a term Veblen invented, differs from the premodern concept of luxury.[2] In courtly societies, the ownership and display of luxury goods reflected a fixed structure of social caste and was tightly regulated by sumptuary laws. Conspicuous consumption, in contrast, is a form of ostentation that expresses pure wealth; its practice is unrestricted except by conventions of taste. By the end of the nineteenth century, anxiety about the breakdown of traditional social structures found its outlet in criticism of increasing profligacy. *The Theory of the Leisure Class* is one of many texts published around 1900 seeking to discipline and regulate wasteful consumption, arguing from dual economic and aesthetic points of view. From this focused study, Veblen went on to construct an all-consuming theory of the leisure class, a phrase already in common use, which he now employed to advance a novel theory of economic nonproductivity. As Veblen explained in his book, membership of this class was apparent not only in the elaborately corseted dresses that constricted the movement of well-off women, but also in activities as varied as competitive sports, financial speculation, politics, religious devotion, and academic study. Beyond the sociological, *The Theory of the Leisure Class* supports multiple other disciplinary readings. Common to many is the theme of Veblen's prescience, the way in which he seemed to anticipate or predict a society yet to come. In the field of design, Veblen's book is read as a commentary on the need for aesthetic reform, the rejection of waste, and the recovery of a latent "instinct of workmanship."[3] Providing an economic rationale for the rejection of ornament in favor of plain and unpretentious consumer goods, it appears to echo the arguments of European design critics Adolf Loos and Hermann Muthesius. Like them, Veblen argued that the denial of superficial and "primitive" adornment in favor of functional simplicity was the true marker of modernity. Veblen's praise for industrialization as a social force made him a prophet of technocracy for American engineers and scientific managers in the period between the world wars. Members of this group, including critic Lewis Mumford and architect Frederick Ackerman, shared Veblen's abhorrence of waste in the industrial system and his belief that productivity driven by scientific principles rather than profit was the path to social progress.[4] For exiled Frankfurt School scholars, however, *The Theory of the Leisure Class* seemed to anticipate not a coming technocratic state but the emergence of mass culture. According to Theodor Adorno, Max Horkheimer, and Herbert Marcuse, the deplorable triumph of the leisure class was to fully integrate working people into consumer culture. A generation later, the book seemed to support a neo-Marxist critique of American architecture in which Chicago played a central role: it had produced a technical and aesthetic revolution, independent of a social one.[5] More recently, Veblen's text has been recovered as a commentary on luxury, one that anticipates late twentieth-century reassessment of modern architecture in terms of fashion.[6] Veblen's writing has continued to be influential for social historians, particularly scholars of the postwar period, when consumerism reached its apogee as a dominant cultural force in the United States. Within this historical framework, scholars have deployed

4   *Introduction*

The Theory of the Leisure Class in their analyses of the architecture of modern consumer culture, from the department store to the hotel to the movie theater to the amusement park and the shopping mall. Central to all these readings is the backdrop of the modern American metropolis, what it was in 1899 and what it had become by the middle of the twentieth century.

*

The urban context of Veblen's theory is explicit. In large cities, he wrote, where most people are strangers to one another, external markers of status assume special significance. Where the German sociologist Georg Simmel wrote of the role of fashion and flânerie in European metropolitan culture, Veblen wrote of invidious comparison and emulation among American city dwellers, the concern with appearances that differentiates city people from rural folk. The mobility of this population, he wrote, "expose[s] the individual to the observation of many persons who have no other means of judging his reputability than the display of goods."[7] As a result, "Conspicuous consumption claims a relatively larger portion of the income of the urban than the rural population, and the claim is also more imperative."[8]

Yet, despite numerous fleeting appearances in histories of modern architecture and urbanism, Veblen remains an enigmatic figure. *The Theory of the Leisure Class* was published the same year that Louis Sullivan's new premises for the Schlesinger & Mayer store (later Carson Pirie Scott & Co.) opened on State Street. Both Veblen's book and Sullivan's building deal with the material manifestation of the invisible forces of capitalism. Both are products of the nineteenth century, yet they stand on the brink of the twentieth. Both men were interpreted first as prophets of functionalism, and later as shrewd interpreters of the social value of ornament, and of the complexities of modern aesthetics. In this way, they may be seen as Chicago's two great contributions to modern design culture. But while Sullivan has always been seen as indelibly *of* the city in which he lived and worked, as an intellectual figure Veblen is much less grounded. Even as Veblen's European counterparts noted the special economic condition of the United States (in

1906 Werner Sombart noted drily, "The United States is a country especially adapted to the development of capitalism"), in historiographic terms it is easier to situate *The Theory of the Leisure Class* in relation to their work than to any narrative of the midwestern metropolis.[9] And although recent scholarship has sought to expand our understanding of the landscape and architecture of modern Chicago, Veblen's firsthand account of it has not yet been considered worthy of examination.[10]

Given the book's complex language and theoretical orientation, it is perhaps perverse to try to find Chicago in Veblen's work or to locate Veblen in Chicago. While he described Chicago as "this representative city of the advanced pecuniary culture," Veblen is largely removed from the city that inspired him.[11] He spent fourteen years there during his unorthodox career, and yet traces of his life in the city are few. In 1892, in time for the university's opening semester, Veblen enrolled in the University of Chicago as a thirty-four-year-old graduate student of economics. Though he spent much of his adult life in academia, he had an uneasy, if not adversarial, relationship with university life. Born to Norwegian immigrant parents in Wisconsin in 1857, Veblen grew up on a farm near Nerstrand, Minnesota. Before arriving in Chicago, he had studied at Carleton College, Johns Hopkins, Yale, and Cornell, and had already earned a PhD in philosophy. Despite these impressive qualifications and his early success as a junior academic, his tenure at the University of Chicago was turbulent. At first, though, his life there was conventional: he taught classes on American agriculture, social economics, and socialism; he became managing editor of the university's *Journal of Political Economy*; and he published articles in learned journals such as the *American Journal of Sociology* and the *Quarterly Journal of Economics*. He gave lectures as part of the University Extension program and at public venues such as the Rev. Jenkin Lloyd Jones's Unitarian All Souls church and Jane Addams's Hull House settlement.

When *The Theory of the Leisure Class* was published, it was seen by sociologists and his fellow economists as an original, though contentious, contribution to scholarly debate. Unusually for such a dense theoretical book, it was generally well-reviewed in the popular press and found a wide readership. By 1899, Veblen had achieved academic success. In 1904 he published a second book, *The Theory of Business Enterprise.* While *The Theory of the Leisure Class* was critical of the social elite, the new book took aim at corporate power, including the influence of business on the administration of American universities. Despite the promise of his early career, in taking up these uncompromising positions, his professional life began to unravel.

Why Veblen fell out with the administrators of the University of Chicago is subject to debate. Though he was promoted through its academic ranks, by the mid-1890s he came to feel his employers had not sufficiently recognized his achievements and were unfairly withholding further rewards. Around this time, Veblen's complex personal life—his separation from his first wife, Ellen Rolfe, his emotional relationships with other women, and Ellen's reaction to those relationships—led to rumors of infidelity. Biographers have claimed that these domestic dramas hindered his career prospects. But, like other aspects of his life at the University of Chicago, these claims are now contested.[12] Veblen's dismissal was more likely due to his criticism of the academy than to his personal conduct. In 1906, he left Chicago for Stanford University, staying there only a short period before again departing under a cloud. Veblen's subsequent career was nomadic, including brief stints at the University of Missouri, the federal government in Washington during World War I, and as a writer and editor at *The Dial,* an influential literary magazine recently relocated from Chicago to New York. Throughout his life, Veblen continued to write, expanding on the themes established early in his career. In 1914, he published *The Instinct of Workmanship,* in which he presented his solution to the social and economic crises of modern America: the inevitable recovery of the primitive urge to create for the sake of making rather than profit. According to Stephen Edgell, Veblen considered this his "only important book."[13]

Cementing his reputation as an iconoclast, Veblen published an expanded condemnation of contemporary academia as *The Higher Learning in America* (1918), a book whose argument is summarized in its subtitle: *A Memorandum on the Conduct of Universities by Business Men.* Presciently, this book argued that the university, as it was presently organized, was simply another social institution beholden to the market economy. This position aligned Veblen with other academic iconoclasts. After leaving mainstream academia for good, in 1919 he became a founding member of the New School for Social Research in New York, which was started as an alternative university by former faculty members of Columbia University and other institutions. Veblen's ideas found traction among New York intellectuals and in popular culture too, despite his estrangement from mainstream economics. During this time, he developed an idea, first proposed in *The Theory of the Leisure Class*, that engineers might be the true social leaders for modern times due to their "immanent revolutionary consciousness."[14] This argument was the basis of *The Engineers and the Price System*, published in 1921. Four years later, Veblen retired to Menlo Park in California, where he died in 1929. Though never conventionally successful, he had established an enduring reputation beginning with the publication of his first, remarkable book.

Early biographers positioned Veblen as an outsider, an observer rather than a participant in the world around him. This characterization began in the decade following his death, when ex-students, ex-colleagues, and other admirers sought to promote his ideas and to capitalize on their association with him. Beginning with Joseph Dorfman's 1934 biography, *Thorstein Veblen and His America*, Veblen has been cast as an intellectual antihero. Drawing on interviews with former colleagues and students, Dorfman's book paints a portrait of Veblen as elusive and unknowable, a self-constructed persona disguising his background as a social misfit. At Yale and Cornell, Dorfman notes, Veblen's speech and dress communicated a frontier rurality amusing to his more sophisticated peers, who described him as a "foreigner" or a "Scandinavian or German from the Middle or North West."[15] In Chicago, a more mature Veblen was known for his reticence and nonconformism. While his graduate students appreciated his sharp mind and lack of pretense, he was not popular with undergraduates. As Dorfman put it, they thought Veblen was "colourless and unimpressive, with clothing that just escaped shabbiness, a carriage that barely missed being slouchy, and a voice that spoke in a slow monotone, without accent on any phrase. He never seemed to raise his eyes from the seminar table." Mumbling through his whiskers, and "looking thin and pale, he seemed to have insufficient strength for the course. He appeared to pay little direct attention to the class, and at times seemed almost asleep. The direction of his discourse was seldom clear, his digressions were numerous."[16]

Since the publication of Dorfman's biography, a considerable library of academic writing has been dedicated to attributing Veblen's theoretical perspective to these complex personal characteristics. For example, in 1953 David Riesman claimed it was Veblen's triply alienated state, as the son of rural immigrants, an academic maverick, and a social subversive, that made him such a perceptive critic.[17] For many, this attitude is captured in a portrait of Veblen taken around 1902 by photographer Eva Watson-Schütze, the wife of his University of Chicago colleague Martin Schütze, a professor of Germanic languages and literature.[18] T. J. Jackson Lears has described this photograph as follows: "A portrait of Thorstein Veblen in the faculty lounge at Yale University shows him leaning back in his chair, one leg tossed easily over the other, smoking a cigarette. He is surveying the passing scene of academic pomp with just the hint of a twinkle in his eye. Despite his mythic marginality, Veblen looks more bemused than embittered. And were he alive today, Veblen might be pardoned some bemusement. The ideas of the celebrated iconoclast have become part of the conventional wisdom about American society and conspicuous consumption."[19]

Veblen's disdain for Chicago is embedded in this "mythic marginality." Almost all biographies repeat the assertion, reportedly made by one of his students, that Veblen "disliked the confusion of the city of Chicago, now a melting pot of 1,100,000 people. ... He compared it to ancient Rome and spoke particularly of the architectural jumble."[20] According to this mythology, Veblen internalized his outsider background into an intellectual position: his disdain for the city and city people was born out of a nostalgic longing for the simple agrarian world of his Norwegian peasant forebears. While this psychoanalytic view may be simplistic, there is evidence that Veblen himself may have contributed to its construction.

Near the end of his life, Veblen appeared to draw a parallel between what he described as the social marginality of Jewish scholars and his own academic experience. In 1919 he published an essay on "The Intellectual Pre-eminence of Jews in Europe," written in response to the growing Zionist movement, which promoted the foundation of a Jewish state.[21] Arguing in favor of the diversity of European cities, Veblen spoke of the significant intellectual contribution Jewish people had made to the formation of modern Europe. Echoing the dominant academic belief of the era, in which psychological traits were associated with distinct racial groups, he attributed the leadership of the Jewish scholar to his position as a hybridized transplant in the gentile world. "It is by loss of allegiance, or at the best by force of a divided allegiance to the people of his origin, that he finds himself in the vanguard of modern inquiry," Veblen wrote.[22] Noting the importance of skepticism to scientific thought, he argued that a sense of rootlessness freed Jewish academics to become productive "wanderer[s] in the intellectual no-man's-land." This experience results in research and criticism that is original because it "presupposes a degree of exemption from hard-and-fast preconceptions, a skeptical animus. *Unbefangenheit* [impartiality], release from the dead hand of conventional finality."[23]

A few years later, in 1925, Veblen's comments were echoed by his contemporary Sigmund Freud, who described his experience at the University of Vienna as a form of productive discomfort. Despite being a secular Jew, Freud noted, he was constantly made aware of his otherness: "at an early age I was made familiar with the fate of being in the Opposition, and of being put under the ban of the 'compact majority.'" For Freud, this exclusion laid the foundations for a "certain degree of independence of judgment."[24] According to Dorfman's biography, published less than a dozen years after Freud's autobiographical essay, Veblen's insight grew from a similar experience. On entering the elite universities where he undertook graduate study, the young man from a rural immigrant family was made to feel like an outsider, unversed in unwritten codes of dress and behavior. In this sense, Daniel Bell has written, Veblen's 1919 essay may be read as "a revealing self-portrait of the Norwegian farm-boy who had left his own hermetic culture."[25] We cannot now know if Veblen's essay reflected his feelings while he was at Johns Hopkins, Yale, Cornell, and the

Figure 0.1
Eva Watson-Schütze, Thorstein Veblen, c. 1902.

University of Chicago, or whether this sense of alienation grew on him later in life. Nevertheless, his comments have contributed to the view of Veblen as an outsider. Promoted first by Dorfman and then taken up by others, this account removes Veblen from his immediate surroundings even as his physical and cultural displacement from his rural familial homestead into the big city is defined as the explanation for his insight.

More recent scholars have challenged the outsider narrative: in a recent biography, Charles Camic argues that, at least until he left Chicago, Veblen was not marginalized at all but deeply embedded in his academic milieu and well respected within it.[26] Rejecting the charge of iconoclasm, Camic and others have repositioned Veblen's writing at the center of contemporary debates within economics. But although the alienation narrative has been criticized as at best an exaggeration and at worst a pathology, it persists.[27] Whether fact or fiction, central to the characterization of Veblen as an outsider is a psychological divide between rural and urban life, between the immigrant farmer in Minnesota, on what was then the western frontier, and the privileged urban Yankee. Yet, throughout numerous exegeses, whether canonical or revisionist, the urban context in which *The Theory of the Leisure Class* was written is seldom considered: the focus remains on Veblen's intellectual environment at the expense of his physical world.

*

Like Freud, Veblen found echoes of the mythical past in the everyday life of the present. Drawing on psychology as much as ethnology, he claimed the motivation behind his economic inquiry was to uncover "the survival of archaic traits of human nature under the modern culture."[28] *The Theory of the Leisure Class* approaches its subject tangentially. Using an ethnographic categorization of human history and racial divisions commonly employed in anthropology, the book is structured as a sweeping portrait of human development spanning all periods and all peoples, from Mongol hordes to Andaman islanders, from Indian Brahmins to Icelandic communities, from Japanese feudal lords to modern-day captains of industry. Its aim, which Veblen pursued through fourteen densely written chapters, was to argue for the historical and evolutionary contingency of economic relations, and for the important role of "waste" (nonproductive expenditure) in certain societies. His reputation for iconoclasm rests on his strident assertion that, far from being exceptional, contemporary Americans were the last remnants of a stagnant "barbarian" culture whose origins dated back centuries.

Particular to no specific place, he argued, the barbarian age began when previously peaceful and unified communities gave up subsistence living and became predatory, venturing beyond their territory to plunder the resources of neighboring tribes. The result was the fracturing of the social unit into two distinct and unequal classes, one dedicated to warfare and one tasked with domestic labor. In the predatory scheme of life, to work at the production of food or goods was a mark of inferiority. As in South Pacific island societies—cultures that were a frequent subject of study for nineteenth-century anthropologists—the association with work was taboo for the highborn or those who aspire to that status. Within this barbarian social structure, relationships became based on invidious comparison, or what Veblen called "pecuniary emulation," with one's neighbor.[29] As Veblen described at length, while barbarism has a long historical trajectory, it has assumed a particular and sinister character in modern times. Over time, as warfare became less and less common, the predatory instinct of the fighting class became sublimated into business, sports, and other competitive enterprises. In Veblen's lexicon, "leisure" does not necessarily connote idleness. Rather, it signifies nonproductive behavior, expressed most explicitly in the wasteful expenditure of time and money.

In writing *The Theory of the Leisure Class*, Veblen believed he was producing something entirely new: a theory of economics written from the dual perspectives of everyday "homely facts" and "ethnological science," or anthropology.[30] The book's more prosaic original subtitle, *An Economic Study in the Evolution of Institutions*, explains his method of inquiry. Influenced by the German historical school, he joined other American economists as a practitioner of what became known as "institutional economics." Rejecting classical economics, with its basis in a philosophical understanding of individual actions understood abstractly and ahistorically, members of this group saw economics as intimately tied to the dynamic "ecology" of society. Echoing ideas the English sociologist Herbert Spencer popularized in the mid-nineteenth century, they understood human institutions as being made up of collective habits of thought and behavior. While these institutions are always evolving, adapting to new conditions, they change slowly. Fundamental to Veblen's theory is the belief that institutions are inherently conservative and tend to reinforce the interests of the dominant social group. His influential and acerbic book portrayed a culture dominated by what he called predatory capitalism, in which systems of production were driven by the need to display wealth rather than to serve pragmatic necessity.

It is difficult to overstate the importance of race science to all aspects of academic research during the nineteenth century. Though this aspect of his writing is seldom remembered today, Veblen based his theory of the leisure class on the belief that human progress might be understood as the evolution of racial types. While contemporary Americans were genetic hybrids, he wrote, the ruling "leisure" class was predominantly composed of the descendants of northern European "dolicho-blonds," a barbaric race prone to predatory, competitive behavior contrasting with the peaceful and cooperative spirit of southern European "brachycephalic brunets." Although he inverted the dominant hierarchy of accepted racial types in which Americans categorized as "white" were considered superior to and more developed than nonwhites, he did not reject the basic premise of evolutionary progress. Throughout his writing, he reacted positively to the demographic mixing found in cosmopolitan cities, seeing the hybridization of once-distinct racial groups as part of universal progress toward a modern outlook.

Echoing his Progressive Era peers, Veblen's *Theory of the Leisure Class* describes a world of social and industrial stasis, poised between barbarism and modernity. Above all, it is notable for its astute understanding of the essential symbiosis of the efficiencies of industrialization with the wastefulness of capitalism, the ways in which mass production served the expansion of consumer markets, and the proliferation of consumer societies. Despite its unusual approach, the book turns on an argument familiar in nineteenth-century intellectual thought: the possibility that advanced industrial production might operate outside the framework of capitalism.[31] Although Veblen paints a mostly pessimistic view of American culture, he concludes with a tentative optimism. Rejecting radical political solutions, he turned instead to psychology, suggesting that Americans might evolve into a peaceful, cooperative, and happier tribe if they rejected material pleasures and learned to recover what he called the "instinct of workmanship." Borrowing from contemporary theories of "primal instincts," he argued for the existence of an innate psychological urge, suppressed under barbarism, to create.[32] With the rise of predatory culture and the shunning of productive labor, he claimed, this instinct or urge had almost disappeared. However, it had never entirely died out and might be nurtured back to life. While conservative social institutions were holding back progress, he argued, they were beginning to buckle under the influence of modern industrial processes. Practically, these processes would improve working and living conditions. Psychologically, they would inspire people to behave more rationally. With the competitive drive overcome, society would revert to a cooperative form of existence. The divide between the leisure and laboring classes would, at last, be eliminated.

However, despite this utopian aspiration, *The Theory of the Leisure Class* is not a manifesto. Veblen's analytical temperament and inveterate skepticism did not allow him zealotry. His vision of a recovered instinct of workmanship was not dissimilar to the concept of "industrial democracy" popular among his reform-minded peers. Like them, he imagined systems of production organized and managed collectively, culminating in a national cooperative system created through the merger of government and industry. But although he was deeply interested in socialism as a system of economic organization, he was not a believer in the inevitability of revolution or the desirability of absolute state control of resources. Rejecting Karl Marx's version of evolutionary economics, with its dependence on an inevitable working-class uprising, Veblen's version of collectivism was aligned more with that of the journalist and reformer Henry Demarest Lloyd, a vocal supporter of the moderate labor movement. Yet, unlike Lloyd, Veblen had little faith that existing producer cooperatives would grow, peacefully and organically, to challenge the power of the "business enterprise" (the term he used to describe capitalism). Although his beliefs were progressive, and he is often described as a Progressive Era intellectual, he was as suspicious about the motivations of the movement as many later-day academics.[33] His critique of what he called programs of social amelioration had two parts. First, he cast membership of reform organizations as an essentially leisure-class activity: to have time to work on the project of civic reform meant a removal from the world of making, the ability to step away from the workings of the city to observe and manage it. Second, he saw links between various reform activities and the capitalist imperative to improve the health and productivity of the urban population. He was not convinced by the agenda of liberal reformers like Jane Addams, for example, describing it scathingly as part of a "propaganda of culture" designed to control the thinking and behavior of working-class people.[34]

Veblen's lack of faith in human agency to enact meaningful change frustrated his early twentieth-century followers. Although he believed in the possibility of an equitable future, he failed to offer a concrete image of it. According to some biographers, Edward Bellamy's utopian novel *Looking Backward, 2000–1887* (1888) had been a powerful influence on Veblen and his first wife, Ellen Rolfe, whom he met at Carleton College.[35] But while Bellamy offered a detailed description of an idealized collectivist industrial metropolis (supposedly the city of Boston in the year 2000), Veblen ventured no such clarity. In the same period, he and his wife were also inspired by the writing of William Morris. Like Morris, Veblen believed that human evolution might bring about an advanced industrial society. Still, he considered the emergence of such a society so remote he could scarcely imagine it, let alone describe it in detail. Morris's intermediate solution, a retreat away from industrialization back to the craft methods of the medieval world, did not appeal to Veblen: *The Theory of the Leisure Class* contains a stinging assessment of the Arts and Crafts movement. With its reverence for expensive and labor-intensive handmade goods, the movement seemed to him merely an annex of the luxury market.

*

At the University of Chicago, Veblen was witness to the formation of what would become known as the first "sociological laboratory" in the United States. Here he was surrounded by academics who undertook studies on topics as varied as municipal reform, urban sanitation and public health, the sweatshop system, factory legislation, and child labor laws. While these dedicated academics ventured deep into the city's immigrant neighborhoods and far-flung manufacturing districts for hours of close observation and to collect reams of quantitative data, Veblen seldom ventured farther than the University of Chicago library. Fluent in German and French, he read voraciously, though he was happy to reject the conventions of academic citation. His references, he wrote, "should be readily traceable to their source by fairly well-read persons."[36] Drawing on a broad range of textual sources from many disciplines, with examples loosely illustrative rather than rigorously researched, he was an armchair academic rather than a field worker.

Reflecting his literary source material, *The Theory of the Leisure Class* hews more closely to the formidable and dense historic surveys written by mid-nineteenth-century scholars than to the meticulously researched quantitative studies of his academic peers. Together with the looseness of his scholarship, the pointed nature of his commentary raises the question of motivation. Did Veblen intend *The Theory of the Leisure Class* to be taken seriously, or was it satire? When the book was first published, readers found it difficult to decide. Twenty years later, his former colleague Albion Small, dean of the Department of Social Science, described it as "a very subtle book, purporting to be a learned treatise, yet it was a satire on the foibles of the modern rich. I have the idea that Veblen is chuckling all the time if anyone takes his book seriously. It is a sort of cartoon, an exaggeration, and he knows it."[37] This reputation earned Veblen the title of "the gadfly of philosophers." As the *Chicago Tribune* literary editor Elia W. Peattie put it, "he has the trick of making men think along the most disturbing lines. Not only does he compel them to scrutinize their actions, their convictions, and their relationships with other men, but he sweeps his glass—his colossal star glass, swung by the most powerful mechanism of abiding doubt—around the universe. Everywhere it reveals mutations."[38] For readers such as Peattie, the purpose of the comparisons Veblen drew between modern Americans and distant peoples living in far-off places and faraway times was surely to highlight the absurdities of present-day customs and beliefs. While many of his academic peers emphasized cultural difference as an argument for the racial superiority and progressiveness of northern Europeans and their descendants, Veblen pointed out similarities to suggest stagnation, if not backwardness. Reframing everyday things and habits in terms of the primitive and exotic, this device gave the book its subversive appeal. On the surface a complex and learned economic treatise drawing on contemporary ethnology and psychology, it also seemed to spoof the rationality of science.

Complicating the interpretation of *The Theory of the Leisure Class* as either a wholly academic enterprise or a parody is the nature of the evidence it presents. As a twenty-first historian of consumption notes, Veblen's famous theory of conspicuous consumption hardly holds up to sustained attention when seen through the exacting lens of scientific sociology: instead, it is best regarded as social criticism.[39] Veblen made no apology for his lack of conventional academic rigor, noting in his preface, "Partly for reasons of convenience, and partly because there is less chance of misapprehending the sense of phenomena that are familiar to all men, the data ... have by preference been drawn from everyday life, by direct observation or through common notoriety, rather than more recondite sources at a farther remove."[40] Yet, although the book is a theory of economic relations grounded in quotidian objects and behaviors, Veblen's aim was to present a general theory, not an empirical study. He did not dwell on the specificity of what he called "vulgar phenomena," nor draw out their meaning with detailed explanations. Instead, he merely telegraphed the significance of material objects and rituals using a few key words.

The iconographic possibility of Freud's unconscious, where hidden desires are revealed in the imagery of dreams, was fertile territory for early twentieth-century critics, not least the Frankfurt School scholar Walter Benjamin, who employed the Parisian arcade as the metonymic dreamscape of modern urban life.[41]

Although Veblen's book refers to many architectural types—churches, schools, libraries, hospitals, and universities—it is not framed around a single structure, as with Benjamin's arcade, Siegfried Kracauer's hotel lobby, or Michel Foucault's prison, for example. These writers ground their theories in concrete places and things. Their writing turns on images of familiar urban or architectural types which act as stand-ins for ideas, endowing them with vivid and memorable qualities. Sometimes two different material images are contrasted to reinforce antithetical or contrasting concepts. But beyond his evocative discussion of women's dress as a modern-day version of "primitive" adornment, Veblen did not replicate that technique. His failure to provide an image to explain his theory beyond the example of women's clothing has led his writing to be associated, in architectural history at least, almost exclusively with the question of ornament.

If Veblen's unusual book may be said to echo any literary genre, it is perhaps the catalogues of metropolitan types found in early modern broadsheets, prints, and journalistic sketches.[42] Veblen populated his book with a rich cast of characters: the captain of industry and his fashionably dressed wife, the priest, the puffed-up college president, the sportsman, the gambler, and the lowly academic, all representatives of the moribund leisure class; and the emancipated "New Woman" and her male counterparts, the mechanic and the engineer, as emissaries of the world to come. In these vaguely sketched characters, the novelist William Dean Howells found the essential drama of American life: the primal instinct or aspiration to improve one's social position. Reviewing *The Theory of the Leisure Class* favorably, Howells suggested the book had furnished "the material of that great American novel which after so much travail has not yet seen the light."[43] Although the themes of this embryonic novel had been explored in literary form, Howells claimed, the novel fully describing the metropolitan world of fashion, luxury, and leisure had yet to be written. Perhaps thinking of Henry James, he noted that this world "cannot be studied by one who is part of it" because "the procession cannot very well look on at itself."[44] Howells's compatriot Theodore Dreiser is the novelist who came closest to doing this. Literary scholars have sometimes been tempted to use Veblen's complex ideas to illustrate the themes in Dreiser's novels, and vice versa, even going so far as to describe Veblen as a thwarted novelist.[45] Howells's commentary on the literary value of *The Theory of the Leisure Class* is suggestive. In this book, the reader may glimpse not only the cast of characters populating the unwritten great American novel, but also its setting, the landscape of the modern city with its monuments to leisure-class profligacy: the imposing mansions of the wealthy with their ornately decorated drawing rooms; luxurious stores, theaters, and hotels modeled on Parisian precedents; battlemented philanthropic institutions; and even the calm monastic cloisters of the modern university. Here we can also see institutions and structures designed to close the divide between leisure and laboring classes, such as settlement houses and manual training schools. Suggested rather than rendered in detail, this shadowy landscape offers an opportunity for the architectural historian. What if we take seriously claims that *The Theory of the Leisure Class* is important for modern architecture and reexamine it as an original theory of modernity founded in the material substance of a particular place?

Admittedly, to read *The Theory of the Leisure Class* in this way is to continue the long tradition of inferring meaning in Veblen's classic text, a practice encouraged by the book's obtuseness. With its dense prose, sweeping historical perspective, and ponderous, often questionable anthropological basis, the book lacks the exactitude of a sociological report or the suggestive imagery of cultural criticism. And yet underlying all is the argument that the modern city was the site in which conspicuous consumption emerged. Besides Baltimore, where he lived briefly, and the European capitals he visited during the summer, Chicago was the only city Veblen knew well. Although he did not refer to it directly, it was the backdrop and stage for his historic survey of labor and leisure. While the physical landscape of turn-of-the-twentieth-century Chicago—in particular, its iconic skyscraper skyline—has long served as an image of modern life, it is seldom identified with the production of architectural theory. Conversely, in the voluminous literature on *The Theory of the Leisure Class*, scholars have paid relatively little attention to Veblen's immediate milieu.[46] But perhaps it is possible to claim that Veblen's relationship to

Chicago was symbiotic, as central to modern cultural history as the connections of Walter Benjamin to Paris, Marx and Engels to Manchester, or Adolf Loos to Vienna? Looking again at *The Theory of the Leisure Class*, we might argue that in Veblen, Chicago, the first modern city, also produced an enduringly influential critic of modern urban culture.

*

Barbarian Architecture: Thorstein Veblen's Chicago investigates Veblen's place in architectural history and the influence of Chicago on his writing. Looking at this iconic urban landscape through the eyes of one of America's leading turn-of-the-century intellectuals, we gain a new perspective on the architecture of this iconic city, then at the height of its international influence. This is an alternative view, neither the boosterism of the Chicago elite (supported by its architects), nor the projections of an industrial future imposed on the city by European visitors a generation later. The intent is to return to the urban origins of *The Theory of the Leisure Class*, understanding the book as an early attempt to explore the built environment from the perspective of political economy. Seen through Veblen's disciplinary lens, such an approach allows us to rethink the relationship between architecture and capital, shaking off the idea that aesthetics is removed from the pressures of the socioeconomic world. Veblen's theory is predicated on the belief that society is dynamic and that attitudes toward style change as rapidly as the built environment itself.

The focus of this book is the period between the early 1880s, when a post-depression building boom changed Chicago's urban morphology dramatically, and the first decade of the twentieth century, when the city was feted by sociologists as the quintessential modern city, resembling, in the words of the German sociologist Max Weber, "a human being with his skin removed, and in which all the physiological process can be seen going on."[47] In this short period of time, around twenty years, Chicago assumed the form it had in 1906, when Veblen left to pursue what was left of his itinerant career. At the same time, the city became a symbol of modernity across the Western world, a symbol built largely on the reception of its high-rise buildings. A key argument of *Barbarian Architecture* is that Veblen's text is meaningful precisely because his view extended beyond the tall office buildings that lined the streets of the downtown Loop. Even in 1899 this building type was what the city was best known for, yet Veblen ignored it completely, hardly touching on commercial architecture at all. And why should he? According to his theory, the skyscraper was hardly unique. Like all architectural typologies associated with the wealthy and influential, it fulfilled a primarily pecuniary function. Just as much as office buildings and factories, cultural, educational, and residential buildings were all expressions of capitalism.

Throughout *Barbarian Architecture: Thorstein Veblen's Chicago*, contemporary photographs of discrete buildings and urban sites act as prompts to investigate themes that resonate in both Veblen's writing and architecture culture. In them, we see both the world that inspired his theory of the leisure class and a series of built responses designed to overcome the inequities created by the dominance of leisure-class culture. My approach to these photographs varies from chapter to chapter, and from object to object. Sometimes I explore Veblen's direct engagement with the buildings around him (for example, the University of Chicago campus in Hyde Park or the Hull House settlement on the Near West Side); sometimes I investigate the ways in which his writing has become attached to specific building types (the department store in particular, exemplified by the luxurious mercantile palaces on State Street); sometimes I use images to explicate the intellectual basis for Veblen's ideas (for example, anthropological displays of "native" housing at the World's Columbian Exposition, understood by both academics and the fair-going public as stand-ins for evolutionary development). No single approach to reading Veblen's theory through architectural objects is definitive. Only one thing is consistent: the use of photographs to recover the material nature of his analysis.

The choice of Gothic Revival as the dominant style for Chicago's important cultural buildings in the postbellum period is a central theme of the first two chapters. Exploring Veblen's description of the leisure class as a barbarian culture, chapter 1 begins with his belief, common to academics in this period, that architecture reflects racially based evolutionary development. It examines

Introduction

his writing in relation to contemporary anthropological research, particularly as it was displayed at the World's Columbian Exposition. The displays of Native American architecture at the world's fair elucidate Veblen's understanding of evolution as the engine of human history, dictating the relationship between industrial technology, social structures, and the constructed world. This "scientific" understanding of cultural production was the basis for Veblen's discussion of architecture in a leisure-class society, including criticism of what was known as the American eclectic Gothic. The excesses of this style, a variation on the Gothic Revival popular from the 1860s to the 1880s, and the critical reaction to it, are exemplified by the Potter Palmer mansion on North Lake Shore Drive, one of the most prominent buildings in Chicago at the time of the world's fair. As an academic treatise on style as well as economics, *The Theory of the Leisure Class* offered a defining trait of barbarianism—conspicuous consumption—and a theoretical framework to support the charge of "ugliness" made against the Palmer mansion in literature and popular criticism.

The second chapter hews closely to Veblen's biography and academic milieu, explaining the basis of his writing in contemporary theories of political economy, and the deep depression and violent social uprisings of the mid-1890s. It begins with his early attention to industrial efficiency, manifested in the mechanism of the grain elevator. While Veblen did not mention the skyscraper, this typology, an extension of the speculative potential of the grain elevator, illustrates his distinction between industrial and "pecuniary," or financial, enterprises. Chapter 2 discusses Veblen's contentious argument that, as much as any commercial endeavor, the modern American university was the product of the business enterprise and, as such, an essentially capitalist institution. Veblen explicitly frames the collegiate Gothic style popular for institutions of higher learning in terms of the publicity necessary for any modern business.

Chapter 3 focuses on the typology with which Veblen is most closely associated. Department stores have long served as stand-ins for Veblen's theories of pecuniary emulation and conspicuous consumption. The denigration of highly ornamented, mass-produced nineteenth-century design through its association with the feminine is a well-known trope in European criticism around 1900. This chapter looks at the specific parameters of this argument as it was framed in Chicago in the same period, beginning with the central role of women's dress in Veblen's theory, echoed in the rhetoric of European architects and critics such as Adolf Loos. While his analysis of women's clothing was influential, Veblen later turned to a different aspect of leisure-class culture: not the ostentatious displays of the very wealthy, but the basis of modern business in barbaric instincts for competition and predation. The chapter ends by arguing that a Veblenian understanding of department store architecture must apply not only to its ornamental facades and large display windows but also to its flexible interiors. Like other business practices such as advertising, the design of such stores was due to what Veblen called the "perversion of industrial efficiency" hampering evolutionary progress.[48]

The fourth chapter is the most speculative. Comparing contemporary descriptions of the pleasures found in the State Street shopping district with efforts to clean up the Levee, the notorious Near South Side vice district centered on South Clark Street, the chapter explores the moral dimension of Veblen's economic theory. *The Theory of the Leisure Class* strongly condemns capitalism by comparing it to vice. For Veblen, the businessman is scarcely different from the gambler; each seeks to benefit from unearned profit. Moving beyond scholarly concern with ornament, this chapter deals with the relationship between capitalism, consumerism, and urban development in the broader sense. When an alliance of business interests, politicians, and anti-vice activists cleared the Levee in the 1890s, they made the land available for manufacturing purposes; lofts replaced older buildings housing saloons, gambling "hells," and brothels. In the early twentieth century, examples of the loft building type, along with the factory, were celebrated as anti-fashion, the image of pure productivity and industrial efficiency. But in Veblen's terms, the loft type may be seen as equally tainted, a new architectural commodity built to serve the market.

Chapter 5 returns to Veblen's biography by evaluating *The Theory of the Leisure Class* in relation to local efforts to reform methods of production and ennoble labor. This chapter positions Veblen's call for a return to the vestigial "instinct of workmanship" in the context of Chicago's Arts and Crafts workshops and manual training programs, including Jane Addams's Labor Museum at Hull House, Rabbi Emil Hirsch's Hebrew Manual Training School (also known as the Jewish Training School), and the short-lived Industrial Art League founded by Veblen's university colleague Oscar Lovell Triggs. Placing Veblen's writing on the industrial enterprise in relation to contemporary attempts to rationalize and improve the productive efficiency of Chicago, the chapter concludes by addressing the early twentieth-century influence of Veblen's vision of an idealized industrial state, controlled by engineers working in concert with producers.

Barbarian Architecture ends by returning to the question of the image of the modern city. How does Veblen's city compare to the heroic photographs familiar from architectural history? Was it a specific or abstract one, a geographic entity or a psychological realm? Oscillating between the two, his book prefigures the role Chicago has come to play in twentieth-century literature and scholarship, not as a real place but as an eternal stand-in for the modern metropolis, a dream city occupied by transient subjects, perpetually balanced between past and future.

1 *The Ethnology of the Leisure Class: The Fair and the Castle*

Just as architecture and design historians often illustrate the polemical writing of John Ruskin and William Morris with images of London's Great Exhibition of 1851, it is tempting to explain Veblen's theory of the leisure class through the phantasmagoria of the World's Columbian Exposition of 1893. Like the Great Exhibition, the world's fair serves as an illustration of the vulgarity of mass production that all three writers rejected in both moral and aesthetic terms. Geographical adjacency and chronological simultaneity make the comparison apt; when Veblen entered the University of Chicago in the fall of 1892, an army of engineers and laborers, carpenters, and decorators were hard at work erecting the structures that made up the fair only a few blocks away at Jackson Park. Orchestrated by Director of Works Daniel Burnham, the fair's monumental buildings and landscaped grounds were conjured up on a boggy lakeside site in a matter of months. The construction of the university campus took considerably longer. Begun within a year of each other, and sitting side by side, the university and the World's Columbian Exposition are often paired as dual models of late nineteenth-century American cultural advancement.

Designed to celebrate four hundred years of American conquest, the World's Columbian Exposition sat next to the newest American university, a center of educational innovation financed by one of the nation's wealthiest men, John D. Rockefeller. In style, the two institutions offered differing models of civic architecture, the fair nominally classical, the university collegiate Gothic, suitable to its scholarly function. If the world's fair was designed to display the wonders of the city, the nation, and the Western world, the university may be described as an architectural instrument designed for the scientific study of those wonders. One was ephemeral and carnivalesque, the other permanent and exclusive; one was designed for a popular audience, the other to educate the elite. When the world's fair opened on May 1, 1893, Veblen was just completing his first year at the university. Noting that Veblen's extended family visited the fair, presumably in his company, a recent biographer has argued that the World's Columbian Exposition may be seen as a "massive echo chamber in which elements from his long-accumulating intellectual repertoire resounded within earshot."[1] Though he would not start work on the academic essays that became *The Theory of the Leisure Class* for another year, these elements were already beginning to cohere into a study of economics considered as an evolutionary science. Six years later, this abstract perspective would culminate in a treatise on the role of waste, or conspicuous consumption as Veblen would term it, in an advanced industrial economy.

On October 21, 1892, the exposition's Dedication Day, an elaborate ceremony was held under the arches of the still incomplete Manufactures and Liberal Arts Building, attended by over 200,000 people seated on temporary platforms. Designed by New York architect George Post, this was not only the largest structure at the fair but also the largest building ever constructed, or so the organizers claimed. Like its neighbors, it was dressed in a cladding white "staff," a mixture of plaster and cement, a method of construction enabling workers to create elaborately molded neoclassical

Figure 1.1
Manufactures and Liberal Arts Building, World's Columbian Exposition, Chicago, 1891–1893. George B. Post, architect; Daniel H. Burnham, director of works.

Figure 1.2
Dedication Day, October 21, 1892, Manufactures and Liberal Arts Building, World's
Columbian Exposition, Chicago, 1891–1893. George B. Post, architect; Daniel H. Burnham,
director of works; C. D. Arnold, photographer.

facades. This photograph reveals the sublime scale of the vast interior, purposely longer and taller than the celebrated Galerie des Machines at the 1889 Paris Exposition. Inside, the crowd had an unobstructed view, thanks to the massive steel trusses, each weighing 300,000 pounds, that supported the 1,600-foot-long structure and rose over 300 feet at their highest point.[2]

The scale of the building was necessary for its purpose: under this ethereal steel-and-glass roof, part railway shed and part cathedral, Post's building was a self-contained universe celebrating the free flow of goods in the global marketplace. Inside, exhibition booths representing all the trading nations in the world would be arrayed along a kind of "world street" nestled under the artificially engineered sky. Strolling down the axial boulevard, visitors would encounter ornate pavilions conceived of as miniature buildings mimicking the styles of many nations.

This international exposition was to be Chicago's triumph. At the dedication ceremony, the mayor of Chicago, Hempstead Washburne, spoke of his city as typifying the civilization of the American continent and the modern age, with the fair as the image of its "material greatness."[3] The director general of the fair, Colonel George R. Davis, proclaimed: "The ceaseless, resistless march of civilization westward—ever westward—has reached and passed the Great Lakes of North America, and has founded on their farthest shore the greatest city of modern times."[4]

Using Veblen's lexicon, the World's Columbian Exposition may be seen as the enactment of the culture of conspicuous consumption produced by industrialization and urbanization and amplified by the rapid expansion of global trade. Images of the huge crowds touring these displays have prompted scholars to claim that the Chicago world's fair, along with other international expositions held in London, Paris, New York, and Philadelphia, were among the earliest "mass culture" events, places where the culture and purchasing habits of the leisure class were disseminated to a larger consumer class. Across its expansive grounds, it featured numerous examples of what Veblen described as "conspicuous waste," attempts to elevate the products of nineteenth-century industrialization by clothing them in the luxurious garb of past ages. Here, nation competed with nation, state with state, and company with company, to display resources, products, and technological advances to best advantage. Questions of cultural evolution and the appropriate aesthetic expression of modernity were at the forefront.

At the World's Columbian Exposition, a seemingly infinite number of displays mapped human progress through technological innovation and at the same time struggled to find appropriate forms through which to represent that progress. Throughout its many exhibits and congresses, the fair was designed to advertise the idea that the American race had reached the highest level of human development in comparison to the people of the world's other nations. Arranged as comparative displays of human habitation, a multitude of displays made the case for a relationship between a people, the goods they produced, and the dwellings in which they lived. This premise was illustrated by the array of fictionalized vernacular architectures on show. Contrasting with these variously primitive and exotic structures, grand buildings like the Manufactures and Liberal Arts Building were testament to the highest level of human achievement in both style and technological sophistication. These monumental buildings represented the urban character, global reach, and imperial aspirations of the American leisure class.

Produced in the wake of the World's Columbian Exposition, *The Theory of the Leisure Class* may be read as a kind of literary caricature of this bombastic premise, and an anticipation of sociological studies of taste written in the twentieth century. The persistence of a vestigial Victorian appetite for historicist ornament and decoration in the face of rapid industrial development was one of Veblen's principal subjects. With its theme of cultural backwardness, *The Theory of the Leisure Class* lampooned the narrative of national and racial progress that was the fair's driving force and key message. Veblen's book paints a deeply unflattering portrait of the urban elite, the very class who organized the fair. At its heart is the idea that consumer culture is not a modern affliction but a throwback to an earlier evolutionary state.

Extending the anthropological approach to material culture evident in the ethnographic exhibits at the fair to Chicago's leading figures, Veblen subjected the members of the leisure class to the same methods of analysis and classification elsewhere applied to cliff-dwelling residents of the Battle Rock Pueblo or the Kwakiutl villagers of the Pacific Northwest. Using terms borrowed from nineteenth-century race science, he described them as latter-day barbarians, the result of an evolutionary regression triggered by the experience of frontier life. While Veblen was far from the only writer to draw a link between the captain of industry and the feudal warrior, he was unique in creating a comprehensive theory of human production and consumption around it, a theory that accounts not just for the popularity and then decline of the wildly eclectic architecture that signified leisure-class aspiration in the second half of the nineteenth century, but also for the socioeconomic role of aesthetics in a larger sense.

Industrial Evolution on Display at the
World's Columbian Exposition

If the light and airy interior of Post's Manufactures and Liberal Arts Building represented the architectural future, an entirely different structure represented the ancient past of the North American continent. Tucked away in the far southeastern corner of the World's Columbian Exposition grounds, between the Anthropological Building and a series of pens housing livestock exhibits, and adjacent to a display of "The Ruins of Yucatan," a primitive-looking mound sat in contrast with its more obviously constructed surroundings. This mound was a reproduction of Battle Rock in southwest Colorado, the ancient home of a Pueblo Indian tribe. Assembled out of timber planks, iron, staff, and paint, this simulated rock formation was known as the Cliff Dwellers exhibit.[5] Though it was obviously a reconstruction, the exhibit's designer aimed at realism.[6] While not evident in photographs, guidebooks reported that the structure was covered with cacti, yucca, cedar, and other trees. To add verisimilitude to the scene, a herd of mountain animals clambered over the surface. (One source claimed, somewhat improbably, that these were, elk, blacktail deer, moose, and Rocky Mountain sheep, but more likely they were the donkeys or burros reported in another guide.)

Following these animals up along a narrow path, visitors could ascend to a lookout point atop the artificial outcrop. Upon paying the twenty-five-cent entrance fee (the concession to mount and operate the exhibit inside had been granted to Col. Charles D. Hazzard of the H. Jay Smith Exploring Company, which operated it for profit), visitors entered the structure through a cave that led into a faux canyon. Looking up between the steep canyon walls, they could see, sitting in niches, miniature versions of Pueblo cliff houses at one-sixteenth scale. Deep within the structure, an artificial underground cave housed panoramic paintings depicting canyons, cliff houses, and pueblo ruins. Guidebooks noted the exhibition designer's skillful use of lighting and mirrors to make the cave seem larger and more lifelike. Replicating cave interiors at full scale, other rooms displayed weapons, cooking utensils, pottery, textiles, and ornaments created by the cliff-dwelling people. Appealing to those less interested in these worthy artifacts, the exhibit also boasted macabre items such as the mummified remains of a "Pueblo princess."

Ever since the European discovery of the remains of extensive and impressive cliff dweller sites in the American Southwest in the 1870s, the idea of an ancient cliff-dwelling peoples had held a powerful hold on the popular imagination. This exhibit was an opportunity for fairgoers to experience the thrill of discovery, to observe the remnants of the continent's prehistoric past, for themselves. Though the Cliff Dwellers exhibit was one of the fair's more popular attractions, archaeological experts viewed it with suspicion, considering it inaccurate and sensationalist.[7] Despite its dubious authenticity, the exhibit compellingly illustrated not only the ancient past of the North American continent but also the sublime scale of human history.

According to the anthropological schema of the 1890s, the cliff dwellers exemplified the "savage" stage of human evolution, a peaceable society living communally, surviving through a subsistence economy. Following a linear trajectory, such societies would be replaced by "barbaric" and then "civilized" forms of human organization. But for at least one fairgoer, this extraordinary structure induced an uncanny sense of familiarity: the exhibit was the inspiration for Henry Blake Fuller's novel *The Cliff-Dwellers*.

1   The Ethnology of the Leisure Class

Figure 1.3
Cliff Dwellers exhibit, World's Columbian Exposition, Chicago, 1891–1893. Charles B. Atwood, architect; Daniel H. Burnham, director of works; C. D. Arnold, photographer.

Serialized in *Harper's Weekly* beginning in June 1893, a month after the fair opened, this novel drew a comparison between Pueblo cliff dwellings and the "canyon streets" of downtown Chicago lined with vertiginous office buildings faced with rugged stone.[8] In noting this similarity, Fuller poked the conceit of proud Chicagoans. In the year of the World's Columbian Exposition, the city's greatest triumph and a testament to civic and aesthetic progress, he suggested instead they had regressed to an archaic era of social development, exemplified by a return to a prehistoric architecture of mound-building. At the same time, Fuller asked readers to question which culture was rightly labeled civilized, and which savage. The same provocation drives Veblen's *The Theory of the Leisure Class*. While not relying directly on this image of the ancient American past, his book poses a similar question. Though the Pueblo

Indians were an ancient culture, in their collective and cooperative form of social organization, if not their level of industrial achievement, they were perhaps more advanced than the competitive and divided society of the present day. Veblen began drafting the chapters of *The Theory of the Leisure Class* in late 1895. His aim, as he wrote to his former graduate student Sarah Hardy, was to bring economics in line with "modern evolutionary science. The point of departure for this rehabilitation, or rather the basis of it, will be the modern anthropological and psychological sciences." Writing was proceeding slowly, he reported. Though consigning many sheets of paper to the wastepaper basket, he was working his way toward introducing the "doctrine of conspicuous waste," the principle he considered the nucleus of the whole.[9] Rejecting the metaphysical basis of classical economics (for example, the balance provided by Adam Smith's "unseen hand"), Veblen joined a generation of economists seeking instead rational principles or laws to explain changes in those relations, finding them in the evolutionary theory of Darwin and Spencer.[10] In creating an economic equivalent to recent research in biology, he wrote, the answer was to look to the way human society responded to its environment.

Rather than thinking of material resources as inert, a form of capital transformable into objects for human use, Veblen argued that economists should focus instead on the dynamic process through which this transformation took place. As he explained in a 1898 essay, "Why Is Economics Not an Evolutionary Science?," human goods are not passive but "facts of human knowledge, skill, and predilection. ... The physical properties of the materials accessible to man are constants; it is the human agent that changes— his insight and his appreciation of what these things can be used for is what develops."[11] In other words, the level of evolutionary development a society had reached might be tracked through its use of tools and its attitude toward material and property. In this sense, Veblen's rhetoric was conventional: like many of his peers, he believed that the industrial arts, more than any other arena of activity, drove social progress.

Veblen's particular insight lay in the idea that, while technological innovation tends to advance societies, habituated ties to the status quo often mean resistance to the changes that technology brings. This is the argument of the eighth chapter of *The Theory of the Leisure Class*, entitled "Industrial Exemption and Conservatism." In keeping with evolutionary theory, he wrote, progress, or "divergence away from the archaic position," takes place not on an individual basis but through the coordinated actions of the community.[12] Consequently, the process is far from rapid: every change in the way in which material products are conceived and made involves a change in habits and process of thought.

Crucial to Veblen's argument is the assumption that conventional ideas and behaviors are deeply ingrained in the human psyche. Even small innovations are resisted because they imply a threat to the entire social system. In short, social institutions are inherently conservative, and they tend to reinforce the interests of the dominant social group. As a result, the process of social evolution was sometimes suspended, held in stasis by the forces of "cultural lag," as sociologist William Fielding Ogburn later described it.[13] For Veblen, the contradiction of American culture was that an advanced race had realized the most up-to-date methods of production; yet at the same time, it had reverted to a social structure not dissimilar to that of feudal Europe or Japan, a backward state in which the emancipatory potential of industrial production was not properly recognized.

In its most academic incarnation, the science of ethnography was relegated to the far periphery of the exposition grounds. Located in a remote corner encircled by an elevated railway, the Anthropological Building was one of several fair buildings of secondary importance designed by Burnham's employee, Charles B. Atwood.[14] The simple two-story structure at the far distant corner of the fairgrounds was hardly a primary destination for fairgoers. On the first floor, Frederick W. Putnam of Harvard University, the director of the fair's Department of Ethnology and Archaeology, organized an exhaustive display of anthropological exhibits, aided by his chief assistant, Franz Boas.[15] Made up of antiquities and relics gathered from around the world, with a special focus on items illustrating the history of the American continent, this display may have seemed dry and uninteresting to many visitors, certainly less diverting than the fair's other attractions.

Figure 1.4
Anthropological Building, World's Columbian Exposition, Chicago, 1891–1893. Charles B. Atwood, architect; Daniel H. Burnham, director of works; C. D. Arnold, photographer.

Packed full of domestic and industrial implements, the building included a series of laboratories exhibiting the ways in which anthropologists studied cultures and people. Upstairs, the North Gallery housed a model laboratory designed to illustrate the scientific basis of anthropology, drawing upon precise measurement and comprehensive data collection. As Veblen's University of Chicago colleague Frederick Starr recounted, these laboratories displayed "a series of instruments used in anthropological investigation—anthropometric machines, craniometric instruments, instruments for drawing skulls, outlines of the body, etc. ... Composite photography, as applied to finding types and in the study of crania, is illustrated."[16] In the neurology laboratory, Starr showed the results of his own research, a series of impressions taken from the fingertips of Native Americans using Francis Galton's method of categorization by fingerprints. While it was perhaps amusing for visitors to have their skulls measured and fingerprints taken, these laboratories likely appealed to a minority. More diverting than the artifacts sitting in glass cases and the charts, diagrams, and instruments arrayed upstairs, Putnam and Boas staged an "ethnographical exhibit" outside the Anthropological Building on the banks of the South Pond, complete with living human residents.

Illustrating the progress of human development by comparing architectural examples from around the world was a feature of world's fairs in the second half of the nineteenth century. As Curtis M. Hinsley has described, the 1851 London Exhibition and the Paris Exposition of 1867 had set the tone in this respect. Imperialist in conception, they displayed not only "the material culture of an industrial, commercial empire, with an emphasis on manufactured goods derived from colonial raw materials," but also archaeological and ethnological products appropriated from colonial territories: "Virtually all subsequent fairs embodied these two aspects: displays of industrial achievement and promise for the regional or national metropolis and exhibits of primitive 'others' collected from peripheral territories or colonies."[17] Borrowing from techniques of visual display and material comparison developed in museums, ethnographic exhibits became common features in the expositions that followed. The Paris Exposition of

Figure 1.5
Penobscot Indian Camp, Ethnographic Exhibit, World's Columbian Exposition, Chicago, 1891–1893. Daniel H. Burnham, director of works; C. D. Arnold, photographer.

1889 was the first to include "ethnographic villages," designed to teach the history of human societies through full-scale displays of model dwellings from around the world. As Irene Cheng has noted, both anthropologists and architectural theorists believed that the study of "processes of racial evolution, diffusion, and hybridization could help explain transformations in architectural style and, correspondingly, that architecture could be read as evidence of racial history."[18] Considered semi-biological entities registering the progress of the people who produced them along a linear scale from savage to civilized, these replica houses reinforced the exposition's message of European advancement.

In November 1890, the *Inland Architect*, the journal of professional architects working in the American West (the region we now call the Midwest), called for an exhibition similar to the one shown at the Paris Exposition to be included in the World's Columbian Exposition.[19] Plans were already underway: even before the site of the exposition was settled upon, the organizing committee

1   The Ethnology of the Leisure Class

Figure 1.6
Massachusetts whaling boat next to the Kwakiutl plank house, Ethnographic Exhibit,
World's Columbian Exposition, Chicago, 1891–1893. Daniel H. Burnham, director of works.

had commissioned Putnam to "illustrate the early life in America from remote ages before historic times down to the period of Columbus."[20] Besides the Cliff Dwellers exhibit, he and Boas organized what Putnam called a small colony of Indians, who lived in reconstructed versions of their native habitations in a sort of suburban enclave beside the Anthropological Building.[21] The result was labeled on maps as the "Ethnographical Exhibit." Visually separated from the backdrop of the fairgrounds by a screen of white fabric panels, this colony included "the long house of the Iroquois, constructed of bark, and divided into six spaces within, one for each of the Six Nations; the birch-bark tent of the Penobscot Indians of Maine; the skin-covered tepee of the plains tribes; the dome-shaped framework of poles, covered with rush matting, of the Algonkins [sic]; the plank-covered houses of the Kwakiool [sic] of Vancouver Island, and the Haidah of Queen Charlotte Islands with their symbolical paintings and totem posts."[22] After Boas's recent research on Native American peoples of the Pacific

Northwest, the components of a Kwakiutl village had been disassembled and transported from the Queen Charlotte Islands along with a group of fourteen Kwakiutl, who lived in the recreated houses and performed ceremonies for the fair-going audience.[23]

A photograph taken from slightly behind the village reveals the span of history the exhibit was intended to encapsulate. On the right, the carved totems of the Kwakiutl plank house face the *Progress*, a Massachusetts whaling boat moored in the South Pond. Behind that is McKim, Mead and White's Agricultural Building, designed to celebrate the United States as "the first agricultural nation of the world."[24] Though architecture was not their primary focus, the ethnographical exhibit of Native American dwellings depended on verisimilitude for their effect. Only through understanding the "natural conditions of life of the different types of peoples who were here when Columbus was crossing the Atlantic Ocean," Putnam wrote, would fairgoers appreciate the great strides the country had taken in four hundred years.[25] In other words, the supposedly pre-Columbian world (reenacted by contemporary Native Americans) was the baseline from which the exposition measured human evolution. Contrasting with replicas of the small and fragile Native American dwellings, the magnificence and technological innovation of the main fair buildings represented the other end of the timeline of human progress.

Significantly, Putnam originally proposed that these outdoor ethnographic displays would be encountered in a naturalistic setting, on the wooded island at the center of the fairground, set apart from the monumental displays of industrial progress. This plan did not come to fruition. While the Native American villages and the reconstructed Pueblo cliff dwelling were consigned to the southeastern corner, the privileged position on the wooded island was reserved for a different kind of "primitive" structure, one that celebrated the patrimony of white Americans. To the north of the Grand Basin, a lagoon over twice its size provided a naturalistic contrast to the strictly ordered geometry of the Court of Honor. Overlooked and overseen by the Horticulture Building, this lagoon contained two artificial islands dedicated to horticultural displays. The larger one was home to a rose garden and, at the northern end, the famous Japanese Ho-o-den Temple credited with fueling

1   The Ethnology of the Leisure Class

the vogue for *japonisme* in the United States. To the south, a much smaller island was the site of two smaller and more rustic constructions: an "Australian squatter's hut" and a "a reproduction of the cabin of one of America's quaintest characters, David Crocket [sic]," a romanticized reconstruction of American frontier life.[26] Rather than being part of a larger display indicating a wider social world, this second building, more commonly known as the Hunter's Cabin, was singular and individualistic. In frontier style, it was constructed of logs and topped by a pitched roof pierced by a chimney. The magnificent horns of an elk topped the single entrance door, with a covered wagon parked to one side of the door. Despite its rustic simplicity, this simple cabin carried a heavy burden of signification.

Like the Cliff Dwellers exhibit, the Hunter's Cabin was the product of thoroughly urban sensibilities. Far from being the work of a frontier craftsman, it was designed by Holabird and Roche, a large Chicago firm better known for its prestigious commercial buildings, and sponsored by the Daniel Boone and Davy Crockett Club of New York City. Named after two famous frontiersmen, the club and the replica cabin it sponsored promoted the romance of frontier life.[27] The club had been founded by Theodore Roosevelt (then in the early phase of his political career) and a group of prominent hunting enthusiasts. In overtly political terms, the cabin represented the formative role Roosevelt believed the frontier had played in creating a new race—"Americans"—the descendants of northern Europeans who had adapted to this new climate and environment. Born into a wealthy and socially connected New York family, Roosevelt had experienced the life of a western rancher through a series of trips to North Dakota during the 1880s. He wrote three books about his time there, each one exalting the liberating effects of elemental frontier living.[28] The first volume of Roosevelt's four-volume history, *The Winning of the West* (1889–1896), popularized the mythology of the settler frontiersman, equipped only with his weapons and ingenuity to conquer the challenges of a western landscape conceived of as "wild." Freed from the softening and enervating effects of civilization, he and his descendants were hardy, independent, and self-reliant. The Hunter's Cabin featured a representative of this type.

Figure 1.7
Hunter's Cabin, Boone and Crockett Club, World's Columbian Exposition, 1892–1893. Holabird & Roche, architects; Daniel H. Burnham, director of works; C. D. Arnold, photographer.

On entering the Hunter's Cabin, visitors were greeted by an actor in the guise of a frontiersman. Complete with long hair and a wide-brimmed hat, he answered their questions about frontier life. Inside, the cabin was furnished to resemble "the houses of pioneers in timbered regions forty years ago. ... The skins of wild animals covered the floor, and beds and settees were made of stretched skins. A double bunk afforded two wide and easy couches. A stool made from a section of log, and primitive cooking apparatus and tin dishes and candles gave a realistic appearance to the domicile."[29] Besides these domestic implements, the cabin was filled with a collection of rifles and hunting equipment purportedly belonging to celebrated hunters and famous frontiersmen, along with stuffed products of the chase. These weapons were a key technology of progress. Their display communicated the message that the pursuit of territorial conquest was inevitable and natural.

Where the Native American dwellings that surrounded the distant South Pond were positioned at one end of the timeline of human history, arrested at an early stage in the process of human

1   *The Ethnology of the Leisure Class*

Figure 1.8
Hunter's Cabin, interior. World's Columbian Exposition, 1893.

development, the Hunter's Cabin in the center of the fair depicted a people on the brink of an unprecedented century of human evolution. This popular mythology was given academic authority when the University of Wisconsin historian Frederick Jackson Turner delivered his paper "The Significance of the Frontier in American History" to a meeting of the American Historical Association at the world's fair on July 12, 1893. For Turner, the experience of frontier life, a process of adaptation to harsh conditions, had formed a new race. Carried through the "Germanic" germ of their northern European stock, he argued, the traits of rationality, practicality, and resourcefulness allowed colonial settlers to conquer the rugged and dangerous landscape.[30] In the process, this unique environment conditioned a hardy and independent race of "Americans." As David Roediger has noted, this race was coded as "white" to distinguish it from more recent immigrants from eastern and southern Europe and from Asia, as well as from the descendants of enslaved and indentured peoples transported to the United States from the African continent and elsewhere.[31]

By the turn of the twentieth century, settler culture had been reframed as "native" American culture. For example, in 1912, the architecture critic Montgomery Schuyler praised the log cabin and its successor, the timber plank house, as "native and, so to speak, indigenous" types of domestic architecture, entirely modern in their simplicity and fitness to purpose.[32] Published in *Art and Progress*, his article was illustrated with a photograph of the Hunter's Cabin at the World's Columbian Exposition. Though designed and built by a large Chicago architecture firm, the Hunter's Cabin was here intended to demonstrate the innate ingenuity and resourcefulness of its purported creator, the frontiersman, attributes that endowed him with the capacity to progress. In this sense, the simple cabin might be seen as the forerunner of the technologically sophisticated steel-framed structures in which firms such as Holabird and Roche specialized.

Of all the representations of American history at the fair, including numerous representations of Native American life and the culture of various colonial settlers, the Hunter's Cabin came closest to symbolizing the version of American history the fair promoted, illustrating both the nation's noble past and its present-day triumph. Both a single structure and the embryonic American home, it represented in miniature the four-hundred-year history of a new historical episteme, the moment when the United States became a leading global nation. And it reinforced the imperative of continued American expansion beyond the nation's shores now that the internal frontier had been "won."

Although he has been accused of nostalgia for his own pioneer roots, Veblen's background as the son of Norwegian immigrants who settled in Wisconsin and then Minnesota left him immune to the romanticizing of frontier life scripted by patrician Easterners. *The Theory of the Leisure Class* was written, in part, as a counter to this mythology. If he did not challenge the concept of northern European racial supremacy directly, he certainly rejected the idea that it had been achieved in the American West. Against the archetype of the frontiersman, Veblen conjured a different figure, that of the urban barbarian. Undoing Turner's narrative, he told a different story emphasizing not progress but regression.

1   The Ethnology of the Leisure Class

The Theory of the Leisure Class describes a divided society dominated by a leisure class whose latent predatory and exploitative nature was nurtured by the experience of conquest and war. Narratives of degeneration were favorite motifs of nineteenth-century racial theorists and cultural commentators alike. Historian T. J. Jackson Lears has claimed, "Veblen's famous satire of conspicuous consumption ... was rooted in part in republican outrage over sybaritic waste among an over-civilized elite."[33] Theodore Roosevelt is perhaps the best known and most influential of those voices, and yet *The Theory of the Leisure Class* dismantles the mythology of the frontiersman that he popularized. In a deliberate inversion of Roosevelt's claim for the racial superiority of Americans descended from northern European stock, Veblen portrayed the members of the ruling class as latter-day barbarians.

Just as Turner transformed the popular mythology of the frontier into an academic theory of history, Veblen transformed criticism of post-Civil War aesthetic taste into a theory of social degeneration. Grounded in the social unrest of the 1880s and '90s and the severe economic depression of 1893–1894, Veblen's *Theory of the Leisure Class* sought an explanation for the unequal results of industrial advancement in which one class of European immigrants had benefited while another, more recent, immigrant group was exploited (Veblen does not consider non-European races in this book). The central contradiction in American society, he argued, was that an apparently advanced race had realized the most up-to-date industrial methods of production, but at the same time it was reverting to a feudal social system that its forebears had left behind: the barbarian stage of evolutionary development. "In the barbarian scheme of life," Veblen wrote, "the peaceable, industrial employments are women's work. They imply defective force, incapacity for aggression or devastation, and are therefore not of good report. ... In this way industrial occupations fall under a polite odium and are apprehended to be substantially ignoble. They are unsportsmanlike. Labor carries a taint, and all contamination from vulgar employments must be shunned by self-respecting men."[34]

Rejecting the narrative of triumphant progress that formed the basis of the World's Columbian Exposition, Veblen claimed that the American colonists had devolved to an earlier predatory stage, as was sometimes the case "when individuals, or even considerable groups of men, are segregated from a higher industrial culture and exposed to a lower cultural environment, or to an economic situation of a more primitive character."[35] This character was defined by its obsession with the accumulation of wealth in the form of land and property. Veblen explained this relapse in terms of a theory of "instincts" that echoed the work of philosopher and psychologist William James: the colonists had reverted to an instinct toward predation and war, now sublimated into a ruthless competitiveness in business, gambling, and sports.

Veblen's use of the language of late nineteenth-century race science is perhaps the most difficult aspect of *The Theory of the Leisure Class* for contemporary readers. Approached from a less essentialist view than earlier in the century, race was increasingly understood as the product of environment, with its physiological markers and psychological characteristics subject to adaptation.[36] However, debate was not settled, and disputes about the nature of race were evident across disciplines, with many academics maintaining the older, fixed definition, including the French physical anthropologist Georges Vacher de LaPouge, whom both Veblen and his colleague, University of Chicago economist Carlos Closson, quoted as an authoritative source.[37] Rejecting Turner's focus on a singular "Germanic" patrimony, Veblen divided Americans of European descent into two distinct racial groups: the "dolichocephalic blond" originating in northern Europe and the "brachycephalic brunet" from the south.[38] Though both of these races were hybrids, he argued, adapted in response to the climate and geographic environment of the North American continent, they retained something of the instinctual character of their forebears.

Mapped onto the demographic of present-day industrial cities, the racial differences between these two groups helped Veblen's readers understand the basis of the class conflict all too evident in contemporaneous street protests, strikes, and the formation of radical political organizations. Recent immigrants who provided industrial labor, many from southern and eastern Europe, were seen as a separate biological stock from native-born "white" Americans, the descendants of earlier northern European immigrants, who were increasingly understood as the true Americans. The struggle between the grip of fixed racial traits and the capacity of the hybrid American "race" to evolve and change under the positive influence of industrialization is the theme that underscores Veblen's criticism of the leisure class. And, in Veblen's writing as in other modernist rhetoric, progress toward a modern industrial future was always measured by contrast with national and racial groups considered "backward" or "primitive."[39]

Because he disliked using citations, it is difficult to determine the exact inspiration for Veblen's categorization of racial difference. David A. Reisman and Thomas C. Leonard have argued that the source of Veblen's race science was William Z. Ripley, a professor of economics at MIT.[40] Published in 1899, Ripley's book *The Races of Europe: A Sociological Study* was based on a series of lectures he gave at Columbia University in 1896. Drawing on physical anthropology, Ripley "classified Europeans into three distinct races, using a tripartite scheme: cephalic index [ratio of head width to length], color, and stature. ... The northern Teutonic race was long headed ('dolichocephalic'), tall in stature, and pale in eyes and skin. The southern Mediterranean race was also long headed but shorter in stature and dark in eyes and skin. The people of the central Alpine race were round-headed ('brachycephalic'), stocky, and intermediate in eye and skin color."[41] In character, the dolichocephalic Teuton—courageous, self-reliant, freedom-loving, and individualistic—contrasted with the docile, communitarian, and less adventurous brachycephalic Mediterranean. Though the connection was implicit in his text, Ripley's readers would understand these distinct racial characteristics as the source of contemporary conflicts between capital and labor, between descendants of earlier immigrant groups such as the Germans and Irish, and newer groups such as Italians and Russian Jews.[42] But while Veblen employed the same categories as Ripley, he interpreted them differently, describing the persistence of the "dolicho-blond" character as a brake on industrial efficiency and social progress.

It is important to note here that even though Veblen inverted the hierarchy commonly found in scientific literature and popular discourse, in which Americans categorized as "white" were seen as superior, more developed, than nonwhites, he did not reject the basic premise of evolutionary progress. Quite the reverse, his book ends on a cautiously optimistic note by arguing that the hybridization of races in American cities would temper the competitive tendencies that produced capitalist exploitation, ensuring the evolution of American society away from its barbaric phase and a return to communitarianism. But he gave no indication of the timeframe of this evolutionary transformation: for the present, barbarism ruled.

In Veblen's assessment, the descendants of the northern European "warrior" tribes had reverted to barbaric behavior, a tendency visible in recent histories of European migration and colonization.[43] In the present day, they retained a psychological, or instinctual, tendency toward competitiveness, an aggressive trait visible in both "conspicuous consumption" and "pecuniary emulation," the desire to better one's neighbor. The status once conferred by physical strength, by skill in warfare, is now conferred by the spoils acquired. The cultural world of the barbarian is characterized by honorific display. Of all honorific products, Veblen wrote, buildings occupy a privileged position: the "process of the selective adaptation of designs to the end of conspicuous waste, and the substitution of pecuniary beauty for aesthetic beauty has been especially effective in the development of architecture."[44] Flaunting fortunes built on industrial-scale agricultural production, manufacturing, and merchandising, Chicago's mercantile class expressed its dominance through extravagantly eclectic architectural monuments, both public and private.

The Chicagoesque

The Theory of the Leisure Class may be read in parallel with similar criticisms conflating cultural and social barbarism published in the United States around the end of the nineteenth century.[45] This literature often cited the luxurious homes of the wealthy as evidence of cultural and moral backwardness. To single out any individual or individual house as representative of Veblen's barbarian would be antithetical to his approach to economics; political economists concentrate not on powerful individuals but on the social institutions through which the powerful exercise their influence. Nevertheless, the dry-goods and real estate magnate Potter Palmer has often been cited as not just an example of Veblen's modern-day barbarian, but perhaps its inspiration. This is an understandable association, due less to Palmer's biography than to the extraordinary home he erected on Chicago's North Side. One of the wealthiest men in the city, Palmer lived with his wife, Bertha Honoré Palmer, in an elaborate and idiosyncratic Norman-inspired mansion on North Lake Shore Drive. Palmer and Bertha were leading philanthropists and public figures. Major patrons of the World's Columbian Exposition, they were highly prominent in its organization: Palmer was one of two vice presidents, and Bertha the president of the Board of Lady Managers. At the time of the fair, the Palmers' palatial residence was one of the leading sights of the city outside the fairgrounds. For example, *Rand, McNally & Co.'s Bird's-Eye Views and Guide to Chicago* (1893) depicted it as one of Chicago's principal tourist attractions.[46] The Palmers' close association with civic and social reform did not make them immune to his charge of barbarianism. Indeed, Veblen considered philanthropy a consummate leisure-class activity. While he did not refer to the Palmers or their home directly, their extravagant house was the most obvious expression of the barbarian aesthetic in Chicago. When he described the world of conspicuous consumption and pecuniary emulation, he no doubt realized readers would call to mind this highly unusual structure.

A leading member of the mercantile class, Palmer made his name in what Veblen described as "pecuniary employments," business activities concerned with promoting "ownership—the immediate function of the leisure class proper—and the subsidiary functions concerned with acquisition and accumulation."[47] After moving to Chicago from New York state in 1852, he had opened a dry-goods store, P. Palmer and Co., and in the early 1850s he developed State Street, where he owned a substantial number of properties, into the city's primary commercial avenue.[48] In 1856 he sold a "controlling interest in his multi-million dollar dry-goods business to Marshall Field and Levi Z. Leiter. He then built a six-story, marble-clad department store on State Street with Field and Leiter, as well as Chicago's most luxurious hotel, the Palmer House."[49] In

Figure 1.9
Exterior view of the Potter Palmer residence, 1350 North Lake Shore Drive, 1888. Cobb and Frost, architects; John W. Taylor, photographer.

anticipation of war with the South, Palmer bought up bulk supplies of cotton and cotton goods. When supply routes from the South were cut off, his stock increased in value hugely and he made a fortune. After the war he retired from the wholesale business to become an entrepreneur.

Because Veblen was not interested in individuals, Potter and Bertha Palmer serve his theory not as a remarkable couple but as a representative one, typical of the psychology and characteristics of their highly privileged social class. Supporting his focus on the cultural activities of this group, their home was not a lone monument to their own wealth and prestige but the centerpiece of a new residential district on the North Side of the city, designed to replace the old hub of lower Michigan and Prairie Avenues. This area, which became known as the Gold Coast, was one of several significant urban developments for which Palmer was responsible. In early 1882, he had purchased from the Catholic Church a large parcel of undeveloped and swampy land between the northern edge of the business district and Lincoln Park, adjacent to Lake Michigan.[50] In draining, filling, and subdividing the land to make it suitable for the construction of housing, including his own residence, he did for residential splendor what he had done for commercial magnificence along State Street south of the river. Working in concert with the Parks Commission, he transformed the muddy lakeshore into a landscaped suburban enclave, creating a new stage for Chicago's high society, with the Palmers as central players.[51] Like his other projects, this was a success. By 1929, the University of Chicago sociologist Harvey Warren Zorbaugh claimed, "the Lake Shore Drive has come to represent more wealth than any other street in the world save Fifth Avenue."[52]

If Palmer's North Lake Shore Drive residential district was intended as an urban theater for the enactment of conspicuous consumption, his own home was its centerpiece. In February 1882, the *Chicago Tribune* reported that Palmer had commissioned society architects Henry Ives Cobb and Charles Frost to draw up plans for a grand house on one of the largest sites.[53] Occupying a corner lot between Banks and Schiller streets, facing the newly landscaped North Lake Shore Drive, Cobb and Frost's Palmer mansion was an idiosyncratic version of the Norman Gothic. Designed with an unusually high degree of input from their client, the house was controversial from the start. In April 1882, the *Tribune* reported, "It is hard to describe the style of the building, as it is rather an odd one for a residence, but perhaps it may be as well to call it a domestic castellated one."[54] Only partly alleviated by an eighty-foot tower, the building's proportions were squat. Constructed of dark gray-brown, quarry-faced Wisconsin granite contrasting with smooth, pale Ohio sandstone trim, the stone walls emulated the striped effect popularized by English architect Richard Norman Shaw. Shaw's polychromic striation was intended as a rational expression of a building's material makeup. The variegated result in Cobb and Frost's Lake Shore Drive house was less successful, not pleasing to the architects or their client. In the spring of 1883, local newspapers reported rumors that Cobb had advised Palmer against using stone in this way, and that neither were happy with the resulting "violent and distressing contrasts."[55] Likened by some to a layered chocolate cake, among other unflattering metaphors, the huge house provoked "a variety of opinion as to impressiveness or good taste," according to the *Chicago Inter-Ocean*.[56] To locals it resembled nothing so much as a fairy tale castle, and that is the label that stuck. While perhaps not achieving the impressive effect that Palmer was hoping for, the gargantuan structure certainly communicated his social position.

According to Veblen's economics of aesthetics, Palmer's castle fits the definition of "honorific waste."[57] A prime example of the pecuniary beauty of domestic architecture in a leisure-class society, its value lay in publicizing the importance and power of its owner. Besides its fortified style, the type of stone used to construct it is significant. Up until the late 1870s, most prominent buildings in Chicago were built from soft sandstone or white, gray, or yellow limestone of unreliable quality, transported from local quarries. Both materials quickly discolored in the noxious atmosphere of the industrial metropolis, created by the burning of bituminous coal for large-scale manufacturing. In the early 1880s, stronger and more durable granite began to be shipped to Chicago from quarries in Missouri, Wisconsin, Minnesota, and New England.[58] With its fine texture suitable for carving, and availability in several colors including red, gray, and black, this material suited the fashion for Gothic polychromy. Its durability also made it resistant to corrosion. As Thomas Leslie notes, "Granite was expensive for Chicago builders, and its use was restricted to either street-level surfaces or particularly high-end buildings. It was rarely used in the 1870s and only began to see widespread use in Chicago with the more expensive construction that occurred in the mid-1880s."[59] Begun in 1882, the Palmer mansion was one of the first buildings in the city, public or private, to employ granite in large quantities. Another example was the Chicago Board of Trade Building at Jackson and La Salle streets.[60] For a domestic dwelling to compete in magnificence with a civic building of such importance suggests the scope of Palmer's aspiration.

The Palmer mansion was a city house that emulated a grand country estate in its size and situation. Sitting alone on a large corner site, the house faced northeast, away from the smoke and dust of the city and toward Lake Michigan. This was a rare view in a city with few natural landmarks and little topographic variation. When the rest of Chicago baked in the hot, humid summers, the residents of this privileged site benefited from the lake's cooling breezes, scented by the smell of freshly cut grass. Considering its urban site, their house sat in generous landscaped grounds, including an unusually large lawn. Lawns, as Veblen pointed out, were a highly visible example of conspicuous consumption. Arguing on questionable anthropological grounds, he claimed the domestic lawn was particularly appealing in well-to-do communities where descendants of the dolicho-blond predominated.[61] Originally a pastoral people living in a humid climate, he argued, the dolicho-blond was instinctively attuned to appreciate such imitations of agricultural splendor, especially when ornamented by an expensive breed of cow or, better yet, a deer or antelope—any large animal that was decorative rather than useful.

Looking across this expanse of grass, Potter and Bertha Palmer could admire a ribbon of newly improved road between their house and the lake. Lake Shore Drive was part of the Chicago park system, an infrastructure of leisure encircling the city. Extending from the city center north to Lincoln Park, the Drive was at that time just three miles long. Nevertheless, it became a popular site for promenading. At intersections along its length, signs bore the admonitions, "For pleasure driving. No traffic wagons allowed."[62] While Lake Shore Drive was given over to working-class Chicagoans on Sunday afternoons in the warmer months, on weekday evenings it was occupied by the wealthy, who paraded in grand carriages.[63]

When Potter Palmer and his wife set out for a drive, they descended the stairs of their grandly scaled porte cochere and stepped into their fashionable carriage, driven by two well-dressed coachmen. Such an activity, Veblen suggested, was a highly public act of both conspicuous leisure and conspicuous consumption, an act even more wasteful because it involved nonproductive human servitude. At its highest level, he claimed, domestic service fulfilled a "spiritual rather than a mechanical function."[64] The more ceremonial the servant's role, the more highly they were prized. In the highest rung of society, he argued, the function of prominent servants such as the butler or the footman was essentially honorific: their role was to perform vicarious leisure on behalf of their masters.[65] Paraded in the public eye high atop the carriage, the impeccably turned-out coachman, perfectly matched in height with his partner and dressed in matching attire, was the personification of this principle.

The theme of conspicuous consumption continued inside "the Castle," as the Palmers' house was known locally. Just as the mythical frontiersman adorned the interior of the hunter's cabin with the skins of wild animals as symbols of his prowess with weapons, the barbarian captain of industry employed exotic treasures gathered from the far corners of the world as tokens of his acquisitive power. From the entrance vestibule, the Palmers' guests entered a three-story-high octagonal center hall. The focal point of the ground floor, this grand receiving room lined with carved wooden panels was overlooked by a gallery in emulation of the great rooms of European castles. But this was the limit of the Gothic style in the interior. Beyond this cavernous and yet somewhat gloomy space, the architects and designers employed to complete the interior of the mansion abandoned the medieval theme. Finally completed in 1885, the interiors were designed not by Cobb and Frost, but by another Chicago firm, Silsbee and Kent, as well as New York City decorators, the Herter Brothers.[66]

1 The Ethnology of the Leisure Class

Figure 1.10
Potter Palmer residence, Chicago, 1885. Cobb and Frost, architects; Kaufmann & Fabry Co., photographer.

The rest of the house was a symphony of aesthetic incoherence, with public rooms decorated in a variety of different styles: an Indian parlor finished in carved teak, a Moorish reception room lined with bird's-eye maple, and a Flemish Renaissance library. A more refined version of the eclectic exoticism of the fair's midway, this decorative scheme expressed both luxury and a determined frenzy of accumulation.

Widely publicized in the local and national press, the Palmer mansion exemplified a style that a waggish journalist for the *Chicago Tribune* dubbed the "Chicagoesque." Combining elements of the Gothic, the Romanesque, and the Queen Anne, the style was characterized by its porches and porticoes, loggias, and galleries, all constructed of roughly cut stone.[67] According to the *Tribune*, the Studebaker Building on Michigan Avenue (later known as the Fine Arts Building) was Chicagoesque, as were the Adams Express Building on Dearborn Street, the Pullman Building on Michigan Avenue and Adams Street, and the Chicago Board of Trade on

Figure 1.11
Potter Palmer residence, library, Chicago, 1885. Cobb and Frost, architects; Kaufmann &
Fabry Co., photographer.

LaSalle Street. While Potter Palmer's castle was the epitome of the residential Chicagoesque, it was far from the only example to attract attention. The Gold Coast was a showcase for aesthetic experiments, both successful and less well regarded. Lake Shore Drive was lined with grand houses, each seeking to outdo its neighbor. Boston architect H. H. Richardson had popularized the Romanesque style, and the Drive boasted its own Richardson house, completed in 1887 for Franklin Mac-Veagh, who made a fortune in the wholesale grocery business. Built at the same time as Richardson's better-known Glessner House on Prairie Avenue, and almost dwarfed by the Palmer mansion, its neighbor to the south, the MacVeagh House exhibited the famed architect's simplified Romanesque style, including his signature heavily rusticated exterior constructed of quarry-cut stone centered on an oversized arched entrance door. The Richardsonian Romanesque style influenced many houses constructed in the neighborhood, including many of the nearly one hundred houses Palmer commissioned. While some were no more than modest rowhouses, all were realized in large blocks of dark-colored stone.[68]

For journalists, novelists, and cultural commentators alike, grandiose structures such as these embodied the deep social, economic, and racial divide between Veblen's leisure and laboring classes, between the established class of "native" (Anglo) American capitalists and recent European immigrants. As the social toll of unchecked economic growth became evident in the late nineteenth century—three decades of devastating depression, strikes, and widespread economic hardship—lavish homes built along Prairie Avenue and Lake Shore Drive contrasted markedly with the humble wooden structures on the periphery of the city, the homes of the workers whose labor fueled the industrial city.[69] Combining elements cobbled together from the marketplace of history, these magnificent homes represented a lack of taste and discernment, material acquisitiveness run rampant. For example, a version of the Palmer mansion features in Upton Sinclair's 1906 novel *The Jungle*, where it is described as "an enormous granite pile, set far back from the street, and occupying a whole block ... it had towers and huge gables, like a medieval castle." The novel's protagonist, a poor

Figure 1.12
Residences on the 1400 block of North Lake Shore Drive, including homes of Franklin MacVeagh, S. E. Barrett, Mrs. F. E. Ogden, V. C. Turner, Mrs. Barbara Armour, and G. A. Armour, c. 1905. Charles R. Clark, photographer.

Lithuanian immigrant, finds it "inconceivable ... that any person could have a home like a hotel or the city hall."[70] Infamous rather than well regarded, the Palmer mansion was seen as a monument to bad taste, a gaudy spectacle divorced from the city's progressive cultural aspirations.

To others, the castellated Palmer mansion looked less like a civic monument, and more like its original architectural model, a defensive castle keep. The journalist responsible for the label "Chicagoesque" joked, "There should be a deep moat around the castle and access to the main door should be over a drawbridge. In front of the castle should be a broad lawn where the retainers could gather on festive occasions and fire off Roman candles and drink beer. In times of war or when Anarchists are out loose, the portcullis or whatever the thing is called, can be barricaded and a Gatling gun fired from one of the turret loopholes."[71] This satirical remark was far from unusual. The 1886 Haymarket bombing had taken place a year after the Palmer mansion was completed, and during these years fears of anarchist attack were real among the wealthy and the middle-class alike.[72] Though Palmer was one of those who argued for clemency for the accused, his grand home was the most prominent of the obviously defensive mansions built at a time of deep social unrest.

Criticism of the extravagant excesses of the Chicagoesque had its basis in the emergence of a reformist political order in Chicago after the upheavals of the Haymarket bombing and the Pullman strike of 1894, resulting in the election of Carter Harrison Jr. as mayor in 1897. Harrison's tenure as mayor was defined by the desire to create shared monuments rather than individual ones, with the World's Columbian Exposition as the ultimate expression of the reformed and reorganized city. In this context, Veblen's argument about the barbaric nature of contemporary culture provided a moral and economic rationale for both social and aesthetic reform.

The true problem of grandiose and archaic structures such as the Palmer mansion, Veblen suggested, was not the strict divide between labor and leisure classes they embodied but the example they provided in a culture of pecuniary emulation. In a city of nearly a million residents, the mansions of the wealthy were the ultimate point of invidious comparison. Veblen was far from the

1   The Ethnology of the Leisure Class

only commentator to speak of American architecture in terms of evolutionary conquest, the survival of the fittest: the theme was commonly repeated in the architectural press. For example, in 1890, prominent architect John Wellborn Root, designer of many grand houses in the Gold Coast, published an essay in *Scribner's Magazine* entitled "The City House in the West." Here, he described the progress of western houses from the mythological "log hut" that served the American frontier to the simple but functional balloon-framed timber house that made up most of the homes in cities throughout the western states, to the ornately decorated timber and stone homes of Root's time. In his boosterish assessment, the development of architecture in this region was unique in history, the result of a "restless wave of progress ... crushing down primeval obstacles in nature and desperate resistance from the inhabitants."[73] As frontier cities grew in prosperity and population, he wrote, their houses grew in aesthetic ambition. While praising the awesome power of progress, Root also expressed dismay at the result when the tastes of the urban elite trickled down to those of more modest means.

Significantly, Root took aim not at the homes of the wealthy (who were, after all, his clients), but at the eclectic houses put up by real estate speculators. Emulating styles made fashionable by Chicago's leading citizens and playing on their customers' desire for novelty, speculative builders conjured up effects both bizarre and startling. Three years later, the New York journalist Julian Ralph echoed Root's criticism, writing, "A peculiarity of the buildings of Chicago is the great variety of building-stones that are employed in their construction. Where we would build two blocks of brownstone, I have counted thirteen varieties of beautiful and differing building material." In the grandest of these homes, "the rich display evidence of a tasteful and costly garnering of the globe for articles of luxury and virtu."[74] Yet he praised the hospitality Chicagoans offered; while their society was crude, they were welcoming, open, and honest, and in this way more truly American than their counterparts in the cities of the Atlantic coast.

Though architects and critics were forgiving of aesthetic excess, seeing it as the relatively harmless result of untutored enthusiasm, the germ of an American culture yet to mature, Veblen saw something more sinister. Their summary of the state of Chicago housing reflects his idea of "pecuniary standards of taste." In modern cities, he wrote, the size and mobility of the population means one often meets people one does not know. Conspicuous leisure (where the privileged pay or command others to labor on their behalf) is no longer as effective, and a new method is needed to display rank. In cities, both dress and the size and character of one's home assume special prominence. Urban life encourages invidious comparison and pecuniary emulation as members of the growing population seek the approval of their neighbors. Conspicuous consumption has utility as a way to establish good repute, and the practice extends across the community from its highest to its lowest ranks.[75] Although middle- and lower-class households are not part of the leisure class, they aspire to the taste of the elite. In this sense, the grand homes constructed by leading social figures like Potter Palmer and his wife Bertha, and the fashions they followed, set the standard for reputability for the lower ranks. According to the logic of invidious comparison and emulation, where status could be achieved only by outdoing others, the Palmers promoted practices of conspicuous consumption far beyond those who could afford it.

With the publication of *The Theory of the Leisure Class*, dissatisfaction with what Veblen defined as "conspicuous consumption" moved from the discursive public sphere of criticism and literature to the established authority of academic theory. Grounded in economics and anthropology, the book provided academic grounds for the rejection of a style, the Chicagoesque, already described as ugly.[76] Far from the moral signification of the Gothic Revival promoted by mid-nineteenth-century architects, or Richardson's attempt at authentic American expression, the Chicagoesque could be understood by Veblen's readers as the exaggerated expression of the warrior phase of social evolution, now transposed into business. Just as the designers of the ethnographic exhibits at the World's Columbian Exposition employed Pueblo cliff dwellings, birch-bark tents, and animal-skin-covered tepees as markers of savage primitiveness, the lithic mansions that lined the streets of the Gold Coast served as architectural signifiers of the backwardness of the barbarian class. Rather than honest and vigorous interpretations of historical styles adapted to the environment of the American West, as Richardson's work was often regarded, the residential examples of the Chicagoesque seemed to express only lack of education on the part of local architects and lack of taste on the part of their owners.

If these Chicago houses represented the result of the most recent phase of barbarianism, what was the alternative? In his brief remarks on urban housing, Veblen not only disparaged the profligacy of ornamental variety, but he also hinted at his own material preference. In a fleeting comment, he gave a glimpse of the possible aesthetic of a highly evolved industrial future. In an often-quoted passage of *The Theory of the Leisure Class*, Veblen wrote:

> It would be extremely difficult to find a modern civilized residence or public building which can claim anything better than relative inoffensiveness in the eyes of anyone who will dissociate the elements of beauty from those of honorific waste. The endless variety of fronts presented by the better class of tenements and apartment houses in our cities is an endless variety of architectural distress and of suggestions of expensive discomfort. Considered as objects of beauty, the dead walls of the sides and back of these structures, left untouched by the hands of the artist, are commonly the best feature of the building.[77]

This remark no doubt raised a particular image in the minds of Veblen's readers: the plain walls of "common" brick used on the sides of buildings where they were not intended to be seen. The opposite of luxurious granite, the common brick party wall is a common feature in late nineteenth-century American street scenes, visible when an adjacent building was being erected or demolished, as in a photograph of an unknown street in Chicago taken in 1905 (figure 1.13).

In contrast with the freestanding houses on North Lake Shore Drive, which emulated the scale and splendor of country estates, and the wooden-framed houses forced out of the city by building codes after the great Chicago fire of 1871, the row house and the tenement were the new model of urban living, efficient

Figure 1.13
Apartment building in Chicago, c. 1905. Charles R. Clark, photographer.

architectural mechanisms for occupying expensive city lots. While their street facades may have featured the decorative eclecticism Root described, the basis of these buildings was common brick, an industrially produced, standardized, and relatively cheap building material.[78] The party wall facing the empty lot next door indicated a never finished, always expanding, urban building project. For Veblen, the humble common brick was the building material of the industrial era. In stating his aesthetic preference for the "dead walls of the sides and back" of tenements and apartment houses, he seemed to disavow aesthetics. Yet at the same time he demonstrated a thoroughly modern taste, one in which beauty was defined as the unity of form and function.

*

Palmer's Castle was demolished on a cold day in February 1950.[79] Just days before, the family had hosted a party to celebrate the debut of one of Palmer's great-granddaughters. The last event held at the Castle, it served as a farewell to the mansion that had been the center of Chicago social life fifty years earlier. Though the house was hardly a ruin, it had been occupied infrequently in recent times. Potter Palmer died in 1902, followed by his wife in 1918. Rumors of pending demolition began circulating soon afterward. In 1930, their son and his family deserted the overscaled house for a more up-to-date residence in an apartment building on nearby Astor Street.[80] While the Gold Coast remained a wealthy neighborhood, by the mid-twentieth century the typology of the rusticated stone mansion was all but extinct, replaced by luxury apartment buildings. Apartment living had gained popularity among wealthy Chicagoans dating back to before the turn of the twentieth century. Introduced in the 1890s, the new residential type was made possible by high-rise technologies developed for commercial buildings in the Loop.[81] As the *Chicago Tribune* noted in 1907, "To live in the country during the summer, to spend a part of each year in Europe, and the craze for long motor trips over our own land has caused a demand for apartments in fashionable buildings and family hotels which hardly can be supplied. The idea of the modern family is to be as free as the air we breathe, to go

1 The Ethnology of the Leisure Class

when and where fancy may wish, without leaving behind a score of responsibilities such as a large house imposes."[82] Providing the comfort and convenience of the luxury hotel, high-rise living was now a status symbol for the leisure class. Unfashionable and obsolete, the baronial Palmer mansion was out of step with contemporary taste, a piece of Chicago's architectural past about which historians were ambivalent, if not embarrassed. A remnant of the Gilded Age, the excessive house signified the height of nineteenth-century barbarianism. In Veblen's terms, it was an obvious image of conspicuous consumption.

In architectural histories written in the mid-twentieth century, the ostentatious residential architecture of the Gold Coast served as a stark contrast to twentieth-century modernism in terms of both style and materials. For historians like Thomas Tallmadge, the Castle represented the end of the era dominated by historical eclecticism, while innovative commercial buildings such as William Le Baron Jenney's Home Insurance Building, almost exactly contemporaneous with the Palmer mansion, signaled the beginning of a new one. In 1927, Tallmadge described the Home Insurance Building, completed in 1884, as the first "true form of skeleton construction for a large portion of the building."[83] In the postwar era, Chicago had taken on the persona of the first city of modern architecture in the United States, a reputation that depended on innovative early skyscrapers designed by Jenney and others. According to the mythology of the Chicago School of architecture, the Home Insurance Building was the starting point for the evolution of architectural form away from a lithic past toward a sleek steel-and-glass future, the first in a sequence of innovative structures leading, eventually, to the American work of German émigré architect Ludwig Mies van der Rohe. Indeed, the ground for Mies's iconic 860–880 Lake Shore Drive apartment buildings was broken in December 1949, only two months before the Palmer mansion was demolished. Mies's twin Lake Shore Drive towers embodied a new model of metropolitan living, not ostentatious and public but minimalist, anonymous, internalized, and private.[84] Supremely elegant, his curtain walls were illusions of pure technology "left untouched by the hands of the artist," in Veblen's words.

The mythology of the birth of modern American architecture in Chicago rests on technological innovation. This innovation is embodied not by the private house but by the steel-framed elevator building, a type offering an original aesthetic expression based in new materials, structural technologies, and functional needs. In this narrative, attention to the wealth of individuals in the form of grand houses is diverted into the expression of regional and national wealth, with capitalist expansion understood as implicitly beneficial for all. If the eclectic Chicagoesque style is mentioned, it is as a precursor to the "nearly modern" Richardsonian Romanesque or as a foil to the Wrightian Prairie house, a negative example against which the aesthetic progress of the early twentieth-century American architecture might be measured. In many ways, Veblen's writing supports this modernist historiography. Quoted selectively by mid-twentieth-century critics and historians, *The Theory of the Leisure Class* serves as a critique of an era of stylistic confusion and excess, one that prefigured the introduction of the modern style known as functionalism.[85] Veblen's utility to this narrative is as the consummate theorist of aesthetic waste. However, in the process of historiographic interpretation, the specific terms of his narrative of social, industrial, and aesthetic progress have been elided.

Veblen arrived at the University of Chicago as a graduate student in 1892. Published in 1899, *The Theory of the Leisure Class* reflects the academic and urban context of the midwestern metropolis poised between the nineteenth and twentieth centuries. This influential book was based on the same evolutionary model of human progress that underpinned the exhibits at the World's Columbian Exposition. Like the anthropologists who organized exhibits for the fair, Veblen understood architecture and other forms of cultural production as the collective product of a people defined in terms of race, evidence of their place on a linear scale from savage to civilized. If a society's industrial arts were an indicator of its evolutionary progress, the preference of the leisure-class descendants of the northern European dolicho-blond race for the obsolete styles and obviously expensive building materials epitomized by the Chicagoesque was surely a sign of cultural regression. Like Henry Blake Fuller's novel *The Cliff-Dwellers*, Veblen satirized the fair's premise

1 The Ethnology of the Leisure Class

of progress: his characterization of the captain of industry not as the descendant of the hearty frontiersman but as a present-day barbarian challenged assumptions of American superiority. Finally, in searching for the aesthetic expression of Veblen's theory, it would be a mistake to give too much weight to the extravagant mansion, or even to the typology of the house. According to political economists, social change is driven not by individuals but by institutions. Veblen's charge of cultural barbarism was not an attack on capitalist millionaires alone. Rather, his book was a condemnation of the class that financed and supported the World's Columbian Exposition, and that operated the city as a predatory machine at the expense of agricultural and industrial producers. As long as control of industrialization remained in their hands, he implies, the transformation of architectural taste expressed nothing more than the continued dominance of that class in a new guise. *The Theory of the Leisure Class* employs as the ultimate architectural image of the leisure class not the Palmer mansion nor any other private home, but the very institution in which he worked, the modern American university.

As an archetype, the university represented the sublimation of the power of the barbarian warrior class into the power of the corporation, the essential organizational unit of the modern leisure class. Organized according to business principles, it played a central role in preserving conservative social ideals, tastes, and behaviors. The following chapter explores the refinement of the University of Chicago's version of Gothic architecture from the crude and castellated style popular in the middle of the nineteenth century to the more cultured and scholarly version it employed during the 1890s. As Veblen showed, this aesthetic transformation represented the persistence of leisure-class cultural values in modern American society.

2 Pecuniary Culture: The Elevator Building and the University

When Thorstein Veblen came to the University of Chicago in the fall of 1892 following periods of study at Cornell and Yale, the new campus hardly matched those East Coast institutions in size, splendor, or situation. After a year in Ithaca, New York, the Minnesota native had traveled west again to take up a position as a graduate fellow in the Department of Political Economy. Passing through the grand arched entranceway of Silas Cobb Hall on the first day of classes, Veblen entered a building that was not yet complete. As an early historian of the university noted, "students entered the building over temporary boards and under the scaffolding on which worked stone-cutters carving the name of the structure."[1] Indeed, several weeks after the university's opening, students, faculty, and administrators were still sharing Cobb Hall with masons, carpenters, plasterers, and painters. Workers had broken ground less than a year earlier on an empty site in the newly annexed suburb of Hyde Park, six miles south of the city's commercial center. Cobb Hall was one of three conjoined buildings that made up the university on its opening day. These buildings were the first manifestation of what was to become an expansive academic landscape organized around six neo-Gothic quadrangles. The others were Divinity Hall, a dormitory for theological students, and Graduate Hall, where Veblen, a mature graduate student of thirty-five, lived in room 22G. Built of blue-gray Bedford limestone quarried in Indiana, his new home was an imposing masonry pile adrift on a sandy plain covered in immature oak trees. Turning away from the spectacular buildings and expansive grounds of the World's Columbian Exposition being erected a few blocks to the east, the university buildings faced west across Ellis Avenue toward the great plains that had made Chicago's fortune.

Despite their archaic appearance, these buildings were the first steps in an ambitious plan for a new kind of university modeled on medieval Oxford but oriented toward the American city. With its lonely aspect, Cobb Hall housed the university's administrative offices, the Divinity School, the traditional academic departments of Languages, Classics, History, and English, and the emerging disciplines of Sociology and Political Economy, along with a recitation hall. With no premises of their own, the science departments (Biology, Physics, Chemistry, and Geology) occupied rented rooms in a nearby brick tenement house at 55th Street and University Avenue, with residential apartments above.[2] Simultaneously monumental and makeshift, this embryonic academic world was to become a significant subject of Veblen's writing during his fourteen years in Chicago. Part of a generation of American political economists known as "institutionalists," he witnessed a new institution of higher learning emerging.

Veblen's position within this world has long been considered precarious and peripheral. The frequently repeated refrain of Veblen scholarship is that his academic and social marginalization made him such a perceptive critic. Beginning with Joseph Dorfman's 1934 biography, successive writers have painted a portrait of a nonconformist and an intellectual antihero, an identity confirmed by Veblen's rural background, gruff manners, and social insularity. Emulating Bartleby, the titular clerk in Herman

Figure 2.1
Cobb Hall entrance, University of Chicago, c. 1891. Henry Ives Cobb, architect.

Melville's short story, the mythological Veblen preferred not to bend to the social conventions of the day. Reserving his energy for late-night writing sessions in which he skewered his peers, he wrote from the position of an outsider looking in, arguing that the true American barbarians were not unsophisticated rural people or recent immigrants but the newly wealthy members of the leisure class. Describing the members of this class as descendants of a warlike race, enriched by fortunes built on trade and manufacturing, he portrayed a culture dominated by materialism and competitiveness. Most damning of all, he depicted the university as an institution designed to maintain leisure-class interests. Scholars have often attributed Veblen's dyspeptic view of academia to his failure to advance in his career. Indeed, his uneasy personal and professional relationship with academic life occupies a large part of the several biographies written about him.[3] As his student Wesley Mitchell later wrote, "Doubtless the difficulty of obtaining an academic appointment reinforced Veblen's critical attitude toward American seminaries of the higher learning. Hope deferred is a bitter diet."[4] While Veblen's personal motivation has been subject to lengthy analysis, few scholars have discussed his novel critique in *The Theory of the Leisure Class* of the modern university as fundamentally "ornamental," both literally and metaphorically.

If Veblen's famous book may be read as a discourse on style as well as economics, its argument rests on the link he drew between barbarism and the obsession with medieval culture and architecture pervasive in American society during the postbellum period. But while the elaborate fortress-like mansions of the city's mercantile elite such as Potter Palmer's Lake Shore Drive folly may have influenced him, his primary mnemonic was not the castle-like residential dwelling but the modern university campus. Veblen's negative assessment of collegiate Gothic architecture was influenced partly by his academic discipline, political economics, and partly by his dissatisfaction with his own position. Promoted from graduate student to instructor in the fall of 1893, his salary was never raised, much to his annoyance. Employed under sufferance on the recommendation of Prof. J. Laurence Laughlin, his advisor and the head of the Department of Political Economy, Veblen always felt his tenure at the university was insecure. From his place on the lower rungs of the academic ladder, Veblen had an intimate view of the rituals of academic life. Still, he was far enough down to appreciate their absurdities. In published form, his criticism of the university was pointed and offensive to his academic employers: founded and financed by a new mercantile class, the modern American university was the cultural expression of the "business enterprise," Veblen's term for capitalism. Even in the guise of a progressive institution, the university was essentially conservative. Here, the essential stratification of society into leisure and laboring classes was preserved as older forms of elitism were transformed into new ones. In its way, the university was as much a capitalist enterprise as an educational one. A product of the leisure class, it was a supplement rather than a counter to the elevator buildings rising in the downtown Loop.

Modeled on the cloistered medieval monastery, the brand-new University of Chicago campus was the palpable representation of Veblen's argument about the role of architecture in a pecuniary society. Like other cultural critics, he took aim at the fashion for the eclectic Gothic Revival style, a trend exemplified in different ways by the hulking form of the first University of Chicago (1869), a fortified Norman-style building designed by William W. Boyington, and its more refined successor, designed by Henry Ives Cobb beginning in 1891. According to Veblen's anthropological schema, these simulated trappings of medieval scholasticism, both vernacular and learned, were the most obvious symbols of the cultural regression of post–Civil War American society.

Veblen's disdain for nineteenth-century collegiate Gothic architecture resonates with the reception of the university in architectural history. Beginning with New York critic Montgomery Schuyler's politely dismissive assessment published in 1896, Cobb's campus has been largely overlooked in surveys of Chicago architecture. Seen as overly mannered, not in keeping with the university's progressive academic mission nor with the refined new style being explored in downtown commercial buildings, it has never been part of the canon. In many ways, Veblen's idiosyncratic book supports this erasure, offering an academic rationale for the rejection of historicism. Yet his criticism of the university also subtly undermines the narrative of modern American architecture in which Chicago was to play such an important role. Understood through Veblen's theory, the Gothic Revival architecture of the second University of Chicago represents not the vestigial remains of an archaic canon of taste but the transformation of leisure-class aesthetics under the logic of capitalism. In this formulation, civic institutions, as much as skyscrapers, may be considered expressions of capitalist development.

Productive and Pecuniary Landscapes

Traveling north from the suburban station at Fifty-Seventh Street, passengers on the Illinois Central Railroad approached downtown Chicago along an elevated track. To the right, goods trains parked in rail yards almost blocked the view of boats plowing across the gray water of Lake Michigan; to the left lay an almost barren plat, landfill set aside for public use but not yet developed into a landscaped park. Peppered with scrubby trees, this was the "lakefront," the urban fringe where the city met incoming ships and trains. Beyond, a row of tall commercial buildings faced east across Michigan Avenue. Ranging from the sturdy Auditorium Building to the Fine Arts Building and the slender clock tower of Montgomery Ward and Co., they formed the basis of the city's skyscraper silhouette. Behind these symbols of Chicago's prosperity lay gridded streets filled with tall office buildings, manufacturing houses, and lofts. Further west, across the two branches of the Chicago River, lay mile after mile of unassuming neighborhoods filled with wooden-framed houses and brick apartment buildings, the homes of the workers who served the industrial metropolis. This was the field in which many of the University of Chicago's academics chose to work, mining the gridded terrain of the industrial city for quantifiable patterns of meaning.

Incorporated in 1890, the University of Chicago was one of the first examples of a new kind of American university, different in intellectual scope and material design from its predecessors. In the historiography of the university, the close relationship between the institution and the city is considered essential to its

Figure 2.2
Lakefront from Illinois Central Railway, Chicago, c. 1900.

identity and success. A virtue is made of its outward-looking perspective, of its contribution to the study of the American city as a unique modern landscape, with a diverse population and basis in industrial production. Under the direction of President William Rainey Harper, the University of Chicago signaled a new direction for higher education in the United States, a modern research university for a modern American city; a vision realized not through the construction of a single building, but through the development of an expansive university campus. From behind the ornate facade of Cobb Hall, Veblen, like many of his academic peers, made the thriving industrial city the subject of his research. A diligent student of political economics, he began his career collecting quantitative data and drawing up charts to illustrate the growth of the region's agricultural economy. But as time went on, he turned to a different area of economic relations, focusing not on farms and farmers but on the class of wealthy urbanites who were the university's patrons.

The Elevator Building and the University 83

Inspired by the German research universities where many prominent American academics had pursued higher degrees, the University of Chicago joined Columbia University, Johns Hopkins, and Cornell in introducing a new curriculum. Augmenting the traditional classical education, they placed new emphasis on the sciences, graduate research, and professional schools. Like Columbia, the University of Chicago made a virtue of its urban location.[5] In common with the leaders of other research universities, Harper expected his faculty and students to conduct theoretical and practical or applied research. He also encouraged them to participate in social reform movements and organizations.[6] Under the direction of Albion Small, a Baptist minister and the founder of the Department of Social Science, the original members of the Chicago School of Sociology undertook an industrial-scale collection of data to match the tremendous industrial productivity of the stockyards and the grain and timber trade. They gathered statistics on the lives of working people, many recent immigrants, in the service of a wide range of reform programs spanning education, housing, public health, and workplace safety, among other initiatives.[7] Passed into the hands of the managerial class, the knowledge produced would, they believed, increase the efficiency and productivity of the city and improve the health and happiness of everyone living in it.

Led by J. Laurence Laughlin, members of the Department of Political Economy were similarly concerned with research into industrial and social questions. Though Veblen was not actively engaged in the reform efforts of some of his colleagues, in his early research he was similarly concerned with collecting empirical evidence. The first essays he wrote in Chicago were sober and detailed discourses on the price of wheat. Published in the *Journal of Political Economy*, the university's first academic publication, these long-forgotten essays were the product of a veritable academic factory of reports, complete with tables and charts, that the university produced in this era. As Laughlin, the journal's first editor, explained in the inaugural issue of 1892, the purpose of the journal was to provide accurate data to support effective social policy.[8] He was especially interested in correcting what he saw as the sentimental and unscientific efforts of philanthropists and labor activists, pursuing instead an approach to economic policy based on data.

Following his advisor's example, Veblen took an empirical approach, concentrating on the cost of wheat production. Wheat farming was one of the earliest forms of agriculture to be industrialized in the United States. Together with lumber and pork, the grain trade was the foundation of Chicago's economy and a major source of the city's wealth. Veblen's earnest analysis was a response to Laughlin's call for the collection and classification of "industrial facts."[9] "The Price of Wheat since 1867" tracked wheat prices against other agricultural products, illustrated with a series of impressive graphs.[10] Though his focus was prices, Veblen described the industrial improvements that had made wheat farming and the wheat trade more efficient and productive, including the invention of the mechanized reaper (in which Chicago's McCormick Harvesting Machine Company played such a significant role), along with improvements to railroad transportation, and bulk grain storage and handling. Six months later, he followed up with a second article, more speculative than the first, assessing how prices might change during the next decade.[11] Concluding with optimism, Veblen argued that American agriculture had become an industry in the modern sense of the word, enabling the cost of production to remain steady or even decline as global demand increased. Though he did not express the idea in this article, the potential for even greater industrial efficiency through the nationalization of agricultural production was to become a central theme of his later writing.

The grain elevator was one of the industrial inventions that had transformed the grain trade and made Chicago an agricultural trading center.[12] Seen from Lake Michigan or from the bridges along the branches of the Chicago River, grain elevators were an imposing sight for visitors. In the two decades following the Civil War, they were the largest and most prominent structures in the city. Chicago's great contribution to grain elevator design was automation and aggregation. By 1893, the city housed twenty-seven elevators with a total capacity of over thirty-two million bushels. Older elevators near the mouth of the Chicago River had gained competitors along the river's north and south branches. The two

Figure 2.3
Armour Elevator A, Goose Island, Chicago, c. 1890. J. W. Taylor, photographer.

largest, each with a capacity of three million bushels, were owned by the Armour Elevator Company.[13] Known chiefly as a meatpacking magnate, Philip Armour had made his fortune in Cincinnati, the center of the pork trade before the Civil War, and then moved his business to Chicago, where he diversified into grain.[14] The elevator complex he built at Goose Island, a mile up the north branch of the Chicago River, was part of the second generation of elevators constructed after the great fire of 1871, which had destroyed many of the older ones.

Constructed in 1888, the timber structure known as Armour Elevator A was the largest grain elevator in the world. Once unloaded from railcars on a series of "elevating belts," grain was sorted in the taller attic section pierced by small windows, and then stored in vertical bins in the great windowless chamber below before being sold and transferred via oarlike chutes to railcars or ships that pulled up alongside. The economic advantages of this system were enormous. Not only was the cost of grain handling significantly lowered, but mixing grain of the same grade into common bins allowed buyers and sellers the assurance of a consistent product. As Veblen marveled, the efficiencies of "bulking graded grain" kept transportation costs and prices low, even as global demand increased.[15] With these technological advances, wheat farming was, in theory, relatively immune to the dramatic booms and busts of the national and global economies, even in years when the harvest was poor. But the efficiencies of the grain trade created new economic complexities. The Armour elevator complex was a mechanism connecting farmers in ten states to a global market.[16] These structures signified not only the enormous value of grain as a commodity, but also the potential of the grain trade for speculation.

If Veblen thought about the grain elevator as a type, the ascetic economist surely approved of its design. While not yet the monumental concrete silos that would so impress European visitors from Erich Mendelsohn to Walter Gropius and Le Corbusier, the grain elevator had a simplicity of form and lack of aesthetic pretense that suggested disdain for considerations of culture.[17] In 1926, Mendelsohn described the type as a "visible expression of an intent to organize, emblem of productive action. A bare practical form becomes abstract beauty."[18] Yet the grain elevator was not just a functionalist machine; its aesthetic was the sublime of both technological innovation and investment potential. Over time, grain traders capitalized on the efficiencies of the grain industry to open a secondary area of trade, one whose profits soon eclipsed those made from sales of the original product. This was the trade in futures. As William Cronon explains in *Nature's Metropolis*, his essential environmental history, "changes in Chicago markets suddenly made it possible for people to buy and sell grain not as the physical product of human labor on a particular tract of prairie earth but as an abstract claim on the golden stream flowing through the city's elevators."[19] Effectively, this was a kind of gambling, where traders bet on future prices.

The trade in futures was a form of capital accumulation that Veblen abhorred. Distanced from the pragmatic function of offering a tangible product for sale, the futures market rendered production secondary to speculation. Removed from direct interest in trade, he wrote, the speculator "may stake his risks on the gain or on the loss of the community with equal chance of success, and he may shift from one side to the other without winking. ... His traffic is a pecuniary traffic and it touches industry only remotely and uncertainly."[20] This distinction between productive and pecuniary employment, between *making goods* and *making money*, formed the basis of Veblen's book *The Theory of Business Enterprise* (1904), his deeply critical assessment of modern capitalism. Essentially an extension of *The Theory of the Leisure Class*, this book focused on work rather than leisure. Here Veblen concentrated on the appearance of new kinds of work that he defined as essentially nonproductive. In contrast to praiseworthy industrial jobs such as farming, construction work, and engineering, pecuniary employments included the predatory activities of business managers, lawyers, bankers, real estate agents, and advertising men. Veblen considered these activities parasitic on the strength of the industrial economy.

The central figure in this narrative was the "captain of industry." Closely aligned with the financial trader or stockbroker, the captain of industry manipulated the capital markets which had replaced older goods markets. As Veblen noted in *The Theory of*

2 *Pecuniary Culture*

Figure 2.4
The Pit of the Chicago Board of Trade, 1896.

Business Enterprise, the speculator profits from changes to market prices in a way that is totally dissociated from the farmer's profit or the cost to the consumer.[21] In Veblen's view, to pursue this kind of trading meant being divorced from ethical obligation. In the laissez-faire economy, businesses exploited the efficiencies of industrialization to manipulate the market for the benefit of the few. While he did not discuss it in aesthetic terms, the grain elevator may be seen as an unintended monument, symbolizing both the agricultural productivity of the American West and Chicago as a center of capitalist speculation.

While the grain elevator was the first architectural emblem of capitalist speculation visible on the Chicago skyline, it was soon followed by another, the tall office building, which appropriated the name "skyscraper" from its agricultural forebear. In 1885, the opening of the Chicago Board of Trade's magnificent new premises at the juncture of Jackson and La Salle streets inaugurated a new era of commercial development in Chicago.[22] The building was the work of William W. Boyington, a pragmatic builder turned architect of the old school. After learning the carpentry trade from his father in Massachusetts, he became a builder's apprentice and then established his own building firm before moving to Chicago in 1853. In 1868, a biographical sketch measured Boyington's output not in single buildings (though he had already designed many important public buildings and impressive private residences), but in linear miles of marble-fronted retail and brick wholesale stores.[23] One of his professional skills, he liked to claim, was his ability to adapt any style to suit his client's purpose. Setting the pace for a generation of Chicago architects to come, he designed and built at an industrial scale for a city growing exponentially.

Taking advantage of the new availability of richly colored stone imported from quarries across the region and from the northeast, Boyington designed the Board of Trade in the highly ornate and polychrome Gothic Revival style, signifying the importance of this institution to the city. Its riotous color scheme, elaborate ornament, and complex massing led the architecture critic Montgomery Schuyler to label it the "American eclectic Gothic."[24] The interior appeared equally disordered. In the giant trading hall, crowds of buyers and sellers converged in the "pit" to shout prices and make trades, supported by telegraph operators and settling clerks, with spectators observing from a gallery above. The symbolism of this extravagant building escaped no one. On its opening night, it was picketed by members of the International Working People's Party, political activists who saw it as a built representation of the inequities of capitalist development.[25]

The completion of the controversial Board of Trade Building ushered in a new era of real estate development at the southern end of the Loop. From an area densely populated with the worst elements of the city, it became a new financial center, the place where leading local architects experimented with new technologies and forms of aesthetic expression for commercial buildings of all types.[26] During the 1880s, architects experimented with new construction technologies and more inventive facade designs. As described in *Industrial Chicago* (1896), an essential compendium of the city's expansion, the elevator and the new system of skeleton-framed "Chicago construction" played leading roles, allowing the "architect, the decorator and the remodeler" to produce "a revolution in the building arts."[27] Freed from the burden of creating facades that could bear structural weight, architects experimented with light-weight facades in a variety of new materials designed to appeal to their prosperous clients.

The Board of Trade was the focal point of La Salle Street, the north-south spine of the business district, and Jackson Street (now Jackson Boulevard), the east-west street that demarcated the southern end of the Loop, the boundary between the business district and the emerging railway and manufacturing district. Nearby, the Gaff (1884), Counselman (1884), Imperial (1885), Rialto (1886), and Brother Jonathan (1887) buildings housed the offices of grain merchants, stockbrokers, and insurance and railroad men.[28] Each of these structures taxed the ingenuity and expertise of their architects to find a form appropriate for an unprecedented building type. As these skyscrapers proliferated, they became less individually significant, experienced as cliff-like facades within a cavernous streetscape rather than singular monuments. As Carol Willis has shown, strict real estate formulae dictated the form of the type in service of the building developers' goal, to maximize financial returns.[29]

Defined by architect Cass Gilbert as "machines to make the land pay," skyscrapers were not permanent monuments but expendable, replaced by more profitable versions almost as quickly as they were erected. For example, seen in the right foreground of figure 2.5, the twenty-two-story neoclassical Insurance Exchange Building replaced the six-story Brother Jonathan less than twenty years after the latter was completed. In the distance, the sixteen-story Monadnock block, the tall building visible on the right, its square windows reflecting the sun, established a new aesthetic for the skyscraper. Largely abandoning traditional ornament, architects Burnham and Root emphasized the building's scale. With massive purple-brown brick walls, the Monadnock would become one of the central references for visitors searching for the origins of modern architecture in Chicago.

In architectural historiography, many linear meters of library shelving are given over to assessments of these unusual buildings, including their technological development and the manipulation of materials and historical forms used to enhance their cultural value.[30] Though he never mentioned the type, Veblen's proximity to the monuments of Chicago School architecture has led historians to apply his concept of conspicuous consumption

Figure 2.5
Jackson Street (now Jackson Boulevard), looking east at Fifth Avenue (now Wells Street), 1914. From right to left, Insurance Exchange Building and Board of Trade. Charles R. Clark, photographer.

to their variously ornamented facades, sometimes implying that these unusual structures inspired him in some way, and sometimes seeking commonalities between his provocative theories and the stated aims of Chicago School architects.[31] Yet, while the skyscraper has often served as the architectural image of capitalism and capitalist excess, it ought not to be seen in isolation. One of Veblen's primary arguments was that all institutions in the American city were essentially driven by business interests. To single out the skyscraper for particular attention would be to suggest that other forms of construction were somehow less tainted. In his assessment of the economic function of philanthropic and cultural institutions in pecuniary societies, Veblen disproved that illusion.

What happened between the publication of Veblen's optimistic view of the industrial future expressed in his essays on wheat prices and the pessimistic critique of consumer culture that characterizes his subsequent writing? Like other University of Chicago academics, Veblen was increasingly concerned with economic inequity and profoundly shaken by the events of 1893–1894: both the devastating depression that left the streets of Chicago crowded with homeless people and the Pullman railway strike, with its associated riots that took place just a few miles from the university. As he noted in his studies of the agricultural economy of the Midwest, while industrialization increased productivity through new methods of production and transportation, it also reduced the producer's dependence on skilled labor and favored the expansion of business to create economies of scale. The transformation of the national economy from a mercantile to an industrial one led to the centralization of capital and investment as small businesses were subsumed by bigger ones. Pitted against each other, increased competition for profits among large firms became cutthroat. As prices fell, so did wages. By the early 1890s, the social costs of competition had become apparent.

The disparities between labor and capital were all too evident on the streets of Chicago.[32] During the winter of 1893–1894, unemployment was so severe that the Harrison Street Police Station and City Hall were opened each night so that homeless men, then known as tramps, could sleep in the cells and corridors.[33] In response, labor leaders organized mass meetings around the

Figure 2.6
Two men foraging along shoreline, Chicago, 1894. Ray Stannard Baker, photographer.

Columbus monument at the north end of Grant Park. Nearby, the Central Relief Association set up a soup kitchen where, a national journalist reported, they fed four thousand people every day. The lakefront east of Michigan Avenue was a liminal space, no longer "natural" but not yet urbanized. As seen in a series of photographs held at the Library of Congress, hobo camps appeared along the shoreline. Compared to the monumental landscape of grain silos and skyscrapers to the north and west, these makeshift structures were highly visible signs of social and economic degeneration. Dressed in ragged metropolitan attire, the unemployed men who gathered around these shacks were a source of great anxiety for those more comfortably off, a wasted labor force with nothing to expend their energy on except agitation.

These unhappy events changed Veblen's approach to academic research and writing. While some of his academic colleagues sought to show the human face of economic deprivation through statistical studies, Veblen focused instead on broader

Figure 2.7
Living conditions among the poor during the depression and Pullman strike, Chicago, 1894. Ray Stannard Baker, photographer.

themes of economic evolution and mass psychology. Although he was too much of a skeptic to believe in the socialist utopia, he was drawn to socialism as an economic theory of social organization. In 1895, he lectured at the liberal Unitarian All Souls Church on the South Side on "Tendencies of the Socialistic Movement."[34] Founded in 1882 by the Rev. Jenkin Lloyd Jones (Frank Lloyd Wright's uncle), All Souls was a center of progressivism in Chicago. It offered a wide program of lectures and social activities for the middle-class community of Oakwood, with an emphasis on civic and social reform.[35] Under the leadership of Jones, members of the church held the standard progressive position, seeking to solve the problem of social inequity by reinforcing the civic responsibilities inherent in liberal democracy.[36] While there was plenty of fiery radical talk in Chicago during these years, Veblen's lecture was likely dry. He did not advocate for socialism; rather, he dissected it. In his talk, he described the appearance of the world-wide socialist movement influenced by Karl Marx and Friedrich

The Elevator Building and the University

Engels's *Communist Manifesto*. Like Marx, he understood economics as an evolutionary science. He also agreed with Marx's assessment that the current state of human evolution had resulted in a deep divide between producers and consumers. But despite his critique of capitalism, Veblen disagreed with Marx on the inevitability of revolution, rejecting the classic Marxist analysis of an insurmountable divide between classes based on their relationship to the means of production.

Both Marx and Veblen understood the urban environment as a geographic accelerator of the modern condition, a condenser of advanced industrialization supported by global-scale colonization and migration.[37] As a site of unprecedented resource gathering, production, and trade networks, the modern city drew on the unprecedented availability of mass labor to create not just goods but wealth, or "capital." In such cities, Marx noted an immense productive capacity controlled by a bourgeois social organization. Though the phenomenon had a long historical build-up, it was only on the western side of the Atlantic, Marx wrote, that the abstraction of labor, its dissociation from skilled individuals into a lumpen resource, which was the starting point of modern political economy, had become realized in practice.[38] With the discovery of gold in California and Australia, the bourgeois economy entered a new stage of development. Notably, Marx produced the first volume of *Capital: A Critique of Political Economy*, published in 1867, in the context of the wild fluctuations of the febrile American economy and the Civil War, on which he had written as European correspondent for the New York *Tribune*.[39] Marx saw in the outcome of the Civil War the potential for working-class emancipation: the freedom of "wage slaves" would follow from the abolition of chattel slavery.

But whereas Marx focused on what he saw as the inevitable revolutionary consequences of rigid capitalist control of the means of production, Veblen saw the restraining effects of ingrained habits of consumption. Although the country had been sorely tested, Veblen noted, there was no sign in the United States of the absolute social revolution that Marx believed would be the inevitable result of this divide.[40] Veblen was doubtful that any form of state socialism would take hold in the United States. Americans wanted greater control over their labor, not centralized cooperation, he argued, and greater access to private property, not its abolition. To institute such radical change would be a step backward from the democracy instituted by the American Revolution, a return to a different sort of despotism, not of the aristocracy but of the State. Veblen was not a radical like some of his university colleagues, but the events of 1894 shook his faith in the inevitable progress of industrial society. He left the world of agricultural production and food prices behind, returning to the topic only during the First World War, when he briefly worked for the federal government as part of the Food Administration.[41] For the remainder of this time in Chicago, Veblen took up a very different subject. Turning from the agricultural economy and the practical economic research promoted by the University of Chicago, he began a broad historical study of the evolution of social institutions. He was one of a group of academics based at the university who were trying to reimagine the study of aesthetics outside the traditional disciplines of philosophy and the fine arts.[42]

Late in 1894, Veblen published his first exploration of the concept of conspicuous consumption: "The Economic Theory of Woman's Dress." This change of subject was more than just an academic diversion, it was the first marker of a new intellectual position he expanded upon further in "The Barbarian Status of Women," published in 1899.[43] Together with "The Instinct of Workmanship and the Irksomeness of Labor" and "The Beginnings of Ownership," both published in 1898, these essays were drawn from early drafts of *The Theory of the Leisure Class*. Along with academics from other disciplines, including economics, anthropology, and sociology, he reconsidered art and design in its social and economic context, framed by Darwinian ideas of racial development and Spencerian theories of social evolution. This was the position of the new generation of economists, who defined the value of an article not as the cost of its production, as in classical economics, but according to the importance it held for potential buyers. Rejecting classical economics as ahistorical and unscientific, members of this school focused on the role of social institutions in shaping economic behavior and cultural development.

The Theory of the Leisure Class was a contribution to a debate about the distribution of wealth, the central topic among this new school of economists in the 1890s.[44] Veblen's new focus was the social world of the urban elite, their appearance and behavior, and the institutions they erected. As T. J. Jackson Lears has written, Veblen added a cultural dimension to Marx's distinction between use-value and exchange-value: "much of what passed for exchange-value, [Veblen] noted, was also a form of symbolic value."[45] This was a significant change of direction, not only of subject but also of method. While other scholars used the investigative tools of the social sciences, Veblen's approach was impressionistic, based on the observation of dominant modes of behavior and forms of aesthetic expression. Qualitative rather than quantitative, his work no longer focused on the specifics of the local economic situation but expanded to place that situation within a broad theory of human history and development. Although he turned from statistical data to aesthetics (in the form of the material evidence of clothing, domestic objects, and architecture), he still viewed his subject from an economic point of view. In characterizing contemporary American society as barbaric, he found ample evidence in the numerous archaic expressions of the eclectic Gothic that continued to proliferate as markers of Chicago's cultural aspirations. But when he chose an architectural type to illustrate his combined theories of the leisure class and the business enterprise, it was not an overtly commercial institution like the skyscraper but another uniquely American typology, the modern university campus, a monument designed not to make money but to waste it.

Higher Learning as Conspicuous Consumption

While sociologists, reformers, and muckraking journalists studied the rough and squalid parts of Chicago—its tenements, stockyards, sweat shops, saloons, and gambling houses—describing such places as evidence of the social cost of capitalist growth, Veblen turned his attention to different built manifestations of inequity. In a pecuniary society, he wrote, the primary function of cultural buildings was to preserve the interests of the dominant class. Throughout *The Theory of the Leisure Class*, he expressed special antipathy for philanthropic institutions such as "schools, libraries, hospitals, and asylums for the infirm or unfortunate," and churches, about whose "austerely wasteful discomfort" he was scathing.[46] However, he reserved his lengthiest and most vitriolic rhetoric for the institution with which he was most familiar. If the grain elevator and the skyscraper were architectures of capitalism, exploiting industrial processes to maximize profit, the typology of the university was an architecture of capitalism in a different way. Indeed, one might speculate that the academic environment, rather than the grand homes of the city's captains of industry, was the impetus for Veblen's theory. While he no doubt drew on his experience at other universities, the University of Chicago, where he wrote the book, was his primary inspiration and target.

The Theory of the Leisure Class concludes with an eyebrow-raising chapter entitled "The Higher Learning as an Expression of the Pecuniary Culture," which describes a college education as the ultimate expression of conspicuous consumption. Curiously, this chapter is also the only place where Veblen describes the historic origins of the American leisure class, which he defined as a discrete social group dominated by conservative practices and linked to a specific racial identity.

It would be difficult to find a more fitting illustration of Veblen's economic theory of aesthetics than the building erected to house the first University of Chicago. Designed by William W. Boyington and planned in conjunction with the Illinois Central Railroad's first suburban line, this massive and foreboding structure owed its existence to that other mechanism of Victorian expansion, the railroad. Opened in 1856, the rail line ran along a six-and-a-half-mile track between Randolph Street and Hyde Park. Located on a swampy plain near the Lake Michigan shore three miles south of the city, with no streets laid out and few other buildings in sight, the early university resembled nothing so much as a medieval castle rising out of the flat prairie landscape.[47] Visible in the foreground of figure 2.8, the Illinois Central's tracks and small, pitch-roofed train station are the only outward sign of the university's connection to urbanity.

Executed in rock-faced limestone with white cut-stone trimmings, the heavily castellated first University of Chicago shared stylistic similarities with another structure by the same architect,

Figure 2.8
Douglas Hall, Old University of Chicago, 34th Street and Cottage Grove Avenue, c. 1869.
William W. Boyington, architect. Demolished in 1890.

William W. Boyington. On North Michigan Avenue, Boyington's Water Works Tower monumentalized in Norman Gothic form a novel engineering enterprise, a pumping station designed to draw fresh water from Lake Michigan. Local boosters called it a "monument to the ever-progressive, ever-growing West."[48] Though it served quite a different purpose, the university was also an emblem of frontier advancement. Dating to 1857, a print illustrating Boyington's original design depicts a rather delicate building, with shades of Alexander Jackson Davis's picturesque neo-Gothic.[49] But as constructed, it was somewhat less refined. Boyington's university was built in three sections beginning with the small southeast wing known as Jones Hall, completed in 1858. In the fall of that year, instruction started for a small group of students, and the building was dedicated the following summer. However, the Civil War delayed construction of an enormous central wing, topped by a tall tower. Known as Douglas Hall, this wing was finally completed in 1869.

Veblen's attack on architecture's function in a pecuniary society targeted the exaggerated ambitions of buildings like Douglas Hall, named for the university's primary benefactor, Illinois Senator Stephen A. Douglas. With its ambition and aesthetic crudity, it illustrates Veblen's argument that when a wealthy man endows a philanthropic institution, he wants not only to help others but also to signify his beneficence publicly through a highly visible expression of honorific waste. In such cases, Veblen asserted,

An appreciable share of the funds is spent in the construction of an edifice faced with some aesthetically objectionable but expensive stone, covered with grotesque and incongruous details, and designed, in its battlemented walls and turrets and its massive portals and strategic approaches, to suggest certain barbaric methods of warfare. The interior of the structure shows the same persuasive guidance of the canons of conspicuous waste and predatory exploit. The windows, for instance, to go no farther into detail, are placed with a view to impress their pecuniary excellence upon the chance beholder from the outside, rather than with a view to effectiveness for their ostensible end in the convenience or comfort of the beneficiaries within; and the detail of interior arrangement is required to conform itself as best it may to this alien but imperious requirement of pecuniary beauty.[50]

With its massive bulk and fortified walls, and its public site adjacent to a railway line, Douglas Hall can easily be seen as just such an example. But beyond its ungainly appearance, Douglas Hall affirms another aspect of Veblen's theory of the leisure class, his contention that the American leisure class originated in a generation irreparably marked by "the psychologically disintegrating effects of the Civil War."[51] As Douglas Hall rose high above the flat prairie skyline, it overlooked Camp Douglas, a sixty-acre military camp established by the Northern Military District of Illinois to train its volunteer army.[52]

Hastily erected and utilitarian in the extreme, Camp Douglas was a lonely and desperate place. After the battle of Fort Donelson near the Tennessee-Kentucky border in February 1862, part of the complex was converted into a military prison to house nearly nine thousand captured Confederate soldiers, many sick and wounded. Conditions were terrible. The chimneys seen poking up above the horizon line heated the simple buildings during the harsh winters, but inadequate sanitation, including failure to implement a drainage plan drawn up when the camp was founded, resulted in disease and thousands of deaths. This set of simple wooden barracks surrounded by a stockade presented an extreme contrast with the Gothic Revival university building immediately to the south. Yet, for Veblen, the extravagance of institutions such as Douglas Hall was best understood in the context of this military landscape: their fortified appearance was evidence of a shared psychological reaction to the trauma of war.

For Veblen, the rapid growth of Chicago in the postbellum era presented a curious paradox. Chicago had experienced an economic boom during the Civil War and its aftermath, yet not all were benefiting.[53] The city became a national supply center after trade with the South was cut off. Stimulated by government contracts, the market for readymade clothing and packaged foodstuffs exploded. After the war, the city's population tripled in a decade, from 100,000 to 300,000, and Chicago became an international trading hub for the distribution of grain, livestock, and packed

Figure 2.9
Group portrait of Confederate prisoners at Camp Douglas during the American Civil War, c. 1863.

meat, as well as textiles and agricultural machinery. Capitalizing on the opportunities offered by the trading city, entrepreneurs amassed vast fortunes, and at the same time aspired to lives of higher culture.[54] As Veblen argued, this aspiration included the emulation of ancient markers of status: "the generation which follows a season of war is apt to witness a rehabilitation of the element of status both in its social life and in its scheme of devout observances and other symbolic or ceremonial forms. Throughout the eighties, and less plainly traceable through the seventies also, there was perceptible a gradually advancing wave of sentiment favoring quasi-predatory business habits, insistence on status, anthropomorphism, and conservatism generally."[55] As Chicago's mercantile class grew, it sought to differentiate itself from newcomers who flooded into the city to work in meatpacking plants, manufacturing houses, factories, and wholesale stores. Rather than building on industrial advances for the benefit of all, this society became more stratified. In demographic terms, the emerging leisure class adopted archaic tastes and habits that set them apart from more recent immigrants from Ireland, Sweden, Norway,

Poland, Bohemia (a region in what is now the Czech Republic), Italy, and Russia, whom they regarded as racially "other" and on whose labor they depended. The dominance of this class in late nineteenth-century Chicago society was visible not only in the grain elevators and skyscrapers that punctuated the skyline, new building types that indicated wealth and industrial progress, but also in cultural institutions.

Of all the institutions dedicated to maintaining conservative social values, Veblen believed the university was the most privileged. The new adherence to medieval academic rituals evident in American institutions of higher learning after the Civil War was a sign of regression rather than progress: the more "strenuous observance of scholastic proprieties ... floated in on this post-bellum tidal wave of reversion to barbarism."[56] Higher learning held value for the newly wealthy as a form of conspicuous consumption, evidence of the honorific waste of time and money. "It is in learning proper, and more particularly in the higher learning," he wrote, "that the influence of leisure-class ideals is most patent."[57] For this class, a classical education was the ultimate luxury product.

Phrased in anthropological terms, the final chapter of *The Theory of the Leisure Class* begins with a discussion of the origins of higher learning in the occult, in pre-Christian religious rituals. From shamanism to the priesthood, Veblen argues, the possession and protection of esoteric knowledge marks a social divide that endures into his present day. The key to maintaining power as a respected shaman is to convince the "vulgate" that one has special powers with which to communicate with higher beings. These powers are expressed through the exercise of priestly rituals. Not far removed from these ancient rites, academic rituals ("the cap and gown, matriculation, initiation, and graduation ceremonies") echo an early stage of human history.[58]

In Veblen's provocative formulation, higher education was not dissimilar to household decoration. The basis of this comparison lay in the distinction he drew between two kinds of knowledge: the esoteric (by which he meant priestly or scholarly) and the exoteric (applied knowledge with industrial or economic effect). Though contemporary universities were introducing scientific departments, he argued these areas of knowledge were not yet considered equal to older, privileged forms of knowledge. A classical education was still the most desirable because it was an expensive form of adornment equivalent to an elaborately ornamented but useless item. As evidence of wasted time and effort, knowledge of the classics served "the decorative ends of leisure-class learning better than any other body of knowledge, and hence they are an effective means of reputability."[59] As an instrument of class formation, the purpose of such an education was to reinforce conservative canons of taste. Veblen described this canon as the result of "race habits, acquired through a more or less protracted habituation to the approval or disapproval of the kind of things upon which a favorable or unfavorable judgment of taste is passed."[60] For him, the desire to recreate the medieval university was evidence of a retrograde state of cultural development aligned with regressive tendencies of postbellum American society.

In the construction of an elaborate monument to higher education, Chicago's leisure class overreached itself. Ultimately, the magnificence of Douglas Hall was fatal to the university it was built to house. Heavily mortgaged, the institution could not overcome the financial burden incurred by the construction of this grandiose building. Though the university amalgamated with a Baptist theological seminary to reduce costs, the debt became insurmountable, and it closed in 1886. Within four years, this troubled building, now owned by an insurance company, was demolished. Mismanaged financially, the construction of Douglas Hall had been fatal to the university it was built to serve. Yet even before this ignominious end, the American Baptist Education Society launched plans to revive the institution. Within a few years it was reestablished on a new site three miles further south. Although the cult for medievalism was fading, tradition required the use of the Gothic Revival style for the resurrected university, even as the institution dedicated itself to progressive causes.

The University of Chicago and the Business Enterprise

In 1901, a photographer captured a view of the University of Chicago campus taken from the top of the new heat, light, and power

Figure 2.10
Aerial view, University of Chicago campus, c. 1901. E. W. Martyn, photographer.

plant. This panoramic image shows a scattering of stone buildings marking a new territory on the unremarkable flat and muddy site, a new campus a decade in the making. It takes in, on the far right, Silas Cobb Hall and the men's dormitories, the university's earliest buildings on the south side of the campus. Their linear form is mirrored by the women's dormitories, forming a perimeter wall facing the surrounding streets. The Kent Chemical Laboratory, notable for its distinctive octagonal lecture hall annex topped by a spire, is visible in the middle of the photograph. Kent's partner, the Ryerson Physical Laboratory, may be seen just behind it. On the north side of the campus, to the left, the four linked buildings that make up the Hull Biological Laboratories (one each for botany, physiology, anatomy, and zoology) hint at a systematic planning program. To the left in the foreground, a new men's dormitory is a sign of the university's continued growth. Across the road, on the far left side of the photograph, a football stadium is flanked by tall bleachers. Though organized by a grid, this is far from an urban scene.

2 Pecuniary Culture

Beyond the campus, sparsely populated lots extend in all directions. Within, the spaces in between buildings are unimproved quagmires waiting for new construction to begin. From this vantage point, there is little sense of a coherent whole beyond the common material used for the buildings (gray limestone) and their style (a variation on the English Gothic).

The origins of the revived University of Chicago lie in a drawing by architect Henry Ives Cobb reproduced in the *Inland Architect* in August 1894.[61] Though only pen on paper, this drawing represents the impressive scope of the university's ambition. Henry Ives Cobb was appointed architect in 1891 by the Trustees' Committee on Buildings and Grounds following a limited competition.[62] A noted society architect, he was responsible for several cultural institutions in Chicago, including the Newberry Library and the Chicago Historical Society, as well as the Potter Palmer residence. Unlike Boyington, Cobb had impeccable architectural and social credentials. Like the other entries to the competition, his initial design had been Romanesque, a style that had recently replaced the Gothic Revival as the preferred choice for civic buildings.[63] However, when they selected Cobb as their architect, the Trustees bowed to a canon of taste established by prestigious American colleges and universities on the East Coast two decades earlier, telling him they preferred the Gothic. This style lent the authority and credibility of ancient tradition to their new enterprise.

As published in the *Inland Architect*, Cobb's drawing depicts a cloistered campus modeled on the English universities at Oxford and Cambridge, rendered in a version of late English Gothic of his devising. The building that became Cobb Hall features picturesque turrets, a gabled red-tile roof ornamented with lacy crenellations and finials, and a vertical entranceway flanked by octagonal towers. Arranged symmetrically around six quadrangles, the architectural ensemble is punctuated by the soaring spire of a chapel. Medieval-inspired ornament adorns a design perhaps more Beaux-Arts than Gothic in its attention to symmetry and rational planning. Depicting not a single building but an urban-scaled complex, the drawing had incremental expansion built into it. Indeed, Cobb's plan and aesthetic directed the university's growth long after their relationship ceased.

While Cobb followed architectural tradition for academic buildings, his drawing featured a caption that set this university apart from its medieval forebears. A prominent legend on the bottom right corner, "Founded by John D. Rockefeller," signifies the unusual nature of the institution. The University of Chicago depended on the patronage of a very modern businessman. Rockefeller, the multimillionaire founder of Standard Oil, had given $600,000 toward the university's endowment on the condition that a further $400,000 be raised, the first of several huge donations he made to the university. Rockefeller did not have strong connections to Chicago, but he was a devout Baptist and a generous benefactor to Baptist institutions, as the university had become when it merged with the Baptist theological seminary. Persuaded by the university's trustees, Rockefeller saw the benefit of supporting a new institution of higher learning in the Midwest.

With its collegiate Gothic styling and acknowledgment of Rockefeller's role as founding benefactor, one may read Cobb's master plan as a graphic illustration of the theme of Veblen's 1918 book, *The Higher Learning in America*: namely, the transformation of the modern American university into a business. Subtitled *A Memorandum on the Conduct of Universities by Business Men*, this book, which was largely written while Veblen was living in Chicago, has been described as "one of the great unread books of modern social science," and one that "shows Veblen to be the consummate sociologist."[64] As he admitted, in writing it, he "necessarily drew largely on first-hand observation of affairs at Chicago, under the administration of its first president."[65] Directed by governing boards made up of businessmen, the twentieth-century university operates according to business principles, he wrote. Though it preserved the rituals and ceremonies derived from the medieval tradition, in its reliance on financial support from wealthy mercantile families, it is motivated not by social transformation, as its administrators and patrons liked to claim, but by the continued dominance of the leisure class.

The Higher Learning in America continues the theme of *The Theory of the Leisure Class* and adds new commentary on the value of campus architecture for the institution. Veblen's initial focus was the almost totemic value that medieval architecture held for the American leisure class as a material connection to the barbarian forebears from whom the modern captain of industry was descended. In this new book, he subtly refined that argument. His attention finely tuned to the reliance of American business on reputation, he employed the typology of the modern American university as his primary example of architecture designed not for functionality but for publicity. Perhaps inspired by President Harper's commitment to realizing his ambitious campus plan, Veblen dedicated the fourth chapter of *The Higher Learning in America* to the subject of "Academic Prestige and the Material Equipment." The continued expansion of what Veblen described as the university's "plant" was vital to its success, he wrote. As an institution, the university's publicity budget must be significant, much more than in a commercial enterprise of a similar size, because the worth of the academy is expressed not through its profit, which is small if it exists at all. Instead, its status must be communicated in other ways. Related to "salesmanship" more than the university's work proper, the construction of new buildings gave the institution a competitive edge over rival seats of learning.[66]

As much as any speculative enterprise, building a new university was an expensive and risky exercise.[67] In 1893, a journalist compared the opening of the University of Chicago to the birth of Minerva, the Roman goddess of wisdom, "complete and radiantly equipped" from the brain of Jupiter.[68] But in fact, its realization was far more difficult. Though Cobb's drawing does not indicate context, the university lay on a parcel of land in the suburb of Hyde Park, three miles further along the Illinois Central railway line than Douglas Hall had been. In an act both philanthropic and self-serving, the dry goods magnate Marshall Field donated ten acres between Fifty-Seventh and Fifty-Ninth streets and Ellis and Lexington avenues for the new campus. Part of the vast southern tract annexed by the city in 1889, Hyde Park had been established in the 1850s as a resort at the end of the railway line but was at that time still largely undeveloped. Driven by the urban growth machine powered by the coordinated efforts of land speculators, utility companies, private institutions, and the municipal government, the planned university was both a civic amenity and a spur to real estate development.[69] Cobb's design offered the right balance between aesthetic appeal, leafy suburban attractiveness, and urban concentration for the university's trustees.

Despite its ambitious start, underwritten by Rockefeller, and supported by Field and other members of Chicago's elite, the university was on unstable footing in its early years.[70] During this time, the specter of the first University of Chicago, bankrupted by the high cost of its extravagant building, hung over the enterprise. Though the first faculty appointments were made in July 1891, by early 1892 many vacancies remained, and rumors spread that the university was in a precarious state. In the year before the university opened, as Harper worked to hire prestigious faculty members away from wealthier and more established universities, and as his Board of Trustees oversaw the construction of the first university buildings now occupying an enlarged twenty-four-acre site, he fought persistent rumors that the enterprise would never get off the ground.[71] Mindful of the disastrous example of Douglas Hall, Harper was in a state of continual anxiety as the cost of the first three buildings ballooned far beyond the initial budget. Yet, throughout the university's challenging first year and the severe economic downturn of the following eighteen months, President Harper and the trustees did not limit the scope of Cobb's master plan. Though later buildings were less ornate, they pressed ahead with the building campaign.

By the turn of the twentieth century, seventeen new buildings had been constructed on the emerging campus, including new dormitories for both male and female students, and eight buildings dedicated to science departments, a significant improvement on their original premises in rented rooms in nearby tenement houses.[72] Curiously, while Veblen regarded science as the only true form of knowledge, he was largely dismissive of the university's support for the scientific disciplines. Although the construction of these impressive facilities appeared to indicate the value the university placed in scientific research, he argued that they were designed primarily for show. Describing the new science buildings as "conspicuous extensions," Veblen claimed their purpose was not to advance knowledge but to advertise the university's ability to attract first-rate researchers.[73]

Cobb's additions were variations of his collegiate Gothic style. Some, such as the Kent Chemical and Ryerson Physical laboratories, were stand-alone buildings. This was perhaps Cobb's ideal, a picturesque ivy-clad structure made up of two wings with steeply pitched roofs, flanking a turreted central hall that was ornamented by an asymmetric stair tower. Elsewhere on the campus, he designed two museums, one dedicated to the natural sciences and the other to the "oriental" arts and religions, and new dormitories for men and women. Variously ascetic and extravagant, each of the new university buildings was sponsored by a wealthy donor, many of whom were second-generation members of Chicago's leading mercantile families.[74] However, the cost overruns that plagued early building projects forced compromises to Cobb's vision. Built on tighter budgets, subsequent buildings were simpler in form with less ornate decoration. For example, the Hull Biological Laboratories consisted of four buildings grouped around an enclosed court, connected by covered passageways. With their cubic forms and sober, gridded facades, Gothic references were

Figure 2.11
Ryerson Physical Laboratory, University of Chicago, 1894. Henry Ives Cobb, architect.

reduced here to little more than picturesque rooftop dormers and ornamental details surrounding the entranceways. The leafless saplings and muddy morass in the foreground suggest that landscaping was an unaffordable luxury.

From an early period, commentators noted a delicate balance if not a contradiction between the claim that the University of Chicago used the city as its laboratory and the siting of its campus on the urban periphery, housed in a set of quadrangles that preserved its autonomy within an elite suburban enclave. Writing in the *Architectural Record* in 1894, Charles Jenkins remarked on the deliberate seclusion of the campus, noting that "the entire plot is surrounded by a series of buildings which form a complete barrier to the outer world."[75] The reason for this arrangement, he concluded, was to, "as far as possible, exclude all outside conditions from the student when he had once entered the university grounds and so, likewise, was the style of architecture selected made as far as possible to remind one of the old English Universities of Cambridge and Oxford; in fact, to remove the mind of the student from the busy mercantile conditions of Chicago and surround him by a

Figure 2.12
Hull Court, c. 1897. Henry Ives Cobb, architect.

peculiar air of quiet dignity which is so noticeable in old university buildings."[76] While some have suggested the campus mimicked the city, with its grid of large-scale buildings and studied picturesqueness, even as it stood apart from it, others have described the university's design as purposefully distanced from both the busy city to the north and the rapidly developing residential and commercial neighborhood surrounding it.[77] Housed in a series of inward-facing courtyards, the University of Chicago benefited from its adjacency to the city as both a source of capital and an object of study, even as it sought to keep the city at bay.

Veblen's reading of the university complements that criticism. However, he was less interested in siting or master planning than he was in aesthetics. In particular, he overturned the association between the Gothic style and morality promoted by the art critic John Ruskin and his followers. For Ruskin, Gothic architecture represented a lost era of social unification and cooperative endeavor. It expressed the nobility of labor in the way it was lovingly made by skilled craftspeople, and the divine nature of beauty in its naturalistic ornamental forms. A taste for the Gothic indicated an aspiration to reject industrial methods of production and return to spiritually fulfilling practices of handicraft. These ideas were just as appealing in the United States as they were in Ruskin's United Kingdom, especially in cities where the pace of industrial change seemed overwhelming.[78] In Chicago, architects such as Peter B. Wight promoted Ruskinian belief in the necessity of material truthfulness, and the complementary ideals of creative and social freedom. By the 1890s, they were also influenced by the French architect Eugène-Emmanuel Viollet-le-Duc, who promoted Gothic architecture as a style suitable for adaptation to modern construction methods, including the use of cast-iron structural elements.[79] But for Veblen, uninterested in aesthetic philosophy, a taste for the Gothic represented something else entirely, a conformity with a canon of leisure-class taste designed to express nothing more than social reputability and exclusiveness.

If a university operates as a business, Veblen claimed, then the primary role of its architecture is advertising. The Gothic Revival style lent prestige to new institutions of higher learning through its long-established and well-understood cultural associations. It gave the university a "reputable exterior," an image designed to impress prospective students and their parents as well as potential donors.[80] For these members of the leisure class, the Gothic was not original and expressive, as Wight and others argued, but conventional, part of the socially sanctioned "canon of taste" that the university embodied. Operating according to business principles, Veblen argued, the governing boards of universities favored expensive real estate ventures over the mundane day-to-day activities of teaching and research. In part, this was due to their dependence on patronage: donors wanted to see their money spent on highly visible named buildings in a style they appreciated, rather than books for the library.

Much has been made of the differing motivations of these patrons of higher learning. Were their actions prompted by altruism or self-interest? For example, Helen Culver, who financed the Hull Biological Laboratories, was one of the major sponsors of the Hull House settlement, to whom she gifted her cousin's house for its original premises. A respected philanthropist, her character was above reproach. The streetcar magnate Charles Yerkes, on the other hand, used his gift of an observatory seventy miles away from the main campus at Williams Bay on Lake Geneva in rural Wisconsin to rehabilitate his reputation for corruption.[81] Yerkes's involvement is the most obvious expression of Veblen's charge that the university was tainted by its association with business. But for a political economist, more significant than the character and motivation of the individuals involved was the university's heavy reliance on private donations to fund its seemingly continuous expansion. As Veblen put it, "To the laity a 'university' has come to mean, in the first place and indispensably, an aggregation of buildings and other improved real-estate."[82] While impressive facilities were expensive, they were essential in providing tangible evidence of the university's prestige. In Veblen's opinion, their primary function was not to enable the basic operation of the university but to increase its reputation and attract future donors.

In these terms, it was vital that the university's architecture reflected nothing new and adventurous, only the ruling canon of taste. For the "successful men of affairs to whom the appeal for funds is directed … wasteful, ornate, and meretricious edifices" were necessary as "a competent expression of their cultural hopes and ambitions."[83] Though architecture critics were politely unimpressed by Cobb's work for the university, seeing it as lacking the technical innovation and aesthetic originality expressed by many of his peers, this *retardataire* style exactly fulfilled its intended purpose.

Little more than a footnote in histories of the University of Chicago, another building constructed in this period highlights the prescience and the contradictions in Veblen's characterization of the university as the ultimate leisure-class institution. Following the construction of Cobb Hall, the next building erected, known as the old gym, was very different in style and appearance. Begun in September 1892 and completed by the end of the year, this long, low brick structure was designed to house a gymnasium, the university press, and the library. A contemporary photograph shows an unusual wooden truss roof structure and simple brick walls punctured by large windows. Utilitarian to the point of muteness, this building requires handwritten annotations to indicate its purpose. University archives do not record the architect

Figure 2.13
Old Gymnasium and Library, University of Chicago, 1893.

of the old gym, but with its plain appearance, it was unlikely to have been Cobb. Described as a "blot on the landscape" by one of the university's early historians, it was always intended to be temporary. Standing alone in the middle of what was to become the northeast quadrangle, it was "built as cheaply as possible, without permanent foundations, of common brick, one story in height and with a flat roof. The roof was supported by trusses standing above it, framed of large timbers, appearing like monstrous sawhorses holding it down."[84] Inside, the gym was more spacious and attractive than the exterior suggested: deep exposed wooden roof beams spanning halfway across the building's hundred-foot width supported a mezzanine running track that ran around the men's gym, creating a circuit twelve laps to the mile. The building served a variety of purposes when a large space was needed; for example, the university's second convocation was held here on April 1, 1893. In its way, it was the inverse of Veblen's criticism of the rest of the university, built not to impress but to serve a variety of pragmatic functions.

Demolished in 1903, this temporary building was remembered fondly by alumni but was not well loved at the time. Veblen's view of the old gym is unrecorded, apart from grumbling remarks about the delay in constructing a proper library, which he saw as evidence of the administration's skewed priorities.[85] He was especially acidic in his criticism of the university's focus on sports and athletic culture, in particular the attention lavished on the Department of Physical Culture under the direction of Professor of Physical Culture and Athletics (and head football coach) A. Alonzo Stagg, a former star player for the Yale football team. As he detailed in a chapter of *The Theory of the Leisure Class* entitled "Modern Survivals of Prowess," for Veblen, an interest in sports was a key marker of membership of the leisure class.[86]

The dual focus of barbaric culture on capitalist acquisition and competitive sports was all too evident at the University of Chicago. If the academic side of the curriculum was intended to inculcate students in accepted, conservative canons of taste, the athletic program was designed to promote the interest of the leisure class in a different way. Sports and physical culture were not only a form of conspicuous consumption; they also sublimated the barbarian predatory instinct into a literal fitness for corporate conformism. As manifested by the helmets and padded uniforms sported by members of the football team, the athletic program transformed the instinct for warfare into preparation for careers in the highly competitive ranks of American business.[87]

The Higher Learning in America contains an unexpected passage connecting Veblen's economic theory of aesthetics with the most forward-thinking architects in the United States and beyond. In the chapter on the academic plant, he gave his support for strategies of architectural design favored in commercial and manufacturing buildings, including a seldom-noted commentary on modern construction methods. The archaic architectural forms that university architecture preserves, Veblen wrote, are ill-adapted to modern materials and methods of building. These curiously specific remarks include commentary on the desirability of skeleton-frame construction:

> Modern building, on a large scale and designed for durable results, is framework building. The modern requirements of light, heating, and ventilation and access require it to be such; and the materials used lend themselves to that manner of construction. The strains involved in modern structures are framework strains; whereas the forms which these edifices are required to simulate are masonry forms. The outward conformation and ostensible structure of the buildings, therefore, are commonly meaningless except as an architectural prevarication.[88]

Combined with Veblen's withering dismissal of Gothic Revival architecture as "edifices of false pretenses" entirely unsuited to an institution dedicated to the "quest of truth," this comment echoes the rhetoric of truth to materials and the expression of function that underpins modern architecture. Efficient and honest, unburdened by acquiescence to the canon of taste, the simple framework building is the opposite of the elaborately decorated and privately endowed university building.

With these brief remarks, Veblen suggests he saw contemporary frame construction as the built form of industrial progress. In

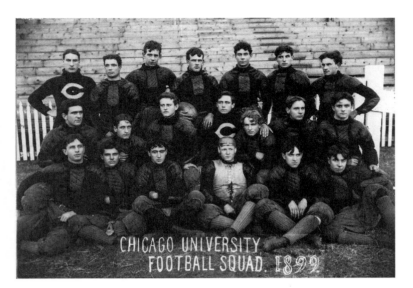

Figure 2.14
University of Chicago football team, 1899.

this way his criticism approaches that of architectural historians such as Sigfried Giedion, who would cite the rejection of historicism and the transformation from masonry to frame structures as pivotal to the formation of modern architecture. *Space, Time and Architecture* (1941), Giedion's heroic interpretation of technological progress as the driver of aesthetic expression, would shape the canonical view of Chicago architecture.[89] In one sense, Veblen's criticism of university architecture in *The Higher Learning* seems to predict this narrative. Explicitly denigrating the Gothic Revival style by making fun of its feudal pretensions and lack of functional efficiency, he praised instead the framework building as a better and more honest way to build. Yet in another sense, through his assessment of the scenographic value of the Gothic university campus, he anticipated a different understanding of modern architecture, one defined not only by its essentially semiotic function but also by its aesthetic fungibility and built-in obsolescence.

The Theory of the Leisure Class presents an industrially developed nation trapped between past and future. Chicago's aesthetic dilemma, disguising ever-innovative construction methods with historicist garb, was evidence of this. Just as he despaired of academic leaders, Veblen remained unconvinced that architects could shake off their status as servants to leisure-class culture. In such a society, he wrote, architecture as a form of cultural expression was not wedded to any particular style, nor did it have lasting value. The Gothic Revival, a signifier of moral authority and political freedom for Ruskin and of rational structural expression for Viollet-le-Duc, was void of meaning except as part of the canon of taste. The collegiate Gothic style used for academic institutions had no enduring artistic merit; "their permanent value in that respect is scarcely to be rated as a substantial motive in their construction."[90] Instead, they must simply "conform to the architectural mannerisms in present vogue."[91] In time the fashion would change, as it does in every society ruled by pecuniary standards of taste. Perhaps thinking of Douglas Hall, he predicted that the "disjointed grotesqueries of an eclectic and modified Gothic" would soon fall into neglect.[92] According to the principles of capitalist real estate development, this neglected state was not a source of disappointment but an opportunity for renewal.

As the constant demolition and construction of commercial buildings in the downtown Loop attested, Chicago excelled at a new form of spectacular architecture, not fixed and stable but subject to the fluid forces of capitalist development described by economist Joseph Schumpeter as the "perennial gale of creative destruction."[93] Subject to the same imperatives, Veblen argued, elite social institutions such as the university fell into the same category. Using the term directly, he prefigured the concern with obsolescence that Daniel Abramson has identified as a central theme in twentieth-century architectural discourse.[94] It did not matter if universities and other civic buildings were cheaply built; rapid physical decay would make them easier to demolish and replace once they had served their purpose. In this way, Veblen's economic theory of aesthetics anticipated by at least five years Chicago property-managers' use of obsolescence in relation to office buildings, though he applied it to a cultural building type supposedly immune to such base pecuniary calculations.[95] The collegiate Gothic was modern, he concluded, inasmuch as its activities were dictated by business principles. Designed according to the

2 *Pecuniary Culture*

prevailing standard of taste, it was intended less to serve essential academic functions than to be a publicity mechanism signifying prestige to a nonacademic audience, especially to potential patrons. Though Veblen did not go so far, his theory suggests that the principle of conspicuous consumption might apply to modern building systems just as much as to its ornate predecessors.

*

The University of Chicago did not build the most monumental elements of Henry Ives Cobb's master plan: the chapel, fountain, and magnificent University Hall he had intended to define the north-south axis of the campus. Significantly taller than any other campus building, the chapel and the great hall would have ornamented the Hyde Park skyline in the same way the skyscraper rose above the downtown Loop and the grain elevator marked the branches of the Chicago River. However, in 1897 Cobb contributed his own, much more modest, finishing touch, donating funds for the construction of a gateway to Hull Court, the quadrangle formed by the four Hull Biological Laboratories. Facing Fifty-Seventh Street, this gateway was flanked on each side by the looming forms of the Anatomy and Zoology buildings. Modeled after the porter's lodges of Oxford and Cambridge, the whimsical structure featured a steeply pointed gable, an arched entrance, ornamental iron lanterns, and a plethora of menacing medieval-style gargoyles. As Edward Wolner has suggested, this entirely ornamental construction perhaps reflected Cobb's desire to have his own contribution to the university recognized.[96] Though it is inscribed with the words "Hull Biological Laboratories," this structure became known as Cobb Gate, suggesting the architect had achieved social equivalence with other, far wealthier, donors to the university.

Purely ornamental, Cobb Gate may be seen as the epitome of Veblen's criticism of university architecture. Theatrical, built for show, it followed the latest fashion but offered nothing to support the actual work of the students and faculty. The gateway illustrates the similar roles played by the architect and the academic in a pecuniary society, at least according to Veblen's acerbic assessment. Both the architect and the academic served the leisure class

Figure 2.15
Cobb (Hull) Gate, University of Chicago, 1897. Henry Ives Cobb, architect.

and sought to be considered members of that class. As cultural reflections of business interests, both higher education and the elaborate architecture of civic institutions had become nothing more than symbols of conspicuous consumption.

The turn of the twentieth century was a turning point for both Cobb and Veblen. Though still in demand by wealthy private and institutional clients, Cobb's mannered historicist style soon fell out of favor. In historiographic terms, this period marks the beginning of what one critic has described as Cobb's "drift into critical irrelevance."[97] Though the University of Chicago was one of his most important commissions, architecture critics and historians saw Cobb's design, a refined version of the Gothic, as failing to capture the university's modern outlook. The progressiveness of the university as an institution appeared mismatched with the conservatism of its architecture. In the twentieth century, Cobb was demoted in importance as the canonical narrative of the Chicago School of architecture took shape, defined by technological determinacy and simplified modern aesthetics. In comparison to the more aesthetically innovative work of his peers, Cobb's was seen as historicist and conservative.

The beginning of this descent is evident in the writing of Montgomery Schuyler, who in 1896 offered lukewarm praise for Cobb's "academical correctness," contrasting it negatively with the work of Dankmar Adler, Louis Sullivan, and Daniel Burnham.[98] Cobb's career exemplified a divide identified by Chicago architect and critic Peter B. Wight. In 1899, Wight argued that the nineteenth-century revival of the English Gothic style had split into two paths in the United States. Rejecting the first, "the extravagant imitation of Gothic forms," he preferred the second, "the rational treatment on constructive lines, and the discarding of ornament in which there was little to suggest medievalism."[99] Cobb's University of Chicago fell into the former category. No longer a progressive aesthetic, the Gothic had come to symbolize social conservatism. For critics such as Schuyler and Wight, Cobb's architecture promoted a vision of American culture modeled on the old world, rather than the new.

The appearance of Veblen's *Theory of the Leisure Class* coincided with these critical assessments. When it was published, Veblen had exiled himself from the center of Cobb's campus to its periphery. From his rooms in the graduate dormitory in Cobb Hall, he retreated first to a series of boarding houses, then to an apartment at the Beatrice Hotel where he lived unhappily with his wife Ellen, and finally to a drafty studio in a converted storefront at the Fifty-Seventh Street Arts Colony, the makeshift home of Ann Bradley Bevans and her two daughters. Recently separated from her architect husband, Bevans would become Veblen's second wife.[100] Situated on the edge of the disused World's Columbian Exposition grounds near the Illinois Central Railroad line viaduct, the Arts Colony was a bohemian enclave, a magnet for Chicago's emerging artistic and literary scene.[101] Here Veblen associated not with academics but with novelists and painters, and it is during this period that Eva Watson-Schütze's famous photographic portrait of Veblen in characteristic bohemian pose was taken. But while this exile reflected his diminished standing at the university, it did not signal the end of his career or reputation. Transformed into an original and subversive theoretical treatise, Veblen's miserable academic experience would make him "the most successful failure in the history of modern American education."[102] His influential first book presented American culture as controlled by predatory capitalism, with consumption driving systems of production, dominated by the desire to display wealth and position rather than to serve pragmatic needs.

Repositioning *The Theory of the Leisure Class* in its historical and geographic context reveals the social conflicts that lay behind Veblen's abstruse theory and the basis of that theory in nineteenth-century anthropology. Inverting accepted concepts of American racial superiority, Veblen described the urban elite as a barbaric people hoarding rather than sharing the advantages of industrial progress. Specifically, he identified Gothic Revival architecture as the expression of the regressive taste of the capitalist elite, descendants of a warlike northern European race. While notorious examples like Potter Palmer's fortress-like mansion may have inspired others, his exemplar was the modern university campus. In his first book and in *The Higher Learning in America*, he presented the University of Chicago (or at least its unnamed twin) as a retrograde institution. In this sense, we might describe the typology of the university as a mnemonic device for Veblen. But perhaps Cobb's university played a more active role, not just as an illustration but as a prompt for his influential theory? The voluminous literature on *The Theory of the Leisure Class* has largely overlooked the significance of Veblen's immediate milieu. Denying any divide between culture and capitalism, he presented the university as a retrograde institution, one that resisted the progressive tendencies of the surrounding industrial world. In this way, *The Theory of the Leisure Class* presents a new image of Chicago's modernity, defined not by technological advances but by the exchangeability of style as a cultural commodity.

3 Mechanisms of Consumption: Fashion and the Department Store

At the turn of the twentieth century, the Marshall Field & Company department store occupied the preeminent block on the preeminent shopping street in Chicago, a colossal white wall of merchandising marked by its famous clock on the corner of State and Washington streets. A photograph captures the scene: contrasting with the white backdrop looming behind them, dark figures populate the broad avenue. The women wear small hats embellished with feathers and veils; their dresses feature tight-fitting jackets over skirts distended by bustles, forming the distinct S-shaped profile created by restraining corsets. Behind them, horse-drawn delivery carts share the road with streetcars. In the distance, the State and Lake El station bridges State Street, transporting a constant supply of shoppers from the suburbs and concentrating the metropolitan economy in Chicago's premier shopping district. Behind, from left to right, are the steep, dual-peaked roofs of the impressively tall Masonic Temple,

Figure 3.1
Marshall Field & Company, State Street, Chicago, c. 1910. J. W. Taylor, photographer.

39851
J.W.T.

briefly the tallest building in the world; next to it, the sober, granite-clad screen wall of the Marshall Field's addition, built in 1902, with restrained classical elements in the style made fashionable by the World's Columbian Exposition, now applied to a monumental commercial enterprise; and finally, the deeper-set, more ornamental windows of the original French Empire-style Field and Leiter store.

The hybrid department store/skyscraper reflects a period of extraordinary economic and urban expansion and the emergence of women as the major consumer class. Ever since 1867, when Field and Leiter moved its dry goods business away from Lake Street, near the main branch of the Chicago River, to the corner of State and Washington streets, Marshall Field's (as it was known from 1881 on) was the magnet that attracted female shoppers to the center of the city and the catalyst that encouraged other similar businesses to grow up around it.[1] Building on the great fortunes the Civil War had created, affluent Chicagoans sought to shrug off pioneer frugality and become cosmopolitan. From its origin as a military outpost, their city had become a manufacturing and merchandising center for the nation, sitting behind only New York in the gross value of products produced.[2] Huge fortunes had been made in industries such as grain processing and brewing, meatpacking, lumber, steel and copper, agricultural machinery, printing, ready-to-wear men's clothing, and financial speculation. Serving a national and then global market, the city's industries were rapidly scaled up and mechanized. The physical and economic expansion of the city was matched by demographic growth, including a tidal wave of immigrants, creating a hungry consumer market. While boosters liked to present their city as a regional center dedicated to marshaling and distributing raw resources, it was also a center for marketing and sales. In a few short decades, the city had transitioned from the production and processing of basic goods to the merchandising of affordable luxuries such as hats, shoes, dress fabrics and trimmings, glassware, china, candy, and many other products from the East Coast and the other side of the Atlantic. Stores such as Marshall Field's were the western outposts of a transatlantic culture of fashion that had Paris as its center.[3]

3 Mechanisms of Consumption

For many early readers, *The Theory of the Leisure Class* conjured up images of these monuments to feminine consumption. Thorstein Veblen's deployment of women's clothing to illustrate his theory of conspicuous consumption is perhaps his most successful rhetorical device. Easily understood by nonspecialist readers, his discussion of women's dress made explicit the relationship between leisure-class men and women central to his account of modern-day barbarianism. The image of the fashionably dressed woman trapped in an unfulfilling social role resonated with advocates of dress reform and female emancipation. When *The Theory of the Leisure Class* was published, journalists seized on Veblen's provocative description of women's dress as a communicator of material waste and physical incapacity.

In 1900, a *Chicago Tribune* article referred to Veblen when discussing department store spring displays. Paraphrasing his argument that the rapid changes in women's fashion produce a form of "aesthetic nausea," the *Tribune* concluded that styles change so frequently because the "ugliness caused by their superfluous cost makes them insufferable to aesthetic senses."[4] Instead, the *Tribune* promoted the shirtwaist dress as a simple and practical alternative, a classic style that remained appealing year after year. In 1901, the same newspaper quoted Veblen when arguing that artists should put their minds to work to create women's dresses that were both beautiful and practical. In doing so, they would become "The Enemies of Fashion."[5] Four years later, the Boston branch of the Woman's Association of Collegiate Alumni urged their Chicago sisters to join them in reforming their spending habits, with Veblen as their guide.[6] Along with the French Protestant minister Charles Wagner, whose recently translated book *The Simple Life* had received much publicity in the American press, the association cast Veblen as a prophet of material abstinence, a "new simple life apostle."

Although he was sympathetic to the cause, Veblen did not intend his book as a response to the debate about women's rights or the dress reform movement.[7] Nor does his book predict the rise of the mass culture in which women play such a significant role. Instead, it focuses on the expensive and archaic tastes of the predatory elite.[8] Rather than positing conspicuous consumption as a modern concept, Veblen understood it as an anachronistic cultural expression with roots in feudal societies, one that the emergence of a true industrial democracy would, in time, overcome. The closest he comes to addressing mass consumption are his statements that the leisure class set the standard of living for all. The American laboring class was not in danger of revolution, he wrote, because transient urban living had made them too much invested in materialism, as they participated in the same commodified form of social relations as the members of the leisure class. But although his name might conjure up images of mercantile palaces filled with mass-produced goods, Veblen's architectural exemplars—the philanthropic institution, the church, and the university—were civic rather than commercial. On retail stores, hotels, theaters, cafes, restaurants, and other places of mass diversion, he is mostly silent.

Like his contemporaries—economists and architects alike—Veblen did not see such buildings as "architecture" in the sense of culturally privileged edifices worthy of sustained commentary. Instead, he referred to them as part of the mechanics of consumption, their aesthetic simply one of the many forms of advertising that were so important to American business. In this way, they serve to illustrate not conspicuous consumption but the perversion of industrial progress under predatory capitalism. Veblen introduces this theme in his second book, *The Theory of Business Enterprise* (1904), where he briefly discusses the department store as both a business model and an architectural type. In this book, the metaphor of dress as a medium designed to communicate good repute is transferred from fashionable women's clothing to architecture, along with other material and graphic products associated with marketing.

When Veblen directed his attention from the domestic to the corporate world, older aesthetic categories of magnificence and luxury gave way to what he later described as the principle of "spectacular publicity," a principle which demanded the adjustment of architectural design to "the current vagaries in decorative art and magnificence."[9] Just as engineers employed more sophisticated technologies to accommodate the scale and complexity of mass production and distribution of goods in the last decades of the nineteenth century, designers and architects developed new

3 Mechanisms of Consumption

technologies and aesthetic forms intended to impress potential customers. These ranged from the open, light-filled interiors and veil-like curtain walls made possible by the new Chicago construction, reliant on the steel frame, to the art and science of merchandising display and window dressing. Although Veblen touched on the typology only briefly, the department store bridges the gap between his abstruse economic theory, early readers who situated *The Theory of the Leisure Class* on State Street and its busy environs, and the rhetoric connecting architecture and fashion that provided a rationale for modern design at the turn of the twentieth century.

An Economic Theory of Woman's Dress

Veblen's 1894 essay, "The Economic Theory of Woman's Dress," was his first published presentation of the concept of conspicuous consumption.[10] Understood in terms of "the dynamic of wants and tastes," fashion was a popular topic for economists, helping to explain the relative roles of production and consumption in the modern marketplace.[11] As editor of the *Journal of Political Economy*, Veblen was aware of recent writing on the topic published in Europe and North America. While many writers took a moralistic approach, condemning expenditure beyond basic necessities, few could overlook the reality of contemporary life. In 1879, Julian M. Sturtevant, president of Illinois College, included a chapter on "Wasteful Expenditure" in his treatise on economics, in which he classed fashionable dress along with stimulants such as alcohol, tobacco, and narcotics.[12] But while Sturtevant claimed the desire for what he called "false modes of ornamentation" perverted the sense of what is truly beautiful, he accepted a heightened awareness of fashion as an inevitable drawback of a democratic society, where the doctrine of equality encouraged people to emulate their social superiors.

During the 1880s, a sociological approach to fashion and dress began to dominate academia. Under the influence of German scholars such as Friedrich Kleinwächter and Friedrich Theodor Vischer, Americans began to explore dress as a mode of social relations, including the importance of what Kleinwächter described as the "imitative principle."[13] But in taking on the subject, Veblen followed the example of not only European academics but also his colleagues at the University of Chicago.

The immediate prompt for Veblen's essay was a paper published in April 1894 by J. Laurence Laughlin, the head of the Department of Political Economy. More pragmatic than philosophical, Laughlin's text was entitled "Economic Effects of Changes of Fashion."[14] Drawing a firm line between the sociological value of dress in "primitive" cultures and the present-day industrial era, Laughlin focused on the benefits of modern production systems. He claimed that machine technology (such as the sewing machine) and the division of labor enabled the creation of more refined products better suited to contemporary market demands. When fashion dictated changes in consumer behavior, he wrote, such systems could quickly adapt in response. Couched in academic language, Laughlin's essay does not touch on the consequences of these industrial production methods or their possible human cost. Yet these questions were not just abstract. Chicago was already an important manufacturing center for the garment industry, specializing in men's and boys' wear. As the enormous sign above Potenberg's Shoe Store on the North Side of Chicago makes clear, the regular introduction of new styles encouraged consumers to think of everyday items such as shoes and boots as purchases to be renewed every season.

Though Laughlin did not make the connection between consumption, economic waste, and social and economic inequity, this was to become Veblen's broader theme. Published just eight months after Laughlin's essay, Veblen's "The Economic Theory of Woman's Dress" balances his teacher's optimistic view of modern industrial efficiency with a warning about the potential corruption of the industrial system, when diverted to serve consumer taste rather than functional necessity.[15] Framed through an anthropological lens, his essay had more in common with the ideas of his colleague and friend, the anthropologist Frederick Starr, than those of Laughlin. In 1891, Starr had published a series of articles on "Dress and Adornment" in *Popular Science Monthly*. Written when he was a curator at the American Museum of Natural History in New York, these essays explored differing definitions of feminine beauty from an ethnological perspective.[16] Drawing on the German

3 Mechanisms of Consumption

Figure 3.2
Potenberg's Shoe Store, 872 North Lincoln Avenue (now 2959 North Lincoln Avenue), c. 1895.

art historian Ernst Grosse's *Anfänge der Kunst* (*The Beginnings of Art*), which he was in the process of translating for an American audience, Starr claimed that while "clothing" may be practical, "dress" should always be understood as a form of ornament.[17] Beginning with practices of body painting, tattooing, piercing, and the binding of skulls and feet, Starr presented these acts of bodily deformation as marks of social affiliation or distinction; in subsequent essays, he addressed dress, jewelry, and religious regalia as developments of these early forms of self-ornamentation.

At the World's Columbian Exposition, where Starr worked as a curator, ethnographic displays ranging from the scientific intent of the Anthropological Building to sideshow spectacles on the Midway Plaisance provided plentiful opportunity to study ethnography practically, as he put it, and to observe the exotic forms of dress he described. Dressed in traditional costumes, the human exhibitors at the replica South Sea Island (Samoan and Fijian), Chinese, Javanese, Laplander, Turkish, and North and West African villages stood ready to enact versions of their domestic and

Figure 3.3
View of the Administration Building, looking south from Wooded Island bridge, World's
Columbian Exposition, 1893.

ceremonial rituals for the entertainment of paying audiences. While he echoed Starr's approach, Veblen's focus was not on the exotic dress of the living ethnographic exhibits at the fair but on the crowds who came to see them.

Monumental and ordered, the primary buildings of the world's fair offered an aesthetic alternative to the eclecticism of the midway. Strolling between the Electricity and Mines buildings, visitors experienced one of the many picturesque vistas laid out by the fair's designers, an artificial boulevard flanked by matching neoclassical buildings, terminating in the magnificent domed Administration Building. For devotees of urban reform and members of the City Beautiful movement, this fantastic scene was an image of the future of the American city. In this photograph, the dark figures that populate the broad avenue contrast with their stark white backdrop. The woman on the right presents an attenuated silhouette, her leg-of-mutton sleeves as wide as her waist is narrow, her feathered toque offering no function except ornament. She is modern in the same way her environment is modern. Yet, for Veblen, she performs no less a signifying role than the human exhibitors at the midway. In his essay, he sought an economic explanation for the absurdity of this dress, focusing on the difference between the striking figure of the elegant woman and her more simply dressed male counterparts, clad in homburgs and overcoats, their collars turned up against a cold Chicago wind.

Though Veblen's writing is often verbose, he came straight to the point: "dress is the index of the wealth of the economic unit which the wearer represents. Under the patriarchal organization of society, where the social unit was the man (with his dependents), the dress of the women was an exponent of the wealth of the man whose chattels they were. In modern society, where the unit is the household, the woman's dress sets forth the wealth of the household to which she belongs." Though society was no longer strictly patriarchal (in anthropological terms, at least), "there is that about the dress of women which suggests that the wearer is something in the nature of a chattel; indeed, the theory of woman's dress quite plainly involves the implication that the woman is a chattel. In this respect, the dress of women differs from that of men."[18] In leisure-class culture, he continued, where the possession of wealth and goods endows social distinction, women's dress takes on an essentially honorific function as a symbol of her household's affluence. Employing an ethnographic parallel designed to provoke his readers, Veblen cited "the extra portion of butter, or other unguent, with which the wives of the magnates of the African interior anoint their persons, beyond what comfort requires. ... So also the pelt of the arctic fur seal, which the women of civilized countries prefer to fabrics that are preferable to it in all respects but that of expense. So also, the ostrich plumes and the many curious effigies of plants and animals that are dealt in by the milliners."[19] With this comparison, Veblen collapsed the apparent distance between residents of the thatched and plastered huts representative of Dahomey in West Africa, or Samoa in the South Sea Islands, and the fashionably dressed women shopping on State Street.

From these observations, Veblen outlined the three cardinal principles of his theory of woman's dress: conspicuous expensiveness, novelty (demonstrating conspicuous waste), and conspicuous abstention from useful effort. This last principle explained the persistence of the high-heeled boot, the floor-length skirt with its cumbersome and complex draperies, and the constraining corset. The corset was a particular target of Veblen, one he would return to in *The Theory of the Leisure Class*. Lowering its wearer's vitality, the corset rendered her unfit for work. But despite its restrictions, she voluntarily accepted physical incapacity, measuring the worth of the garment in "the gain in reputability which comes of her visibly increased expensiveness and infirmity."[20] Modern women wear corsets, Veblen argued, because they must appear idle to be respectable. Even in the poorest homes, he noted, it is the housewife who must fulfil the function of honorific waste, even when her husband makes no attempt at it.

Drawing on anthropological writing on the practice known as "ownership marriage," he associated this gender disparity with the barbarian stage of human evolution. In such societies, women captured from competing tribes during warfare served as decorative trophies, seen as evidence of a man's predatory or accumulative prowess. As Nils Gilman puts it, "ownership, which was nothing but the institutionalization of the right to exclusive consumption, arose directly out of the capture of women in warfare.

3 Mechanisms of Consumption

The subjugation of women was thus the foundational act, one might say, of a consumer society."[21] Exhibiting a startlingly contemporary understanding of gender identity, Veblen conceded that many of the principles he ascribed to women applied also to "a large class of persons who, in the crude biological sense, are men."[22] In this category, he included clergymen with their embroidered vestments and academics with their gowns. Both, he argued, perform unproductive and largely honorific roles on behalf of leisure-class society.

The Theory of the Leisure Class is often cited alongside works by Veblen's German-speaking contemporaries, sociologists Georg Simmel and Werner Sombart, and the Austrian architect and Anglophile Adolf Loos.[23] Common to their writing is the evolutionary argument that metropolitan excess was leading to cultural degeneration (accompanied by an economic rationale for reform), with women's clothing as the ultimate exemplar of cultural decline. Fashion, above all, exemplified the new mode of social relations: mass production had made a cornucopia of goods available, and the anonymity of metropolitan living made it as easy to try on a new persona as it was to try on new clothes.[24] In Veblen's terms, the residents of large urban centers had become beholden to an economy of wasteful inefficiency, in which the demand for constant novelty made production the servant of consumption. Here, Veblen is closely aligned with Sombart, whose 1913 book *Luxury and Capitalism* established the importance of the luxury market for capitalist expansion.[25] But in another sense, his position is closer to that of Simmel, who approached the topic of fashion from a dual sociological and psychological point of view. Emphasizing fashion's role as a signifier of conformity, Simmel understood it as a marker of class distinction and a social institution that satisfies the antagonistic human instincts for imitation and self-expression.[26] Because women have historically occupied a weaker social position than men, he argued, they were more inclined to follow social convention, which explained their greater interest in fashion. Their elaborate dress was a form of compensation for their supplemental social role.

In his discussion of the perversity of female fashion, linking it to the origins of consumerism in barbarian societies, Veblen

Figure 3.4
Jackson Street and Sherman Street, Chicago, c. 1910. J. W. Taylor, photographer.

has particular parallels with Loos.[27] Indeed, Veblen's putative influence on Loos accounts for much of the importance Veblen is given in histories of architecture and material culture, where *The Theory of the Leisure Class* is often discussed alongside Loos's manifesto "Ornament and Crime" (1908).[28] Even Theodor Adorno noted similarities between Veblen's critique of consumption and what he described as Loos's "functionalism."[29] Famously, Loos attacked the inventive ornament of the Art Nouveau movement

3 Mechanisms of Consumption

by comparing it to tattooing and associating it with the primitive, the criminal, and the sexually deviant. Like Veblen, he used the example of contemporary women's dress, restrictive and highly decorative, to argue the need for simplicity in modern architecture and design. And, like Veblen, he inverted the dominant nineteenth-century theory of racial progress, using it as a mechanism to critique present-day culture, though without challenging it as scientific fact. Widely read in the early twentieth century, Loos's polemic captures a key theme of modern architecture and design, the desire to decouple architecture from style, freeing it to exist outside the marketplace. Just as dress reformers called for the release of women from the "slavery" of the corset, Loos called for architecture's emancipation from the consumer system, making it, too, an enemy of fashion.

Anticipating the rhetoric of the avant-garde, Loos's radical proposal involved stripping architecture of any signifier of novelty and employing instead strict aesthetic anonymity grounded in the moral authority of advanced industrial production.[30] For Loos, this meant rejecting bourgeois European culture and wholeheartedly adopting what he called western culture, by which he meant English and American culture.[31] As a twenty-two-year-old, he had been one of the thousands of foreign tourists drawn to the spectacle of the World's Columbian Exposition. His brief visit to Chicago came at the beginning of a three-year stay in the United States, during which he spent extended periods in Philadelphia and then New York.[32] This trip was an epiphany for the young Loos, who enthusiastically embraced the American lack of deference to convention, comparing it favorably to what he saw as the oppressive and backward-looking culture of Austria and Germany. He saw in the cities he visited a landscape of advanced production where consumption was equalized, made available to all in the form of well-designed, mass-produced goods. In later years, he described a moment of revelation. Seeing an elegantly designed suitcase in a New York City store window, a simple leather case bound with copper, he could not stop thinking about it, even the next day: here, he realized, was the modern style.[33]

For early historians of modern architecture, America was the vital mediator between the old and new worlds, and Loos was a prophet of Anglo-Saxon functionalism in the dying Austro-Hungarian empire.[34] At the risk of overstating his importance, he may serve as a stand-in for European visitors for whom the United States represented an advanced industrial society, supported by an egalitarian political doctrine that did away with ideas of class and social difference, a place where immigrants threw off the conventions of the old world. Freed from historical prejudice, they were converted to a new, realist mindset.[35] For many of these visitors, the most modern thing about Chicago was not the pseudo-European enclave of the world's fair at Jackson Park, an artificial city of boulevards defined by manmade lakes, but the wholly original metropolis of towers that dominated the intersection of Lake Michigan and the Chicago River. While Chicago's boosters promoted the neoclassical splendor of the Federal Building with its impressive dome, Europeans were more interested in the imposing masses of the skyscrapers surrounding it. Rising from the sidewalk to dizzy heights, supported by steel-framed armatures and unrelieved by aesthetic modulation, these innovative structures seemed to provide evidence of superior technological progress, the evolution of a new industrial aesthetic. Viewed selectively, with plainer forms privileged and historical eclecticism ignored, these commercial monuments formed the canon of modern American architecture in histories written in the early decades of the twentieth century.

The Theory of the Leisure Class has often been interpreted as supporting this narrative. But although Veblen, like Loos, believed industrial innovation was the basis of evolutionary progress, he was much more ambivalent about the changes he saw taking place around him. His refusal to speculate on the shape of the future indicates, perhaps, that he saw the present moment not as a temporary way station but as an interregnum of uncertain duration.

The two books Veblen published while living in Chicago may be read as two halves of a whole. The theme of his second book, The Theory of Business Enterprise, is "the inherent conflict between 'business,' the financial interests who are concerned primarily with profit, and 'industry,' those forces that are geared to production."[36] From his position as an economist at the University of Chicago, Veblen was well placed to see that conflict at work. Although

3 Mechanisms of Consumption

Figure 3.5
Pedestrians looking in Marshall Field & Company windows, 1910.

essentially regressive, he argued, American society was undergoing an internal evolution. A new phase of barbarism was emerging, he warned, one that took advantage of industrial production to promote the growth of the market economy. In an advanced leisure-class society, barbarism involved preserving archaic aesthetic forms (as in the case of the university) and marshaling the publicity value of aesthetic novelty. Moving its focus beyond the elite members of the leisure class, Veblen's second book approaches the subject of embryonic consumer culture. From the women looking into the windows of the Marshall Field store who advertised their incapacity for work through their pristine white dresses, so impractical in the smoky atmosphere of the heavily polluted city, Veblen turned his reader's attention to the windows themselves.

Architecture as Advertising

In the transition from *The Theory of the Leisure Class* to *The Theory of Business Enterprise*, Veblen's discussion of conspicuous consumption moves from the familial to the corporate, from the private homes and elite social institutions of Prairie Avenue and the Gold Coast to the downtown Loop shopping district. As with modern individuals, he wrote, the businesses that sprang up there could no longer establish their reputation through personal relationships: they must signify prestige and good repute through visual and material language, communicating quality, desirability, and corporate trustworthiness. This drive spurred not only the design of State Street architecture but also the creation of State Street itself. The vision of Field and Leiter's early partner, Potter Palmer, the famous thoroughfare features in numerous late nineteenth-century guidebooks as evidence of Chicago's thriving economy and its aspiration to compete with the largest and most glamorous of the world's cities.[37] Inspired by a trip to Paris in 1867, Palmer lobbied to have the street widened after the model of Baron Haussmann's boulevards so that it might serve as a privileged commercial thoroughfare with his grand hotel, the Palmer House, as its centerpiece. Running six blocks south from Randolph Street to Van Buren, State Street became the premier landscape of consumption in the American Midwest, integrated into the city infrastructure by the circuit of streetcars and elevated railway lines known as the Loop.

On State Street, shopping was a form of leisure. The department stores built there were a new kind of business, not fixed and stable in form but constantly changing. In the 1870s, most businesses that filled the blocks of the downtown Loop were designed as two-dimensional planar facades with little sense of the built volume behind them. This included most retailers, even the large dry-goods emporiums. In line with Veblen's principle of the "canon of taste," the reputation of the businesses within was enhanced by reference to historical forms. As new buildings were constructed, one aside another, companies took advantage of the bare brick of party walls to commission painted signage. On the street facades, businesses incorporated signs into the design of entrances and windows, forming a horizontal band between the first and second stories, and later using reflective gold paint on the windows themselves. This landscape was constantly changing, with buildings erected and demolished in rapid succession as the value of the land increased, and landowners sought to keep up with fashion.

3 Mechanisms of Consumption

Figure 3.6
Marshall Field & Company buildings, view from across the street intersection, c. 1902.

By the turn of the twentieth century, this commercial landscape was in transition. Streets lined with two-dimensional storefront facades built in the post-fire period, known as "shirtfront-style" buildings, gave way to grander structures conceived in the round, most notably Marshall Field's, as seen here in 1902.[38] Each store vied with its competitors to offer a whole world of affordable luxury goods. Modeled on the arcade, these stores needed to be big to deal with the volume of products they offered. They needed to be well-lit and easy to move through. And they needed to be impressive both inside and out, designed with what Veblen called "decorative or spectacular intent."[39]

Fashion and the Department Store 147

Figure 3.7 Interior view of Marshall Field & Company retail store, c. 1900.

Conceived under compulsion of the principle of publicity, Marshall Field's and its competitors incorporated amenities designed to appeal to female shoppers, such as cafes, restaurants, and ladies' lounges.[40] Numerous new technologies, including electric lighting, elevators, pneumatic-tube cash payment systems, and forced ventilation, advanced the business and impressed customers. Encompassing all, a new structural system developed in the 1880s—the "Chicago construction," as *Industrial Chicago* described it in 1896—allowed the "architect, the decorator, and the remodeler" to produce "a revolution in the building arts."[41] Based on the steel frame, this revolutionary system enabled architects to construct enormous structures with light and airy interiors, such as the central atrium of Marshall Field & Company, which featured tier upon tier of goods on display, top-lit by a glazed skylight. Spacious and expansive, with a cornucopia of goods visible all at once, the store's interior was like a "permanent yet ever-changing exposition," as Marshall Field's described itself.[42]

In Veblen's terms, this spectacular environment was part of the "mechanics of consumption."[43] A branch of public relations, the profession of architecture was a business practice aimed at investing value and meaning into inert material. Like Karl Marx, Veblen was deeply interested in the animistic powers people attribute to inanimate objects, principally the power to bestow the good opinion of others on those who possessed particular objects. In this way, Veblen's concept of conspicuous consumption is linked to Marx's "commodity fetishism."[44] The industrial revolution produced a consumer economy in which goods were made not primarily for practical purposes but to display status. According to both Marx and Veblen, the modern age retained aspects of the magical thinking of the archaic period. Influenced by the example of captains of industry and their families, working-class immigrants to the metropolis who were imported as labor to operate the urban production machine quickly learned the habit of acquisition. However, writing in the mid-1890s, Veblen differed from Marx in his belief that this habit held a powerful grip over even the poorest city dweller.[45] For Veblen, the collective psychology of pecuniary emulation—the desire to be seen well in the eyes of one's neighbors—outweighed the rational self-interest that would

3 Mechanisms of Consumption

lead to revolution by the working class. Unlike Marx's theory in which class position was fixed, for Veblen, movement across the divide demarcating the leisure and laboring classes was an ever-present possibility.

The Theory of the Leisure Class proposed that all members of the urban population participate, in some way, in the logic of conspicuous consumption. While the leisure class set standards of taste for others to follow, this taste was on display not only through their own personal consumption, visible as they prome-naded through the streets, but also through the combined efforts of advertising companies, salespeople, and window dressers.

The department store was designed to cater to a wide range of consumer budgets: even the lowest wage earner sought the approval of her peers through the purchase of items such as hats, shoes, gloves, and handkerchiefs. As they expressed in the pages of journals and related publications, department store architects saw themselves as rational-minded professionals, responding pragmatically to the functional requirements of the new business type. In this sense, they might be seen as specialist technicians, members of the class that Veblen believed would lead the way toward the evolution of an industrial society. Yet, as a typology, the department store was far from Veblen's ideal. Inside and out, from frame construction to store window, it was the realization of the mechanics of consumption in an advanced form.

Theory of Business Enterprise argues that, in the years following the Civil War, a new chapter in the operation of American busi-ness began. The barbarian "capitalist-employer" had taken hold of the community's industrial efficiency and, through his ownership and control of its resources and equipment, used this efficiency for his own gain. As Veblen explained, this process exponentially increased when the pecuniary magnate replaced the individual capitalist. Instead of running a single business, this magnate con-trolled many, in the form of trusts, mergers, and other forms of corporate combinations. As corporate empires expanded, all parts of the economy, from manufacturing to shipping to marketing, became tied together, parts of a coordinated whole that Veblen called the "concatenation of industries," the latest step in the evolution of economics which Alan Trachtenberg has called "the incorporation of America."[46] For Veblen, this was an embryonic new phase of capitalism, business enterprise on a higher plane. Still a fundamentally barbarian society, it did not yet exploit the efficiency of industrial systems for the benefit of all. Instead, inefficiencies abound, and both industrial and human progress is arrested so long as consumption drives production.

Veblen condemned the increasingly corporatized organization of industrial production and its associated marketing, which he saw as the height of industrial inefficiency. Controlled by managers and highly skilled salespeople rather than engineers and mechanics, the role of business was now not to make goods but to increase profitability. With its method of selling goods and its physical design, the department store was just such an organization. Here, the producer and the consumer had no direct relationship—a middleman handled selling. The fixing and standardization of the prices of consumable goods "occur in a particularly evident and instructive way in the practice of the department stores, where the seller fixes the price and meets the buyer only through the intervention of a salesman who has no discretion as to the terms of sale."[47] Architecture had a role to play here, both as the "plant," or functional premises, and as a form of advertising.

The primary purpose of advertising, now an essential branch of business, was to continually raise the standard of living. Veblen was one of many turn-of-the-century commentators to address modern advertising methods as an integral part of the capitalist economy.[48] Contrary to popular thought, he argued, the standard of living was not fixed, based on the needs of subsistence and a basic level of comfort; rather, it was a dynamic scale based on the manner of living thought acceptable at a particular moment in time.[49] Because the standard is relative, no amount of technical or mechanical invention would allow universal access to the highest standard of living: even as the standard improves for the lowest, what is thought socially acceptable will increase. Although each class seeks to emulate the standard of living of the class directly above it, the ultimate judges are those in the highest level of society, in other words, the leisure class. (Academics, Veblen noted wryly, are in an especially difficult position because, although they associate with those of a higher class,

3 Mechanisms of Consumption

they are relatively poorly paid. Of all classes, he concluded, they spend the highest proportion of their income on "conspicuous waste.")[50] The role of advertising was, of course, to continually raise expectations:

> It frequently happens that an element of the standard of living which set out with being primarily wasteful, ends with becoming, in the apprehension of the consumer, a necessary of life; and it may in this way become as indispensable as any other item of the consumer's habitual expenditure. As items which sometimes fall under this head, and are therefore available as illustrations of the manner in which this principle applies, may be cited carpets and tapestries, silver table service, waiter's services, silk hats, starched linens, and many articles of jewelry and of dress.[51]

In other words, what was a luxury for one generation became a necessity for the next.

For some of Veblen's contemporaries, the encouragement of consumption was a form of seduction, an appeal to feminine base instincts. But although his initial discussion of consumer culture depended on the unequal relationship between men and women in leisure-class societies, Veblen did not interpret advertising in gendered terms, or at least not explicitly. Instead of focusing on women as a special group, *The Theory of Business Enterprise* highlights the importance of marketing for consumers of all kinds. Citing Marx's *Capital*, Veblen talked of advertising as a crucial part of converting goods into profit: the sale is the last step in the process, the end of "the businessman's endeavor."[52] In other words, advertising was an accepted part of the cost of production. This cost included employing a whole raft of employees, such as salesmen, sign writers, and display artists. It also included architects' fees. In advanced pecuniary culture, Veblen explained, the primary task of the architect was to design a building that communicated or, in business terms, "advertised" reputability. Like other forms of marketing, the work of the modern architect expressed not fixed and eternal values but the ever-changing appeal of the new.

The Display Window

In Chicago, novelty in the form of constant changes to the commercial streetscape was the norm. The disastrous fire of 1871, which destroyed almost all the buildings within the city's compact commercial core, was a dramatic purge that appeared at first to erase all that the city had achieved in forty years. Still, in another sense, it was merely an accelerated version of the process of demolition and rebuilding that was to characterize the Western metropolis for the next hundred years. The rapid and dramatic rise of the city attracted both awe and opprobrium. Foreign visitors were shocked at the result. Walking the canyon-like streets thrown into shadow by the tall towers on either side, they were overwhelmed by the cacophonous noise of crowds, streetcars, and the elevated trains that screeched overhead, and nauseated by the filthy, polluted atmosphere, the product of thousands of coal-fired chimneys.[53] Many also criticized the business practices that formed this landscape. Large companies such as Marshall Field & Company and its competitors achieved dominance by ruthlessly undercutting their competitors, putting smaller stores out of business. Constant renovations and expansions were signs of prestige and success.

As large companies drove smaller ones out of business, they expanded across contiguous rental premises, employing architects to design new frontages and signage to unify disparate buildings. For example, in 1898, the Mandel Brothers store employed Jenney and Mundie to remove the lower-level stonework of three existing buildings and wrap them with a common facade at the first- and second-floor levels, a facade notable for its innovative use of Luxfer prism glass and elaborate ornamental ironwork executed by Winslow Brothers and Co.[54] So rapid was the turnover in commercial premises on this privileged commercial boulevard that photographs of State Street taken even a few years apart capture very different scenes. As successful stores grew, they rented more and more space. Architects and engineers added new stories on top of existing buildings and connected older buildings to new premises next door. They nipped and tucked buildings like a dress on a dressmaker's dummy, uniting adjacent structures with a band of standard store windows and signage, stitching additions alongside,

3 Mechanisms of Consumption

Figure 3.8
Christmas shoppers on State Street, c. 1905. Mandel Brothers department store, with a new facade by Jenney and Mundie, is on the right.

lopping off outdated rooflines to add more stories on top. Like trimming an old hat or gown with a new ribbon each season, the imperative of fashion drove this practice of constant remodeling.

Of all the architectural mechanisms designed to increase sales, one of the most important features of the department store was the street-front display window.[55] From the 1870s, merchants exploited the show window as a "sidewalk sales device," with a strong influence on consumer behavior, converting casual pedestrians into customers. As the *Inland Architect* recognized in 1898, the conversion of older-style commercial facades into transparent show windows was part of a broader trend, one that would have a significant impact on the streets of Chicago: "In place of crude stone carvings of 'after-the-fire' architecture appears a style of architecture entirely American and of commercial origin. This style was invented by necessity. The demand of the window dresser—an artist of recent development—was constantly for a more showy place in which to exhibit his goods; and the buyers demanded more light."[56] Along with New York City, Chicago was a major center of display window innovation. Holidays, changes in season, and important national events were a pretext for new displays. Large stores hired dedicated display staff, including highly skilled window trimmers, or dressers, whose designs communicated the store's prestige and the range and desirability of the goods for sale inside. Members of a brand-new profession, window dressers taught potential customers a new way to engage with goods.[57] Balancing artistry, technological know-how, and a sense of what would sell, they adopted aesthetic forms from the fine and applied arts to give their work authority and appeal. Sculptural stacking, pleating, and draping were an essential part of the window dresser's arsenal. Elaborate in their conception and frequently changed, store windows enhanced the visual and material interest of the items they displayed.

Although the transparent window-wall was to become a fundamental element of modern architecture, an element identified with industrial and social progress in the early twentieth century, it emerged from purely commercial imperatives. With their large display windows, the early department stores came to dictate the form of the buildings constructed to house them.[58] In a 1908 article entitled "On the Nature of Capital," Veblen addressed this architectural mechanism directly.[59] The theme of this article is his lifelong obsession with economic inefficiency. Veblen's larger point is that technological innovation is not inherently progressive; it may be abused, leading to, in his words, the "perversion of industrial efficiency." By "perversion," he meant that the "disposition of the industrial forces entails a net waste or detriment to the community's livelihood."[60] The first example Veblen cites is military production, the case of weapons and armaments. He then moves on to other areas of business where function and waste (which he calls "serviceability and disserviceability") are mingled. These include retail stores, where, again, he notes that advertising is essential. Businesses such as department stores spend vast amounts of money to employ persuasive salespeople whose job it is to secure customers. Outside, they create "convincing, not to say vain-glorious, show-windows that shall promise something more than one would like to commit oneself to in words." The store window is one of the many "appliances of marketing," including "printed matter, sign-boards, and the like with a view

3 Mechanisms of Consumption

to creating a certain body of goodwill," he noted.[61] Ultimately, Veblen argued, marketing was a parasitic industry, one that lowered "the effective vitality of the community" in the same way as expenditure on war.[62]

One of the most celebrated monuments of Chicago School architecture embodies Veblen's idea of the mechanics of consumption: Louis Sullivan's Schlesinger & Mayer department store (later known as Carson Pirie Scott & Co.). An alternative to the photographs published in architectural histories (see figure 3.9) shows Sullivan's famous store in its commercial and human context, sitting across Madison Street from the Mandel Brothers department store. In front of these stores, an early automobile shares the cobbled street with horses and streetcars; full-skirted women and bowler-hatted men brush past each other on the sidewalks, crossing the street without apparent order or pattern. With their glamorous design, lavish seasonal displays, and sophisticated marketing campaigns, we can see why *The Theory of the Leisure Class* may have conjured to mind these stores. Unlike Mrs. Potter Palmer's grand ballroom or the cloistered halls of the University of Chicago, State Street was open to all. As much as the fox-fur stoles or ostrich-feather trimmed hats of the women who peered in their windows and crowded through their doors, the street's glittering retail emporiums were, surely, the obvious and palpable products of pecuniary culture.

In 1891, Schlesinger & Mayer hired Adler and Sullivan to give a unified architectural expression to their original store, located in a series of adjoining buildings in the block bounded by State, Madison, Wabash, and Monroe streets. In 1898, after Adler and Sullivan dissolved their partnership, Sullivan was commissioned to design a new flagship building for the company to replace the existing one on the corner of State and Madison. Constructed in two stages, a nine-story, three-bay building on Madison Street was completed first. The main twelve-story block with three bays on Madison and seven on State was completed in 1903, and the following year it was renamed Carson Pirie Scott & Co. following a change of ownership.[63] Like the newly remodeled Mandel Brothers across the street, Sullivan's building made a feature of its store windows, complete with Luxfer prisms and ironwork by Winslow Brothers and Co.

Figure 3.9
View of the intersection of State and Madison streets, including Mandel Brothers store on the left and the entrance to the Carson Pirie Scott & Co. building on the right, Chicago, c. 1905. Barnes-Crosby Company, photographer.

Drawing on the formula he had established for the tall office building in the early 1890s, Sullivan divided the volume into three horizontal layers consisting of a two-story "mercantile base" decorated in a "sumptuous" way to "attract the eye"; a variable number of office tiers above this; and finally an attic, which signified the vertical termination of the building.[64] Though the upper levels are plain, expressing the scale and rationality of large-scale business production, Sullivan recognized the necessity of advertising as part of this kind of business operation and gave the mercantile base special prominence. Working with his assistant Grant Elmslie, he developed a distinctive dark-green metallic frame for the street-level display windows. The design of these windows was part of an effort to brand the store with a memorable visual identity. Beautiful and intricate, the design consists of a foliated decorative motif within a geometric frame repeated in the store's interior. From the grid of decorative ironwork, a richly ornamented canopy shades the goods on show behind the large plate glass windows. Behind this transparent facade, displays of folded and pleated fabrics suggest elegant dinner tables and future costumes yet to be made.

As Joseph Siry has noted, Sullivan's ornamental motifs became a vital part of the store's marketing, echoed in Carson Pirie Scott & Co.'s newspaper advertising: "the interplay between the architecture and advertising graphics helped cultivate readers' image of the store in the printed medium in anticipation of the experience of the building itself."[65] Here Veblen's description of the marriage of all forms of advertising technology is complete: the cast-bronze window surrounds frame the products on display in much the same way as the controlling grid of the newspaper page. The display window was a built technology of publicity, a material construction that reinforced immaterial expressions of innovation and modishness, and vice versa. A mechanism for communicating modern taste, it abstracted real material objects (rendered temporarily inaccessible behind sheets of plate glass) into desirable, visually consumable commodities.[66] Applied to the street-level facade of Carson Pirie Scott & Co., Sullivan's decorative strategy is Veblen's mechanics of consumption developed into an art form.

But while Sullivan's ornamented windows undoubtedly had a commercial function—to draw attention to the store and establish

Figure 3.10
Carson Pirie Scott & Co. store, Chicago, 1899. Louis H. Sullivan, architect.

an image for the company as a purveyor of affordable luxury—
the architect sublimated that pragmatic function into a broader,
social one. Though he was undoubtedly aware of the social conditions that produced the new building type—real estate conventions, structural technology, its interior program—Sullivan had
no interest in expressing them directly. For him, the new commercial buildings rising on the streets of Chicago symbolized the
power of American business to achieve great things through sheer
will and heroic determination. His ornamental plant motifs were,
above all, a metaphor for growth. In applying them to architectural surfaces, he sought to naturalize the processes of business
and industrial development that produced building types such
as department stores and skyscrapers. Above all, he linked his
unique brand of organic architecture to the concept of democracy, which he understood not as a formal system of government
but as a philosophy of individual freedom and self-reliance particular to the United States.[67] In this way, mass consumption was
a sign of national progress, particularly when compared to less
evolved European culture. It is this quality that Sullivan intended

his ornament to reflect: the image of the new society being forged in the United States.

Though Sullivan expressed these ideas using portentous language (published contemporaneously, his essays are as florid as Veblen's are convoluted), they were far from unusual. Display windows offered the illusion of shared material prosperity, the idea that the standard of living acceptable to the best families might, through hard work, be attained by all. Business owners and social reformers believed shopping was more than a leisure activity; the department store, in particular, was considered an aid to assimilation, a means for personal self-improvement, if not reinvention.[68] In an era of significant social instability, such stores played an important role in the fashioning of new American citizens: here, immigrants from Ireland, Germany, Scandinavia, Bohemia, Italy, or eastern Europe could learn how to dress, behave, and ultimately succeed as Americans.

The settlement house founder Jane Addams echoed the belief in shopping as a democratic institution when she argued it was wrong to judge working-class women for spending a significant part of their income on clothing. Writing in *Atlantic Monthly* in 1899, Addams argued that when immigrant women imitate, "sometimes in more showy and often in more trying colors, in cheap and flimsy material, in poor shoes and flippant hats, the extreme fashion of the well-to-do ... they are striving to conform to a common standard which their democratic training presupposes belongs to us all."[69] When an Italian woman lays aside her "picturesque kerchief" for a "cheap street hat," Addams claimed, she takes her first step toward "democratic expression." To be fashionable was to participate in a common American culture, to fulfil a fantasy of achieving the dream of wealth and material prosperity.[70]

Veblen's *Theory of the Leisure Class* essentially confirms these ideas, though with little enthusiasm for the quality of the national culture being created. Shopping was an important activity within the urban economy of nineteenth-century America. New kinds of stores made fashion accessible to a broad audience of potential consumers from the wealthiest matron to the shop girl and the domestic servant. From Marshall Field & Company, Mandel Brothers, Schlesinger & Mayer, and Carson Pirie Scott & Co. to more egalitarian stores further south on State Street and in the Chicago suburbs, the humblest patron could afford to buy a small item, such as a comb, a piece of ribbon, gloves, or a handkerchief, if not a few yards of cotton to make a dress. Making mass-produced luxury goods available to all, the department store collapsed the distinction between classes and tied workers to ever-more exploitative systems of production and merchandising. While Veblen was not overtly moralistic about this situation, he identified fashion as an essential part of what he called the "propaganda of culture."[71] Such propaganda promoted the instinct for pecuniary emulation. Teaching the laboring class a taste for fashionable rather than functional goods, it encouraged working people to participate in, and thus perpetuate, the leisure-class economy.

Downplaying the threat of socialism to the United States (a threat he considered exaggerated), Veblen mused that working-class Americans living in big cities were conditioned to be aspirational.[72] Expanding on this idea in *The Theory of Business Enterprise*, Veblen reasoned that because modern industries needed a highly mobile labor force, workers were always moving from place to place. They, like the material they handled, became commodified, paid by the hour for their labor and valued by their social peers through their appearance and personal possessions. As a result, he writes, "The working population is required to be standardized, movable, and interchangeable in much the same impersonal manner as the raw or half wrought materials of industry. From which it follows that the modern workman cannot advantageously own a home. By force of this latter feature of the case he is discouraged from investing his savings in real property, or, indeed, in any of the impedimenta of living. ... The conditions of life imposed upon the working population by the machine industry discourage thrift."[73] Discouraged from saving and unable to form stable social bonds, even the lowest wage earners spent a portion of their weekly salary on simple goods, seeking to emulate the style of their better-dressed neighbors. "Under modern conditions, a free expenditure in consumable goods is a condition requisite to good repute," Veblen wrote.[74]

The argument that aesthetics had been corrupted by consumerism was common in this period: the rise of the capitalist economy

3 Mechanisms of Consumption

had resulted in the essential commodification of all social relations, and the status once conferred by luxury goods could now be bought and sold. Along with his academic colleagues, Veblen presented his position in evolutionary terms, associating the profligate display of luxury and ornament with racial devolution. As T. J. Jackson Lears has noted, this position was not unusual in turn-of-the-century American culture, where concern with excessive consumption was part of a wider fear about the overcivilization of the American race.[75] This fear was particularly prevalent among the educated class, where leading thinkers developed the theme of the enervating and degenerating effects of city life, a theme that also had popular appeal. For Lears, Veblen's "critique resonates with a long tradition in Anglo-American Protestant culture: the Puritan's plain-speak assault on theatrical artifice and effete display."[76] The particular susceptibility of women to the lure of metropolitan pleasures is a recurring theme across the discourse of consumption in this period, including in the genres of American naturalist and realist literature. For example, the novels of Frank Norris and Theodore Dreiser evoke the same moral and sexual themes as Veblen's writing and provide vividly described Chicago-based settings, both real and imagined, in which they play out.[77]

But whether due to the puritanism of his Norwegian immigrant background or his rational disciplinary outlook, Veblen was not explicit in his discussion of sexual relations as were Norris and Dreiser, or cultural commentators such as Loos. Deriding efforts to create a modern form of ornament, Loos famously argued that conventional decoration appealed only to the culturally backward, criminals, and primitives. Explicitly linking contemporary women's dress and base sexual instincts in his 1898 essay "Ladies Fashion," he described the present day as "a horrible chapter of our cultural history, laying bare mankind's secret lusts ... dreadful perversions and unbelievable vices." Our obsession with fashion exposes our "only barely repressed sensuality," he wrote.[78] Veblen's writing is often positioned in these terms, and indeed *The Theory of the Leisure Class* supports Loos's manifesto in its essential argument. Like Loos, Veblen believed that men are obsessed with a desire to emulate the upper classes and that women seek out fashionable dress to ensnare a suitable man because she receives her

Figure 3.11
Christmas shoppers in front of Marshall Field's department store, 1905.

social status from her husband.[79] Along with the writer and feminist reformer Charlotte Perkins Gilman, whose *Women and Economics* was published a year before *The Theory of the Leisure Class*, Veblen rejected the association commonly drawn between consumption and feminine taste.[80] Instead, he was resolute in describing women as victims, not perpetuators, of a barbaric economic system. In Veblen's view, the culture of conspicuous consumption was fundamentally masculine and hierarchical. Controlled by a small group of social elites, the practice had a damaging influence not only on women but also on the many different ethnic groups that made up the laboring class.

As Theodor Adorno noted, seen through Veblen's lens, where socioeconomic power structures are entirely one-sided, all aspects of culture, from art to fashion, became suspect.[81] Using anthropological methods of analysis, contemporary scholars have reassessed patterns of material creation and display in terms of more complex social forces, recognizing the agency and autonomy of subgroups of all kinds—from immigrant enclaves with their entrenched ethnic traditions to the power of the demimonde of the brothel, the dance hall, and vaudeville theater—to introduce and influence new standards of dress and beauty.[82] Yet *The Theory of the Leisure Class* remains an essential text as one of the first to focus on consumption as a crucial economic category, perhaps the defining category in modern culture.

Connecting the ideas of Simmel, Sombart, and Loos about the social role of fashion with Addams's pragmatic assessment of working-class female identity formation, *The Theory of the Leisure Class* maintains a strict division between leisure and laboring classes. Yet Veblen also understood that members of the urban working class were far from immune from the pressure of pecuniary emulation. Like Addams, he uncoupled the link between consumption, fashion, and morality that supported popular and academic criticism of women who sought out fashionable clothing. To buy and wear the latest style was not to exhibit "good" or "bad" taste, personal refinement or vulgarity, but to adopt the commonly accepted standard of taste that advertised one's social reputability. For a woman of limited means to wear up-to-date clothing was not a sign of profligacy but a rational economic choice made to attain or maintain a social position. Unlike Sombart, who blamed the rise of capitalism on the influence of the courtesan and her debased desire for luxury, Veblen laid the blame on patriarchal barbarianism, a social structure in which women of status were consigned, against their will, to an honorific role. In this schema, the immorality of women's clothing and the perversion of fashion was due not to unchecked sexuality but to the structure of leisure-class society in which consumption played such an important part.

*

In 1889, the mercantile king Levi Z. Leiter commissioned William Le Baron Jenney's office to design an innovative new retail building further south on State Street, the so-called Second Leiter Building, on a block bounded by State, Van Buren, and Congress streets.[83] Close to the Illinois Central railroad suburban depot, Dearborn Station, Rock Island Station, and several horsecar lines, this seemed an ideal location for a second retail center, one that balanced the hub of Marshall Field's at the northern end of State Street. This ambitious aim was not unprecedented: when Field and Leiter moved their dry-goods business from Lake Street to State Street in 1868, they had succeeded in moving the city's commercial center away from the old market streets near the main branch of the Chicago River.[84] Now Leiter aimed to do the same again. As the 1893 *Rand McNally* guide noted, the shopping public, only two decades after the great fire, had come to regard the older retail stores as crowded and unsafe.[85] The guidebook compared the interiors of such stores to rabbit warrens, and implied that they seemed in danger from disastrous conflagrations or structural collapse. An astute businessman, Leiter sensed an opportunity. In contrast to these aggregate piles, his mammoth building occupied the entire length of its block, and was "instructive and healthy to look at, lightsome and airy."[86]

While the Second Leiter Building was less opulent than its competitors, it was a mechanism for profit in its own way. On the exterior, the eight-story structure was notably plain, its structural iron-and-steel skeleton covered with smooth-dressed gray granite. Solid corner piers of granite supported an almost unadorned cornice. Its most impressive innovation was not stylistic but functional. Internalizing the cycle of perpetual renovation characteristic of older stores, and exploiting the flexibility that the Chicago construction allowed, Jenney designed the Second Leiter Building to accommodate up to nine separate tenancies.[87] When it opened in 1891, it housed a single tenant, the Siegel, Cooper & Co. store, a budget competitor to Marshall Fields. Popularly called "the Big Store," Siegel, Cooper & Co. was a retail emporium known for its wide range of moderately priced goods. In the early twentieth century, Jenney's version of the department store—colossal, internally flexible, and aesthetically mute—became a model modern building type.

Although less well-known than *The Theory of the Leisure Class*, Veblen's *Theory of Business Enterprise* anticipates the critique of ornament that powered the rhetoric of modern architecture and design. And it prefigures the ambiguous reception of Sullivan's Carson Pirie Scott & Co. building by architectural critics and historians. When traditional social boundaries were rapidly loosening, the florid ornament of the Victorian era was damningly associated

3 Mechanisms of Consumption

Figure 3.12
Levi Z. Leiter (Second Leiter) Building, Chicago, 1891. Jenney & Mundie, architects; J. W. Taylor, photographer.

with the bourgeois or middle class: no longer considered a legitimate expression of social status, ornamented goods began to be seen as wasteful, signifying the corruption of culture by feminine taste. For Lewis Mumford and others, Sullivan's design for the highly decorative street-level store windows and entrance rotunda seemed to be in the thrall of a regressive aesthetic tendency. In 1924, Mumford described the ornamental base as the last gesture of traditional architecture, clinging to the highest and lowest stories of the "draped cube."[88] The upper levels of the store were a crucial development in the evolution of the modern style, a refinement of the construction type pioneered by Jenney in the Second Leiter Store, and one of the first conscious expressions of the "articulated frame." In contrast, the ornamented base was a relic of nineteenth-century aesthetics. Decorated with historicizing ornament, this icon of the early American skyscraper was compared to the fashionably dressed woman, her natural form constrained by a corset, draped in heavy folds, smothered by a fur wrap, and topped with an impractical feathered hat.

Around the turn of the twentieth century, the landscape of consumption proliferating in American cities became the focus of programs of social amelioration intended to change consumer behavior and improve the lives of vulnerable, predominantly female, workers, both factory employees and saleswomen. As part of the Progressive Era culture of reform, new sites of production—factories and lofts—became signifiers of modernity within architecture culture. Crucially for architects seeking to escape the imperatives of leisure-class ornament, this new model of architecture—efficient, adaptable, and hygienic—appeared to resist the cycle of fashion. Its structural basis was frame construction, a way of building that Veblen had explicitly described as "modern" due to its simplicity and structural rationality.[89] In theory, frame construction was the opposite of "invidious" social expression. Here, the technological potential of building hidden beneath the facade's false disguise was finally revealed, the built realization of both human and industrial evolution. Designed to make production healthy and efficient, the loft building became a model type for modern architects who rejected ornamented, historicist buildings in favor of the example of structures designed for production. Lofts and factory buildings became the architectural symbol of modernity both in the United States and Europe. Initially, *The Theory of the Leisure Class* was used to support this modernist narrative: ornament should be eliminated because it was wasteful, serving no purpose except social display. Instead, architects should turn to simple, efficient, and technologically sophisticated buildings. Chicago played an important role in this story as the place where the unadorned frame-building supposedly first appeared. In the historiographic framework canonized by architectural historian Carl Condit, the architects of the Chicago School took the industrial building, such as the loft and mercantile building, and elevated it using simple massing and refined materials. Yet Veblen referred to commercial architecture in only a few brief sentences: this typology was never his focus. A closer reading of his economics of aesthetics reveals that the reform of leisure-class culture required more than the rejection of ornament and the adoption of an aesthetic of timeless simplicity and standardization. In the case of the department store, the interior frame, no less than the decorative facade, was part of the same "mechanics of consumption." For example, the Second Leiter Building was designed to meet the requirements of mass merchandising not through a decorative facade but through its adaptable interior. According to Veblen's theory, even this unadorned mercantile building, the model of modern architecture with its structure apparently exposed, remained inefficient, or "perverse," when constructed under the auspices of capitalist production.

4 The Business of Vice: The Levee

Walking south down State Street from Washing-
ton and Madison streets, crossing Van Buren and then Harrison, a
pedestrian at the turn into the twentieth century entered an urban
realm dedicated to myriad forms of conspicuous consumption and
leisure, represented most obviously by the vaudeville theaters
offering popular and salacious entertainments. Opened around
1900, the London Dime Museum and Theatre marked the northern
limit of this world, near the corner of State Street and Van Buren,
directly opposite the Siegel, Cooper & Co. department store.
The two buildings could hardly be more different. The facade of
the austere merchandising building that William Le Baron Jenney built for Levi Z. Leiter was a mute screen of plate glass and
stone. Across the street, the building housing the London Dime
Museum was almost invisible behind a plethora of painted sign-
boards. A form of popular entertainment dating back to the early
nineteenth century, dime museums first appeared in Chicago in

Figure 4.1
London Dime Museum and Theatre on State Street between Van Buren and Congress streets, c. 1912.

the early 1880s.[1] A 1905 city guide lists the London Dime Museum under the heading "Questionable Places for Ladies."[2] Like many other commercial premises in Chicago, it occupied several repurposed, conjoined buildings. The upper floors were dedicated to a "first class" museum of oddities, while the ground floor was a vaudeville theater, with performances given several times daily. Across the facades, cartoonish images and large-type signs advertise attractions, including human freaks and the "original Midway dancers," a testament to the lingering exotic appeal of the World's Columbian Exposition.

The obverse of the respectable culture of consumption, the London Dime Museum served as a gateway to the section of State Street notorious for theaters of dubious reputation. The Trocadero, Folly, and Park theaters specialized in vaudeville acts of low appeal, including burlesque shows featuring women in "artistic" or scanty costumes. These theaters were precisely the kind of business Levi Z. Leiter had hoped to displace when he built his new retail hub directly opposite the dime museum at the southern end of the Loop. Described in guidebooks to Chicago's nightlife as "liberal" or "democratic" and certainly not suitable for ladies, these theaters were a "favorite resort for 'bloods' who, having come to town for fun, propose to see all there is in it."[3] In 1912, the same year this photograph was taken, a book published by the Young People's Civic League named these theaters as some of "hundreds of indecent forms of entertainment that have enough air of respectability about them to exist on the borders of Chicago's loop district. Here they flourish and reap their harvest."[4] These diversions were a few steps to even more insalubrious attractions along Custom House Place and South Clark Street. In 1916, the Juvenile Protective Association, an organization with similar aims to the Young People's Civic League, studied fourteen theaters on State Street and found the results "very discouraging."[5] The performance was rated "respectable" in only two. The dances were "coarse, obscene and vulgar" in seven more. In others, "living models" danced "practically nude." The association reported these theaters to the Morals Division of the City Police Department. But while the police did nothing to shut down such performances, other forces were at work to clear this area of its dubious attractions.

As Chicago grew into an important metropolitan trading center, the principal entrepôt of the American West following the Civil War, so, too, did a secondary economy flourish, the business of vice.[6] Around 1900, descriptions of the city's South Side vice district published in novels, tourist guides, and muckraking journalism reveal anxiety about an imagined relationship between fashion, consumption, and immorality. Each genre featured warnings that the department store was a place where innocent young women were in danger of corruption. As guidebooks advised, fashionable dress should not be mistaken for reputability, nor wealth for moral rectitude. According to the moralistic literature of reform, the worlds of respectability and decadence were separated by inches. As the primary boulevard connecting these two worlds, State Street was as dangerous as it was enthralling, a slippery path to dissolution and depravity for the naive and uninitiated, particularly young working women. Veblen's writing on the economics of women's dress, in which the commodification of women was understood as an integral part of leisure-class society, echoes these contemporary narratives connecting excessive consumption with immorality.

Architectural historians have often discussed Veblen's theory of conspicuous consumption in relation to spectacular department stores. Yet to focus too closely on the department store leaves another aspect of his critique of leisure-class culture in the shadows. *The Theory of the Leisure Class* was published in the context of condemnation, nationally and internationally, of Chicago as a city in which corruption ran rampant, tacitly supported by the police, city aldermen, and business leaders. In the notorious area known as the South Side Levee, hotels, vaudeville theaters, saloons, gambling halls, and *bagnios* or brothels offered hedonistic forms of consumption by day and night. Veblen referred to this world obliquely in a chapter entitled "The Belief in Luck," which focuses on the figure of the gambler, a metropolitan type motivated by his anachronistic and irrational beliefs. Curiously, Veblen's comments on the gambler are seldom discussed in the context of the moral climate in which he wrote the book, a strange omission given Chicago's reputation as a center of illicit entertainment.

Veblen's criticism of the seamier aspects of leisure coincided with efforts to break the so-called vice trust that controlled the

4   The Business of Vice

South Side. As part of this process, the network of streets that made up the Levee, and the businesses they supported, were cast as dangerous and indecent, unsanitary and unsafe. Spread by journalists, social reformers, and business interests alike, narratives of health, safety, and morality supported efforts toward what would come to be known, euphemistically, as urban renewal. By the first decade of the twentieth century, the Levee had been cleared, relocated to a segregated district further south around Twenty-Second Street, making way for more profitable businesses including the large loft buildings of Printing House Row.

Although *The Theory of the Leisure Class* appears aligned with the writing of well-known Progressive Era reformers who took on the scourge of vice, including the English journalist William T. Stead and the settlement house worker Jane Addams, Veblen remained suspicious of all aspects of civic reform. While he participated in the critique of consumption as a cultural force, he also pointed out the hypocrisy that sometimes lay behind proposals to reform unhealthy forms of consumption in the name of modernizing the city and its population. Central to his book is the argument that the economic exploitation of women and labor was institutionalized within business practices and protected by the political and legal systems. In such a society, he implied, one could not hope to reform the vice trade without overturning the dominance of business as the preeminent and most powerful social institution.

The Whitechapel of Chicago

Vice was a leisure-class social institution, an industry just like any other in Chicago, an accepted part of the city's economy and geography, and a highly profitable one. Part of the city's fabric beginning with its founding as a western trading post, saloons and gambling dens occupied less valuable sites, constantly moving as the town grew. While every neighborhood had its saloon, an essential social gathering spot for men and a center of local politics, the city also boasted leisure-time institutions that were aimed at visitors, conveniently located around the Loop area hotels and railway stations.[7] In the decades following the Civil War, the city's agricultural, mercantile, and vice industries grew up in tandem, catering to the same market and packaged for easy consumption.[8] Catering to the demand for illicit entertainment and spatially concentrated for ease of access, businesses such as gambling halls, vaudeville theaters, and brothels made up a significant portion of Chicago's income, some of it filtering through to police and politicians through bribes. In the second half of the nineteenth century, the city was known for being "wide open," as the contemporary phrase had it, with liberal policing of its vice laws, where the illicit was hardly underground, but widely advertised and encouraged. Well-covered in popular journalism, city guidebooks, and later reformist tracts, this decadent world was a source of eternal fascination for readers far beyond the city limits.

While there were several vice districts in Chicago in the 1890s, the South Side Levee was the most famous, located as it was right in the shadow of the city's commercial center. The word "levee," meaning an embankment near a river designed to prevent flooding, is also used to refer to a district adjacent to the river. Often neighborhoods of ill-repute, levees were places where classes and races mixed, and drinking, gambling, and prostitution were tolerated. In his indispensable history of Chicago real estate to 1933, Homer Hoyt notes that in the 1860s and '70s, the vice district lay to the west of the section of State Street then being developed into a commercial boulevard, from LaSalle Street to the south branch of the Chicago River.[9] After the 1871 fire, when many of the wooden shanties around the city's periphery burned down, the value of this land increased, and what Hoyt calls "immoral houses" moved south into a district of narrow streets left untouched by the fire, hemmed in by Lake Michigan to the east and the south branch of the Chicago River on the other side.

By 1880, the border between respectability and disrepute fell around Van Buren and Harrison streets, on the west side of State Street. According to a history of Chicago vice published in 1934, "The Levee of unsavory memories was between Van Buren and Twelfth Streets and from State Street to Pacific Avenue. Within the boundaries of this small district, there were more than two hundred dives, ranging from low brothels to extravagantly furnished palaces."[10] Here businesses such as The Log Cabin Saloon,

Figure 4.2
Saloon interior, Chicago, c. 1905.

Heinegabubler's Palace Saloon, and King Yen Lo, one of the earliest "Chop Suey" restaurants, occupied pre-fire buildings along South Clark Street, Custom House Place, and Plymouth Court.[11] Magnificently fitted out behind its innocuous-looking facade, King Yen Lo featured beautifully carved teak furniture inlaid with mother of pearl and curtains of hand-embroidered silk. According to local lore, the same street offered even more exotic attractions, including opium dens: "Every basement in Clark Street between Van Buren and Harrison was a hop-joint, and the stench of opium in its cooking process assailed the nostrils of the passerby."[12] Beyond Clark Street, the southeast section of the Levee bounded by Harrison, Dearborn, and Twelfth streets, and Fifth Avenue was an African American district, sometimes called the "Cheyenne" or the "Whitechapel of Chicago," after London's notorious red-light district.[13] Employing grotesque racial stereotypes, guidebooks described this area as the most dangerous section of the Levee, a modern-day Babylon, a place that all but the bravest thrill-seekers were advised to avoid.

The South Side Levee reached its peak during the World's Columbian Exposition when illicit attractions, served up on an

Figure 4.3
Chinese-owned businesses on Clark Street between Van Buren and Harrison streets, c. 1900–1910.

industrial scale by day and night, enticed the enormous influx of visitors. As Richard Junger, a historian of Chicago's popular media, has written, this "was the ultimate World's Fair attraction, a cacophony of chanting barkers, confidence men and women, street games of thimblerig and three-card monte, clicking beer mugs, flickering lights, and women advertising themselves in windows and doors mixed with the comings and goings of sporting men, pimps, prostitutes, drunks, greenhorns, and a few police."[14]

4   The Business of Vice

To help visitors navigate this exotic world, Chicago journalist Ransom H. "Shang" Andrews published the evocatively titled *Chicago by Day and Night: The Pleasure Seekers Guide to the Paris of America* (1892). (While the book is attributed to Harold Vynne, Andrews may have been the author.) This was an updated version of an earlier book he had published, *Chicago after Dark* (1882).[15] Both were explicit in their descriptions of the attractions on offer. Even reputable guidebooks published by George E. Moran, Frank H. Richardson, the Rand McNally Company, and others augmented their descriptions of the daylight attractions of the city with carefully worded advice about its dark corners.

State Street had been known for its streetwalkers since at least the 1870s, when "Shang" Andrews wrote a series of novels about Chicago's demimonde, including *Cranky Ann, the Street-walker: A Story of Chicago in Chunks* (1878). *Chicago by Day and Night* devoted a chapter to "Adventuresses" or confidence women, including the story of a "mark" picked up outside Marshall Field's by a "splendid creature" described as wearing "fine clothes" and being "a royal blonde, mayhap, or a plump brunette (either will do for the sake of illustration) peeping shyly at him from beneath long silken lashes and smiling ever so slightly."[16] In later years, a body of reform-minded literature appeared that took on the same subject with a different tone, no longer tolerant but outraged and censorious. For example, in the unambiguously titled *Chicago and Its Cess-pools of Infamy* (1910), Samuel Paynter Wilson compared State Street to the boulevards of Paris. From the Chicago River to Twelfth Street, it was thronged with "restless pleasure-seekers, the good and the bad," he wrote. At noon, families stroll; at night, one might encounter parties of theatergoers, out for an evening of innocent amusement, or a "'gang of roughs,' swaggering along the sidewalks, jostling all who come within their way; here, a party of young bloods, out on a lark." Among the crowd, "a number of flashily dressed women," whose business was to lure men into "many of the so-called 'hotels' in the business district or perchance to the back room of some pretentious saloon," where the luckless victims would be drugged and robbed.[17]

In 1894, the English journalist William T. Stead brought the Levee district to international attention when he published a detailed study of vice and corruption in Chicago. Stead had established a reputation as a leading social critic in his work for the liberal *Pall Mall Gazette*, including a sensational exposé of child prostitution in London.[18] Inspired by the example of Leo Tolstoy during a visit to Russia in the 1880s, he had become convinced of the need to follow the example of Christ by living communally as an act of secular service. Reporting on conditions in the worst corners of modern cities was part of this service, a call to action issued to his many readers. This was the impetus for Stead's six-month stay in Chicago from October 1893 to March 1894, which spanned the tail end of the World's Columbian Exposition and the severe economic depression which followed. Much of what we know of the Chicago underworld in this period comes from Stead and the sociological studies he inspired.[19]

Stead's visit spawned two publications; the first, *Chicago Today: The Labor War in America*, focused on the labor-capital divide, and the second, *If Christ Came to Chicago*, on the city's vice industry.[20] Driven by the message of Christian brotherhood in a way that Veblen's book was not, *If Christ Came to Chicago* shares the same basic theme as *The Theory of the Leisure Class*. Using the terms "barbarians" and the "predatory rich" to describe the ruling elite, Stead pressed the members of this class to confront the profound social and economic inequities rupturing the city they had created. *If Christ Came to Chicago* has become a classic of Progressive Era reform literature. Based on firsthand reporting, it contrasted Chicago's wealth and industrial success with the deep social divisions and political corruption all too evident on the streets of the city. Stead was ruthless in attacking the established church for what he saw as its pious ineffectiveness, along with the city's wealthiest citizens, casting them as "commercial deities" whose personal success came at the cost of Christian ethics. Employing similar language to that Veblen used six years later, he described the department store magnate Marshall Field, the meatpacking king Philip Armour, and the railway carriage empresario George Pullman as modern-day barbarians. But although Stead began by condemning powerful business leaders, he did not make them the focus of his study. Instead, he dedicated himself to mapping the landscape of inequity their power created.

Like the police photographer Jacob Riis, whose studies of the Lower East Side of New York were published a few years later, Stead combined traditional journalism with methods borrowed from the social sciences. Famously, *If Christ Came to Chicago* includes a color-coded map of two blocks in the heart of Chicago's vice district, bounded by Clark, Dearborn, Harrison, and Polk streets. Showing the locations of forty-five saloons, thirty-seven brothels, eleven pawnbrokers, and five lodging houses, this diagram has become an iconic graphic, the image of concentrated vice. While Stead's simple map is presented out of context, the blocks he depicted were only a short stroll away from the State Street shopping district.

Understanding prostitution as part of the urban economy, Stead's effort to map and quantify illicit activity in the Levee was part of a wider progressive agenda to order and control the chaos of the late nineteenth-century city, the same statistical approach elsewhere applied to managing legitimate businesses. In his accounting of vice, he was careful to enumerate its connections to those businesses. While conducting his investigation, Stead stayed at a notorious brothel, Carrie Watson's Place, located above Hank North's saloon on South Clark Street. Here, he interviewed a series of colorful characters, including Watson herself. Describing Watson as an "exploiteur, the capitalist of her class," Stead's investigation of the business of prostitution included the sensational claim that Watson and her fellow brothelkeepers procured many of their employees from among the ranks of department store clerks.[21]

A contemporary photograph sets the scene: deep inside the store, within the various departments such as those dedicated to silk materials, gloves, or handkerchiefs, attentive clerks wait for customers to occupy the empty stools in front of their counters. On the right, glass-fronted cases display handkerchiefs as if they were precious exhibits in a museum. The regimented shelves behind the clerks hold stacks of boxes, ready to package the purchases. Extending back into the building, seemingly infinitely, the supply of attractive goods appears never ending. Waiting attentively behind the counter, the female clerks appeared (to a certain type of customer) to be available for purchase and consumption like the goods on display.

Figure 4.4
Marshall Field & Company department store, interior, Chicago, c. 1892–1914. Daniel H. Burnham, architect.

Prompted by Stead's journalistic exposé, this pathway to prostitution became an object of great popular interest, as well as academic study by settlement house workers and sociologists. Around 1910, these forces combined to combat the scourge of what was known as the "white slave trade," in which naive young women, new to big-city life and separated from their families, were lured into prostitution by unscrupulous but persuasive strangers.[22] With its suggestion of forced miscegenation, the white slave trade was a tremendous boon to the newspaper industry, generating thousands of salacious stories of temptation and ruin.

One of these, published in the *Chicago Daily News* in May 1907, described the story of Mona B. Marshall, an alleged "white slave."[23] Rescued during a raid on a Wabash Avenue apartment building in the Twenty-Second Street Levee district, Mona told police she had been held captive for six weeks, and forced to work at the Casino, a "resort" or brothel on South Dearborn Street. As she told police, and later reporters, she had been befriended by a handsome young man while she was working as a clerk at a counter of Marshall Field's department store. He took her out for a chop suey dinner and the theater, before inviting her to the Prima Dance Hall at Thirty-Fifth Street near Indiana Avenue, where she was drugged and abducted.

The scandalous story of Mona Marshall attracted enormous publicity. The *Daily News* article is accompanied by a remarkable photograph of her, which may have been taken at the newspaper office or perhaps at Mona's mother's house, where she was interviewed. Looking directly into the camera, she clasps her hands tightly, elbows resting on the arms of a plain wooden chair. Her hair and face stand out against the background of a newspaper held up by an anonymous man standing behind her. Represented only by his hands, this faceless figure renders the scene sinister. Yet Mona, perhaps inured to exposure, is guarded in her expression. With her simple blouse with a high-necked collar and a modest bow at the waist, she is an unlikely representative of the dissolute life. But her image and well-publicized story had consequences. The fact that Mona met the man who exploited her while working at Chicago's preeminent department store confirmed rumors that such work was a dangerous employment for young women, and

4 The Business of Vice

Figure 4.5
Mona B. Marshall, an alleged prostitute (called a "white slave"), Chicago, 1907.`

spurred efforts to rescue innocent (and explicitly white) young women who were cast as victims of the vice trade.

The "white slave" scare was one of the prompts that led to the appointment of the Vice Commission of Chicago in 1910, tasked with investigating the "social evil" of forced prostitution. The Chicago Commission was influential in lobbying Congress to pass the Mann Act, sometimes known as the White-Slave Traffic Act, in 1910.[24] Two years later, Jane Addams published a detailed survey of prostitution, *A New Conscience and an Ancient Evil* (1912), written with the help of the Juvenile Protective Association of Chicago.

As part of its work investigating "dance halls, theaters, amusement parks, lake excursion boats, petty gambling," the association collected the "personal histories of 200 department store girls, 200 factory girls, 200 office girls, and of girls employed in one hundred hotels and restaurants." Addams spelled out the dangers of this beguiling environment for naive young women, lured into a dangerous world by more experienced employees or by nefarious men posing as customers.[25] Encouraged by these false friends, the department store clerk might take up lunchtime trysts in the disreputable "assignation hotels" that lined the side streets of the Loop in order to afford the luxuries they craved. In turn, this might develop into evenings spent at racy cafes and, before long, the "unfathomable abyss."[26] In stories such as this, the typologies of leisure—the department store, the vaudeville theater, the café, and the hotel—feature as liminal worlds, thresholds between acceptable and immoral consumption.

An ardent promoter of women's rights, Addams advocated for the separation of male and female social spheres: the workplace and the home. A woman's domestic labor was her Christian duty, just as it was her husband's role to protect her from the world of production and profit. Veblen's economic theory of sexual relations is more complex. In *The Theory of the Leisure Class*, he introduced the subject of female exploitation in more expansive terms than just the subjugation of working-class women. Though Veblen did not discuss the interchangeability of the fashionably dressed woman and the prostitute, as other reformers did, he implied it in his discussion of the anthropological concept of ownership-marriage. According to his theory of women's dress, the display of fashionable clothing might be considered a form of female commodification, to the extent that a woman's worth, judged by her appearance, was measured in economic terms. But while Addams's research on vice, like Stead's, was based on the observation and recording of data, Veblen sought other methods to explain the seemingly irrational marketplace of commodities, whether goods or people. Rather than quantifying the business of vice, he sought instead an evolutionary explanation for the human behaviors that led to the creation of places like the Levee.

According to Veblen's theory of the leisure class, the existence of this debased landscape was due to the persistence of the instinct for predation, the desire to accumulate and consume, even at the cost of exploiting others. In his critique of modern immorality, Veblen focused not on the prostitute but her male counterpart, the gambler, and the wider world of illicit entertainment he inhabited. Where Stead and Addams used maps and statistics to enumerate the business of vice in Chicago, Veblen concentrated on psychology. This approach allowed him a more expansive and critical view than that of his reformist peers. Focusing not just on the most obvious participants in the vice trade, Veblen discussed the pervasiveness of their ruthless and immoral attitude, a holdover from the barbarian stage of human evolution, an attitude that primed predatory consumption of all kinds.

Luck and the Gambler

When Veblen described the modern American university campus as combining inauthentic references to Gothic architecture with the "sprightly and exuberant effects of decoration and magnificence to which the modern concert-hall, the more expensive cafes and clubrooms, and the Pullman coaches have given a degree of authentication," he may have been thinking of the monumental pleasure palaces erected to entertain leisure-class consumers within Chicago's Loop district.[27] Among the most celebrated of these was Louis Sullivan and Dankmar Adler's Auditorium Building, a grand concert hall and hotel built on Michigan Avenue between Congress and Wabash streets. Completed in 1889, the Auditorium was developed by a syndicate of investors organized by orchestra leader Ferdinand W. Peck with the noble aim of being a "locus for culture and politics."[28] Inspired by H. H. Richardson's Marshall Field's Wholesale Store on Adams Street, a free interpretation of the Romanesque, the Auditorium was intended as a "democratic" concert hall in contrast with the socially segregated theaters of Europe. The Auditorium also housed a hotel facing Michigan Avenue. Marked by three arched doorways, the entrance was topped by a ladies' gallery that projected over the street supported by four

Figure 4.6
Pedestrians walking in front of Auditorium Building at 430 South Michigan Avenue, c. 1909. Adler and Sullivan, architects. Fred M. Tuckerman, photographer.

massive corbels, providing unimpeded views over the lake. Inside, modern magnificence prevailed in the form of organic ornament rendered in many different materials, which Sullivan intended to express the flowering of American democracy. As with the Carson Pirie Scott & Co. building, Sullivan set out his aims in a series of high-minded essays that have become critical texts in the canon of American architectural history.[29] However, less commonly referenced is the way in which such spaces were received by their local audience. For journalists and guidebook authors writing at the time of the World's Columbian Exposition, the key characteristic of the Auditorium was its dual aspect, facing the Lake Front Park and the rising sun to the east, and the Levee to the southwest, a district that opened for business after dark.

The Auditorium Hotel was one of several built in the 1880s to compete with older, more staid establishments such as the Tremont, Sherman House, Palmer House, and Grand Pacific hotels. Taking advantage of South Side development, these hotels were located conveniently close to the new railway terminals and the night-time attractions that surrounded them.[30] Published in time for the World's Columbian Exposition, *Chicago by Day and Night* (1892) described the Auditorium, Leland, and Richelieu hotels, which sat on adjacent blocks between Jackson and Congress streets, as the nucleus of the "Blooded District," the headquarters of the "high rolling young men" of the city.[31] According to *Chicago by Day and Night*, the cafés in these three hotels, along with Devine's wine room on the other side of Jackson Street, and Colonel John Harvey's Wayside Inn in a nearby alley, formed a sort of "circuit or beat" around which "rapid" young men traveled long after midnight, when such businesses were meant to be closed. In 1893, the *Rand McNally* guide delicately hinted that they were the gateway to more louche aspects of Chicago's nightlife: "To get a good view of an interesting side of city life, it is best to go not merely into Kinsley's, The Auditorium, The Richelieu, The Virginia (North Side), The Palmer House, Grand Pacific Cafe, Rector's Cafe (five-story), The Peacock, The Frogs, and the basement eating-houses, but also to visit some of the cheapest and plainest resorts of the very poor."[32] In 1912, during the height of publicity over the "white slave trade," the author of a reformist tract claimed that the grand hotels on Michigan Avenue were "infested with men of wealth and time, men of dead consciences, men of diseased moral senses, who are always in search of young, innocent, pretty prey for their decaying passions."[33] Frequented by members of high society and the demimonde, such hotels were a liminal world where identities were fluid and morals suspended; fashionably decorated, they were dedicated to the pursuit of all forms of consumption.

The behaviors Veblen associated with the leisure class—the obsession with appearances, the display of conspicuous wealth, and the ritualized enactment of wasted time—have often been located within the grand city hotel.[34] Veblen himself indicated the role public spaces played in urban society, as places where one's class must be instantly identifiable: "In the modern community there is ... a more frequent attendance at large gatherings of people to whom one's everyday life is unknown; in such places as churches, theatres, ballrooms, hotels, parks, shops, and the like. In order to impress these transient observers, and to retain one's self-complacency under their observation, the signature of one's pecuniary strength should be written in characters which he who runs may read."[35] (That is, one's wealth and social standing must be telegraphed in a quickly and easily understood way.) While the church and the park were places where urban dwellers demonstrated their "pecuniary strength" in conjunction with their propriety, the theater, the ballroom, and hotel had a different character. Predating Siegfried Kracauer's description of the hotel lobby as a profane realm of perpetual stasis, a functionless place for people in a state of eternal transition, Chicago's fashionable hotels were described by journalists, novelists, and social reformers alike as places where morals were flexible and identities uncertain.[36] Open to people from all walks of life, strangers to one another, who signaled their identity through dress and behavior, the hotel lobby not only exhibited modern luxury, it suggested the diverse forms of leisure available to cosmopolitan visitors.

Passing through one of the arched portals that marked the Auditorium Hotel's entrance on Michigan Avenue, visitors entered a large lobby decorated with multicolored onyx wainscoting below and gilded plasterwork above, carved and stenciled in Sullivan's signature foliated ornament.[37] A fan palm in an oversized pot and mysterious hanging balls of vegetation complete the botanical theme. The man who loitered in upholstered comfort might be a member of an identifiable urban type, the "lobby sitter" or "seat warmer" known for lingering in the public areas of hotels to observe the spectacle. But his identity was difficult to discern. Dressed in a standard uniform of suit and hat, he might be a traveling businessman early for his next appointment, a respectable captain of industry waiting to take his wife to the opera, or an adventurous "blood" looking for diversion.

While Veblen never discusses the hotel in detail, a curious chapter of *The Theory of the Leisure Class* entitled "The Belief in Luck" considers the larger group of which these "bloods" were a part. Foreshadowing the early twentieth-century research of University of Chicago sociologists Robert Park and Ernest Burgess and their students, Veblen was deeply interested in the behavior of such urban types. These types included not only the gentleman of leisure but also the athlete, the gambler, and the "swaggering

4 The Business of Vice

Figure 4.7
Auditorium Hotel lobby.

delinquent." Veblen was interested in them less for their geographically distinct social worlds and more for the common archaic traits he believed they shared. Made up of "representatives of the upper and the lowest social strata," members of this type exhibited a fighting temperament, the desire to win or best one's opponent.[38] Operating through force and fraud, they valued ferocity and astuteness, marking them out as "tough." Psychologically, they preserved habits and beliefs associated with an earlier stage of barbaric evolution, including a belief in luck not far removed from anthropomorphic religious cults. Veblen condemned the persistence of this belief, considering it "primitive," an irrational and animistic tendency that hindered positive social progress. The belief in luck, which extended across classes from the wealthiest casino habitué to the lowliest street urchin playing the faro table, was a sign that American culture lagged behind the rationality of its modern industrial systems.[39]

In the years following the Civil War, when the unpredictability and exuberance of the marketplace made success dependent less on knowledge and effort than on chance, it was difficult to distinguish between legitimate and illegitimate speculation.[40] At high-end casinos and racetracks, at backstreet betting shops and pool halls, and in the sober offices of stockbrokers and real estate agents, the successful manipulation of numbers promised endless riches for those favored by fortune. Veblen was one of many late nineteenth-century American critics who argued for the rationalization of production and consumption, along with the stabilization of the market economy. Applying a simple moral equivalency, he argued that the businessman who traded stocks with his broker was essentially the same as the gambler. Because both sought profit without the expenditure of effort, both were equally deviant.

Although Veblen shared with many prominent capitalists what Jackson Lears has called a "morally charged commitment to efficiency," contemporary reviewers often assumed his criticism was motivated by socialist tendencies.[41] When *The Theory of the Leisure Class* was published, the uncomfortable parallel Veblen drew between gamblers and capitalists attracted particular notice.[42] Surely this was a sign of his political sympathies? After all, the comparison was a frequent theme of speeches in labor movement circles. As his University of Chicago colleague the sociologist Charles R. Henderson noted, Veblen's book "is an academic, subtle, and acute phrasing of what the workingmen are saying about us in every shop and Sunday trades council. ... This is the great merit of the book—it compels us to see ourselves as others see us."[43] The trope comparing business speculation with gambling was also commonly repeated in popular journalism. For example, in his popular guidebook, *Chicago by Day and Night*, Vynne advised visitors to Chicago to steer clear of "the polished and gentlemanly professional gamblers" who frequented the gaming "hells" of South Clark Street. Instead, he advised:

> For people of wealth who, afflicted with the speculative mania, desire a larger field of operations than mere roulette, faro, or other trifling games, such a field is not difficult to find. On the Board of Trade, where colossal fortunes are sometimes lost and won in an hour, every facility is offered the stranger who desires to take a "flyer." Stop in any commission house and signify your desire to "play" the market. No introduction is necessary—only sufficient money to "margin" your deal. For the benefit of the uninitiated the system of speculation in grain and provisions may be briefly explained.[44]

In "commission houses," illegitimate trading exchanges sometimes also known as bucket shops, unscrupulous agents posing as brokers fleeced small investors by encouraging them to bet on the market.[45] Labor leaders with socialist sympathies saw little difference between these unsavory activities and legitimate business dealings. While buying and selling penny stocks was far removed from the big deals enacted at the Board of Trade on LaSalle Street, the principle of benefiting from unearned dividends was considered essentially the same.

Nonetheless Veblen, ever the contrarian, was not one of the progressives, among them Stead and Addams, who joined together in the middle of the 1890s to argue that the landscape of iniquity in the South Side Levee must be bought under control, if not eliminated altogether, in order to restore the proper moral order. In a particularly devastating chapter of *The Theory*

Figure 4.8
Harrison Street Police Station on the northeast corner of Harrison and LaSalle streets, c. 1900.
Barnes-Crosby Company, photographer.

of the Leisure Class entitled "Survivals of the Non-Invidious Interest," Veblen described civic reform as a leisure-class activity and progressive politics as the realization of leisure-class values.[46] Stead and Addams's time-consuming accounting of vice signified not only their removal from the world of productive making, but their participation in efforts to manage the chaotic urban environment. In this respect, Veblen's perceptive social criticism was again ahead of its time. As twentieth-century commentators on the Progressive Era have noted, the rise of "managerialism" in both social reform and business reflected a desire to cleanse and control the industrial city and its largely immigrant working-class population. While the desire to eliminate hunger, disease, and abuse was often expressed in terms of the social Gospel, of an urgent need to implement Christian ethics, the project was not unrelated to the goal of making the city more profitable.[47] Often, Veblen claimed, moral indignation about the depravity of vice disguised what were essentially financial motivations.

4 The Business of Vice

The economic basis of Veblen's brand of moralism is evident in a 1908 essay entitled "On the Nature of Capital." Here he addressed the common basis of vice and other seemingly innocuous businesses in their essential wastefulness. Although some forms of waste, such as "the production of goods of fashion, sophisticated household supplies, newspapers, and advertising enterprise," are socially acceptable, others, including "racetracks, saloons, gambling-houses, and houses of prostitution," are not.[48] However, these activities were more similar than different. In Veblen's terms, the murky world of the Levee was no more exploitative than the department stores further north on State Street: both were places where profit was derived from nonproductive consumption. For him, the danger of conspicuous consumption lay not in encouraging vanity, greed, envy, and lust among individuals, but in the exploitative results of predatory capitalism in the wider sense. For society as a whole to change, its most basic institutions would have to change too, not just the cabal of business interests, but also local government and the law.

Corruption and Reform

In Chicago and beyond, it was common knowledge that the saloons, gambling houses, and brothels of the city's vice districts operated freely, owned and controlled by influential businessmen and politicians who paid the police to protect their interests. Of all the money-making institutions in the Levee, the Harrison Street Police Station, or Second Precinct, was one of the busiest. Every night the station was filled with residents who fell afoul of the police, including the unfortunate prostitute or gambler who paid their bail in exchange for release, marks reporting a crime, and tourists who visited to take in the spectacle. Built soon after the fire of 1871, the two-story red-brick station house was police headquarters on the South Side, housing a "police court, cell rooms, inspectors' and captain's offices, sleeping quarters for the men, gymnasium, and bureau of identification."[49] Sitting in the heart of the Levee, the station was at the forefront of the modern science of policing, boasting an impressive Bureau of Identification in its upstairs offices. Organized using the Bertillon system, it was second in size only to the original in Paris. In the early 1880s, French policeman Alphonse Bertillon had developed a system of criminal identification cards involving photographs and measurements of eleven distinct features including height, finger length, and ear length.[50] Coded into a series of shorthand numbers, each criminal's identifying marks could be recorded and disseminated across law enforcement agencies. By 1883, the Bertillon system was in use across Europe and North America. Overseen by Captain Michael Evans, the Chicago Bureau was the first one established in the United States.

Under the direction of Captain Evans, the Bureau of Identification photographed thousands of criminals and responded to requests for information and identification from around the world. In 1900, Evans reported, the Bureau held forty thousand photographs and negatives dating back to 1884, along with police files containing a "detailed statement of each and every case, with names and addresses of witnesses, and criminal records collected from all parts of the world."[51] Early in the century, the Bureau started collecting fingerprints in addition to photographs.[52] As an architectural monument to up-to-date policing methods, the station represented the rule of law. But while criminal anthropology indicated that propensity to certain behaviors was visible, written on the body in the case of the Bertillon system, Veblen's theory of instinctual equivalency meant that the same behaviors were viewed differently depending on the class of the person performing them. The gap between the efficiency of the system and the corruption of everyday policing was another instance of cultural lag, one in which ingrained social habits had failed to keep pace with the new science of social management.

In Chicago, the law had a complicated relationship with the Levee. Here, connections between policemen and the criminal element were unusually close, even for a big-city police department. In a city ripe with business opportunities, police work was a low-status occupation. Still, it could provide a living if one were willing to work within the structure of Chicago's political machine: "in return for protecting the saloon, the gambling den, the bordello, ... the police officer could reasonably expect a degree of job

4 The Business of Vice

longevity and the gratitude of his political sponsor's party, if he was able to maintain its success at the polls on election day."[53] In the 1890s, Chicago was known to practice a loose interpretation of laws regulating petty vice and crime. The Police Association defended its members, claiming a lack of resourcing as the city suffered through periods of economic depression: "In their efforts to cope with the thugs, sluggers, burglars and footpads, the force had been compelled to allow the gambler, the disorderly resort, the confidence men and bunco steerers to go unmolested."[54] This particular passage relates to the depression of the 1870s, but the association repeatedly claimed that police were limited in their effectiveness by underfunding. This leniency was more than neglect; the political machine wrote its own rules, despite periodic efforts at reform.[55] For example, in 1895, the municipal government ordered the police to clean up the city following the disorder of the Pullman railroad strike.Gambling houses and "hop joints" on the South Side were raided, and, in theory, gambling was abolished, as was the practice of selecting men for the police force through political appointments. But these changes made little difference. Sometimes the police raided saloons looking for illegal gambling, but this was mainly for show, little more than window dressing. Even after reformist Mayor Carter Harrison Jr. was elected in 1897, he had little inclination to disrupt the complex economic and social networks that connected the Levee, the financial district, and City Hall.

The Harrison Street Police Station has attained almost mythical status in the numerous historical accounts of the city's nightlife and its denizens, histories as romanticized as they are lurid.[56] An evening spent at the station was a source of guaranteed copy for journalists. Around the turn of the twentieth century, articles about the Second Precinct station offered the thrill of a glimpse into a degenerate world and an alarming example to other municipalities concerned about the spread of political corruption. In December 1897, journalist Franklin Matthews toured the Levee for three days with a police reporter as a guide, and later wrote about the experience in a *Harper's Weekly* article entitled "'Wide Open' Chicago," which included a detailed tableau of a night spent at the station.[57] The article aimed to present Chicago as a negative example for New York City, an illustration of what might happen if voters made the "wrong" choice in the upcoming municipal election, that is, to return the Tammany Hall-controlled Democratic party to power. Illustrated with photographs of notorious figures such as Aldermen Michael "Hinky Dink" Kenna (whose saloon on the corner of Clark and Van Buren shared a building with the King Yen Lo restaurant), John Powers, and William O'Brien, the article reinforced the dominant international narrative about Chicago— that it was the most advanced modern metropolis in the world, bested only by New York, and rotten to the core.

The fact that the police and politicians were complicit with the economy of vice in Chicago was hardly news: Stead had already described this close relationship, and many others had repeated the claim.[58] In one sense, Veblen's writing was part of this reform literature. Yet he never framed his social criticism in local terms, and he never mentioned the specific circumstances of his own city. In *The Theory of Business Enterprise* (1904), he described the connection between the institution of the law and the business interests in simultaneously categorical and oblique terms. In a leisure-class society, he wrote, "modern politics is business politics, even apart from the sinister application of the phrase to what is invidiously called corrupt politics. This is true both of foreign and domestic policy. Legislation, police surveillance, the administration of justice, the military and diplomatic service, all are chiefly concerned with business relations, pecuniary interests, and they have little more than an incidental bearing on other human interests."[59] From a progressive point of view, despite the implementation of advanced technologies of policing, the institution of the law was being held back by entrenched corruption, an older system of ethnic and mutually favorable ties. Business owned both politicians and the police, and business was also responsible for clearing the Levee, under the pretext of cleaning up vice.

After years of the city tolerating the South Side vice district, in the mid-1890s new real estate development began to exert pressure on the Levee's northern boundary as business interests began to capitalize on the area's proximity to railroad stations. The contrast between old and new is evident in a photograph of Plymouth Court, where pre-fire two- and three-story buildings may be seen

4 The Business of Vice

Figure 4.9
Plymouth Court, south of Jackson Street, c. 1908. Great Northern Hotel is visible at rear.
Charles R. Clark, photographer.

overshadowed by D. H. Burnham's sixteen-story Great Northern
Hotel at Jackson and Dearborn streets. As new structures like the
Great Northern were built and landowners sought to benefit from
rapidly increasing land values, they pushed marginal businesses
further south. From the turn of the twentieth century, anti-vice
laws would doom this area to obliteration as the creative destruction of real estate development rolled on.

In 1894, influenced by Stead's shocking exposé, Jane Addams,
Bertha Honoré Palmer, and others founded the Civic Association
of Chicago with a mission to reform city politics. From the late
1890s, the businesses that made up the Levee came under tremendous pressure as police cracked down on beggars, dope dealers,
bookmakers, confidence men, and prostitutes. On a larger scale,
organizations including the National Vigilance Committee, the
American Purity Federation, and the Alliance for the Suppression
and Prevention of the White Slave Trade focused on abolishing
commercialized vice nationwide. In Chicago, these efforts were
concentrated in the work of the Vice Commission. Beginning in

Figure 4.10
R. R. Donnelley and Sons Co. Lakeside Press Building, Chicago, 1897. Howard Van Doren Shaw, architect; Henry Fuermann, photographer.

1910, the commission sought to close brothels, and less than a decade later they were banished to a segregated district near railroad lines on the South Side around Twenty-Second and Dearborn streets, where prostitution was legal within a designated zone. In the early years of the twentieth century, the heart of the old Levee was cleared and rebuilt as an expansion of the neighborhood known since the early 1890s as Printing House Row.[60]

The expansion of Chicago's printing industry into the former vice district illustrates the close relationship between capitalist

4   The Business of Vice

speculation, on one hand, and the seemingly unrelated project of social reform, on the other. When the linotyping process was developed in the early 1880s, the process of printing was transformed from a skilled craft into an automated industry, one that allowed printing to be done on a mass scale at far less cost. The growth of the printing industry and related industrial enterprises changed the morphology of the city. While twelve- and sixteen-story skyscrapers dominated the Loop, the southern periphery was given over to loft buildings intended for manufacturing and wholesale merchandising.[61] For example, one of the earliest American linotyping companies, the Mergenthaler Linotype Company, built new premises on Plymouth Court in 1886, an imposing six-story building by Richard E. Schmidt.[62] Subsequent versions such as Holabird and Roche's Pontiac Building (1891) were developed as rental buildings offering the sturdy structure, large windows, and open interior spaces that printing companies required. Others, such as the Donohue Building (1893) and R. R. Donnelley and Sons' Lakeside Press Building (1897), were commissioned by single companies.[63] Multistory but less ornate than the skyscraper, these loft buildings were a way to organize large-scale manufacturing and integrate it into the urban infrastructure, principally near the railway terminals in the South Side of the Loop. Underground, a system of freight tunnels accessible via basement entrances allowed for the rapid and efficient transportation of goods directly between printing shops, binderies, and railway stations.[64]

By the 1910s, Printing House Row extended south beyond Dearborn Street: most of the two and three-story houses of ill repute along South Clark and the surrounding streets were demolished, replaced with much larger structures. Perhaps paradoxically, even the Harrison Street Police Station was swept away by the reformist broom. In 1898, the *Chicago Tribune* reported on efforts, supported by the mayor, to move the Second Precinct police station further south, claiming it was a "threat to the moral and commercial health of the community," blighting what might otherwise be a prosperous business area.[65] In the summer of 1911, the station was finally closed and its imposing premises demolished.[66] The twenty-year drive to reclaim the Near South Side for "legitimate" businesses had succeeded. While city leaders and the police celebrated, few had any illusions about the motivations behind this urban renewal. Even one of the Harrison Street station's own, former Detective Clifton Wooldridge, noted that the clean-up of the Levee, including the closure of the Second Precinct building, was prompted not so much by moral reform as by the urgent desire of businessmen for land to develop.[67]

*

When the Harrison Street Police Station was demolished in 1911, the way was cleared for a mammoth building, the new headquarters for the Rand McNally publishing company. Designed by Holabird and Roche, the structure covered half the block bounded by Van Buren, Harrison, Clark, and LaSalle streets.[68] Opened in 1912, the Rand McNally Building was a solid ten-story block pierced by an internal lightwell, its facade an array of identical windows topped with a minimally decorative attic of indeterminate style. A photograph taken soon after the building was completed shows the arched shed of the Great Northern railroad company's Chicago terminus behind it. Together, these two buildings—a giant loft and a railway terminal—are modern architectural machines dwarfing the tiny buildings surrounding them. Where the Great Northern is already dulled with smoke, the skeletal form of the gargantuan Rand McNally Building gleams against its dingy and polluted background. A white whale of a building, the longed-for realization of urban renewal embedded in a primitive industrial landscape, this is the image of the modern city.

From the Harrison Street Police Station to the Rand McNally Building, the story of the block bounded by Van Buren, Harrison, Clark, and LaSalle streets may be read as a parable of Veblenian economics applied to real estate development. The police station was built to control illicit trade but also to profit from it. Veblen was one of many contemporary critics to note the hypocrisy of this dual enterprise. As part of the project to clean up the Levee, the station was replaced by an enormous building erected for the publishing industry. This industry had also profited from the notorious vice district, especially during the World's Columbian Exposition, when it produced guidebooks pandering to the

Figure 4.11
Rand McNally building, Chicago, 1911–1912. Holabird & Roche, architects; J. W. Taylor, photographer.

prurient interest in the area known as the Whitechapel of Chicago. Around the turn of the twentieth century, the vice trade moved further south, driven out both by reformers who voiced concern for the victims of the vice trade (particularly vulnerable young women) and by those seeking higher profits than gambling halls and bordellos could provide. Small, pre-fire buildings were razed and replaced by giant loft buildings emblematic of a new aesthetic that was not overtly decorative but sober in appearance. Instead of being dedicated to producing staples (grain or lumber, for example) or consumer goods (men's and boy's clothing), these buildings in Printing House Row produced words and pictures. While Chicago became a hub for the advertising and media industries much later, these businesses represented a new phase of American capitalism. In Veblen's terms, the twentieth-century triumph of the leisure class was to profit from the global promotion of leisure-class values, values embedded in aspirational images of urban modernity sent around the world in books, magazines, and exhibitions, and later film and television. Among them were heroic photographs of Chicago itself, and the city's skyscraper skyline was replicated in cities from Berlin to Brasília to Beijing.

Considered in relation to efforts to clean up Chicago's infamous vice district, the message of *The Theory of the Leisure Class* relates as much to urban development as it does to architecture. In this book, Veblen critiques the rhetoric of progressive social reform as another facet of leisure-class culture. In the case of the Levee, the project of vice reform supported the growth of a different kind of immoral business: real estate development. While Veblen did not discuss the Levee directly, he was explicit about how the institutions of the law and business acted in tandem. Spurred on by reformers such as Stead and Addams, the routing of the vice district was designed to protect vulnerable citizens, but the effort was supported by members of Chicago's elite who were also interested in clearing undercapitalized land for more profitable uses. In the process, old-fashioned buildings dedicated to unwholesome forms of leisure were replaced by larger structures such as lofts, an apparently rational type of architecture. However, seen through the lens of Veblen's institutional economics, the imperatives of moral and aesthetic reform were complex.

Just as much as the department store and the brothel, the businesses housed within loft buildings were inextricably tied to capitalism and its excesses.

Ultimately, Thorstein Veblen's economic theory of aesthetics implies more than a singular focus on the condemnation of the decorative as an expression of economic inequality and exploitation; *The Theory of the Leisure Class* points to a different and more complicated link between architecture and capitalism than Veblen has been given credit for. Rather than just the denigration of ornament, his book reveals the varied architectural and urban expressions and mechanisms of unearned profit within the market economy. The leisure-class city was defined not only by its promotion of mass consumption and wasteful decoration but also by the constant, and profitable, practice of urban renewal.

5 *New Industrial Institutions:*
The Workshop, the School, and the Museum

The Irish playwright and aesthete Oscar Wilde visited Chicago as part of his American lecture tour in February and March of 1882. He told an interviewer that he liked Chicagoans, finding them "simple and strong, and without any foolish prejudices that have influenced East America."[1] Wilde appreciated the hospitality he received, making special mention of American hotels, which he declared much superior to English ones. While in Chicago, he stayed at the luxurious Grand Pacific Hotel, an imposing French Empire-style colossus that occupied half a city block on La Salle and Jackson streets. The Grand Pacific was the height of modern luxury: the six hundred rooms were serviced by two elevators and electric lighting, still a novelty for most guests.[2] Only a few years old at the time of Wilde's visit, the hotel was one of many structures destroyed and reconstructed after the great fire of October 9, 1871. A photograph shows all that remained of the original building, a columnar elevator shaft punctuating the ruins, visible between the crumbling brick walls and fallen cast-iron columns of the Honoré block in the foreground. In the mythology of Chicago as the "phoenix of cities," the fire that destroyed the Grand Pacific and much of the central city was a disaster only in the immediate sense.[3] In the longer term, it was the catalyst that would allow Chicagoans to build a magnificent new city on the charred remains of the old one, financed by the rapidly growing agricultural economy. For Wilde, however, that magnificence was not yet apparent.

Wilde's tour attracted enormous attention in the American press, much of it generated by Wilde himself. Throughout his eleven-month visit, journalists recorded every detail of his movements and his deliberately provocative pronouncements and took a particular interest in his dress and physical appearance. In his room at the Grand Pacific, Parlor 11, the "apostle of the beautiful" received visitors for carefully staged interviews. Dressed in a black-velvet jacket accented with a scarlet handkerchief and socks, he reclined languidly on a tiger-skin-covered sofa, raising his head to deliver the droll remarks for which he was famous. He told a reporter for the *Chicago Tribune* that the actress Sarah Bernhardt had advised him there were only two things worth seeing in America, and one of them was "some dreadful method of killing pigs in Chicago."[4] (The other was the acting of Bernhardt's contemporary, Clara Morris.) However, Wilde did not visit the famous meatpacking plants on the South Side. The weekend before his first lecture, he was taken to see the newly installed State Street cable car and important public buildings, including the Art Institute, the Interstate Industrial Exposition Building, and the Water Tower on North Michigan Avenue. Visitors to these cultural and industrial attractions were encouraged to see them as evidence of the city's remarkable progress. Wilde, however, did not. He told a reporter for the *Chicago Inter-Ocean*, "It is wonderful to think how you have built such a large city in so short a time, especially after such a great calamity as your great fire. But of course, it is a little sad to think of all the millions of money spent on buildings and so little architecture."[5]

For Wilde, the rebuilding of Chicago after the fire was an astonishing spectacle of business confidence not yet matched

5 New Industrial Institutions

Figure 5.1
View from the southwest corner of Dearborn Street and Monroe Street of the Honoré Block (foreground) and Grand Pacific Hotel (background) following the Chicago fire of 1871. Jex Bardwell, photographer.

by artistic achievement. In his lectures, delivered to large audiences at the Central Music Hall on State Street, he offered advice, preaching a practical aesthetics derived from the unity of beauty and usefulness.[6] Paraphrasing Ruskin, he proclaimed: "Without beauty, civilization has no meaning, because industry without beauty becomes barbarism."[7] Speaking in favor of truthful and honest craftsmanship, he argued against machine-made ornament, which he described as worthless and ugly. Above all, he emphasized the necessity for a "lived" aesthetic, declaring that Americans deserve to live in "bright and novel surrounds that you can yourself create. Stately and simple architecture for your city, bright and simple dress for your men and women, and streets clean enough for them to walk across without being soiled—those are the conditions of a real artistic movement."[8]

As a means to achieve this goal, Wilde recommended the creation of art workshops, where attention to "the beautiful things of Nature" would prepare local craftsmen for "a new history of the world, with a promise of the brotherhood of man, of peace rather than war, of praise of God's handcraftsmanship, of new imagination and new beauty."[9] And, appealing to the political sensibilities of his audience, he claimed that "to work at any handicraft produces that sense of individualism which is the keynote of all republicanism." In manufacturing towns such as Chicago, the commercial spirit and the artistic one need not be opposed. Instead, such towns were a vital locus for their unification, engendering "a certain clash of ideas which make men think for themselves."[10] Though delivered in florid terms that some Americans found out of step with the manly pragmatism associated with frontier life, Wilde's address was largely synchronous with the transcendental philosophy of Ralph Waldo Emerson, Henry David Thoreau, and Walt Whitman. In Chicago, the belief that the midwestern city was an ideal nursery for "democratic" and "organic" art and design would become a core belief for local architects, including Louis Sullivan and Frank Lloyd Wright, although their influence was more Whitman than Wilde.

In the most well-publicized part of his February lecture, Wilde offended his listeners by describing the Water Tower as "a castellated monstrosity with pepper-boxes stuck all over it," an abuse

5 New Industrial Institutions

of Gothic art.[11] Designed in 1869 by William W. Boyington, the Water Tower (whose unadorned machinery Wilde found "beautiful") monumentalized in Norman Gothic form a heroic engineering enterprise, the establishment of a clean water supply pumped into the city from Lake Michigan. Amused by the furious reaction his comment received, Wilde repeated the criticism in an interview he gave to the *Chicago Tribune* the following day. Arguing for a modern style reflective of modern functions, he wrote: "If you build a water tower, why don't you build it for water and make a simple structure of it, instead of building it like a castle, where one expects to see mailed knights peering out of every part?"[12] To hear one of the most prominent monuments in the city belittled in this way was deeply hurtful. One of the few structures to survive the great fire, the Water Tower was seen as a romantic symbol of the city's fortitude. However, this monument to the technological sublime held no appeal for the propagandist of Ruskinian aesthetics. Though local boosters claimed the Water Tower was the "eighth wonder of the world" and a "monument to the ever-progressive, ever-growing West," Wilde's comments pointed to the absurdity of disguising a waterworks pumping station as a baronial castle.[13]

Less than twenty years later, Thorstein Veblen echoed Wilde's accusation that America's cultural barbarism was epitomized by the strange conflation of advanced industrial technology with a bastardized feudal style of architecture. In his characterization of Chicago as a backward-looking society, Veblen, like Wilde, found in the numerous expressions of the American eclectic Gothic ample evidence of cultural regression. As a book-length critique of the culture and taste of his contemporaries, *The Theory of the Leisure Class* provoked the sensibilities of its readers in the same way as Wilde's provocative remarks about the Water Tower. But while Veblen has been called the "Oscar Wilde of economics," there is not much else to connect the two figures.[14] Veblen was not a foreign visitor but a resident of Chicago, the son of Norwegian immigrant farmers who had settled in Minnesota. He was not an authority on taste but a lowly academic aspiring to be taken seriously as a political economist. And rather than a follower of aestheticism, Veblen was a critic of the results of the program that Wilde so earnestly espoused. Instead of being a genuine attempt

Figure 5.2
Water Works, Chicago, 1869. William W. Boyington, architect.

at social salvation, late nineteenth-century aestheticism appeared to Veblen as another expression of leisure-class taste.

The publication of *The Theory of the Leisure Class* coincided with the height of the influence of the Arts and Crafts movement in the United States. By the late 1890s, Chicago boasted several Arts and Crafts-inspired organizations aimed at achieving social cohesion and civic rejuvenation through the reform of industrial production. Just as *The Theory of the Leisure Class* offered an academic basis for critical rejection of the Gothic Revival, the book also provided a scholarly grounding for these local projects of social and aesthetic reform. It concludes with the optimistic argument that the future of modern society belonged to the engineer and the New Woman, modern urban types formed through the recovery of a premodern "instinct of workmanship."

Complicating the narrative of alienation that has built up around him, Veblen was involved, though tangentially, with local efforts to encourage the psychological development of these modern people through the founding of new kinds of social institutions. Industrial institutions intended to replace predatory ones, these were progressive variations on the workshop, the school, and the museum. Many were organized by members of the Chicago Arts and Crafts Society founded at the Hull House settlement in 1897, including Veblen's University of Chicago colleague Oscar Lovell Triggs and Hull House founder Jane Addams. Many of these efforts aligned with Veblen's beliefs, in broad terms. However, he tempered his cautious praise for institutions such as the settlement house and the manual training school with suspicion that their supposedly "non-invidious" programs of social amelioration, focused on racial assimilation, the education and health of working-class immigrants, and their conversion to "American" habits and values, were unwitting agents of capitalist expansion. Understood in these terms, reformist institutions were as dangerous as the mainstream universities from which they sprang, perpetuating rather than overcoming leisure-class dominance, and expanding the stranglehold of consumer culture.

The Arts and Crafts as a Leisure-Class Pursuit

When Oscar Wilde stayed at the Grand Pacific Hotel in 1882, the area surrounding it was on the brink of transformation from a district on the fringe of the South Side Levee into a busy financial center. The "very center of New Chicago," as the *Rand McNally* guide to the city phrased it, was where the first group of Chicago's tall office towers was erected.[15] By the early 1890s, a series of towers on either side of La Salle Street had replaced the hotels built immediately after the fire as the city's most notable architectural monuments. Not all were pure commercial vehicles; several attempted to combine profit making with social improvement. One of these was the Woman's Temple at the southwest corner of La Salle and Monroe streets. Designed by the prominent firm of Burnham and Root, this was an unusual building of the type later labeled a "civic skyscraper."[16] Built on a site leased from Marshall Field (a stockholder in the company that financed the building), it was the headquarters of the Woman's Christian Temperance

Union (WCTU), a nationwide group created to lobby for prohibition and to provide support for the "rum-soaked victims of the legalized liquor trade."[17] With an unusual form to match its unique program, the Woman's Temple was the image of corporate philanthropy. Unlike Veblen's description of the typical rugged and baronial philanthropic institution of the 1870s and '80s, its French Gothic style was more refined; with rounded corners and elaborate ornament surrounding the ninth-floor arches, it expressed a romantic, if not feminine persona. Completed in 1892, the heavy masonry building was thirteen stories high, topped by a steeply pitched, turreted roof, giving it the appearance of an oversized medieval château. Besides revenue-generating rental space, the building housed the offices of the WCTU and other organizations dedicated to the moral improvement of the city.

With its focus on temperance, the WCTU was a female-led institution of a new kind, one aimed at overturning the dominance of the saloon in American social and political life. Supported by wealthy and powerful backers, the union could afford to bring other reform organizations along with it. Beginning in 1899, the Chicago Arts and Crafts Society (CACS) held its annual spring show here, a society event reported on in local newspapers and journals dedicated to the applied arts. In room 1301, an attic studio under the eaves of the Woman's Temple, the CACS had its permanent exhibition and sales room.[18] The society was made up of members of the city's higher social echelon, along with settlement house workers, architects, designers, and academics, all seeking to solve what they called the "social problem," the deep division evident in the violent labor disputes that shook the city in the 1880s and '90s.[19] Ranging in their philosophy from moderate to radical, they took their direction from the English Arts and Crafts movement.

In keeping with the dominant intellectual trope of the nineteenth century, members of the CACS assumed there had been an evolutionary progress of human society from primitive peoples who used hand tools, to organized craft guilds, to contemporary methods of industrial production. Influenced by Morris, they agreed that this technological transformation harmed society, creating a deep rift between labor and capital, and between producer and consumer. Aligned with the Progressive movement, the

Figure 5.3
Woman's Temple, Chicago, 1892. Burnham and Root, architects; Chicago Architectural
Photography Co., photographer.

society sought a return to the principles of democracy on which the country had been founded, tempering individualism with the doctrine of community cooperation. Within this grand vision, the Arts and Crafts workshop served as a highly effective model of self-government in miniature.

Despite their noble aims, however, the WCTU and the CACS were forms of philanthropic enterprise that Veblen scrutinized with suspicion. In the penultimate chapter of *The Theory of the Leisure Class*, entitled "Survivals of the Non-Invidious Interest," he voiced strong reservations about social enterprises such as temperance organizations, settlement houses, and neighborhood guilds and arts clubs—enterprises in which leisure-class women were leading actors. The chapter ends with an extended tribute to the positive influence of the figure known as the New Woman, who, "by force of youth, education, or temperament," sought emancipation from her unproductive life as an honorific marker of status for her family; possessing a well-developed impulse to take on active social roles, Veblen wrote, such women longed to enter the "sphere of usefulness."[20] Confronting the problems of modern industrial life, she dedicated herself to social welfare. Veblen was sympathetic to women of this kind, seeing in their actions the hopeful recovery of a long-repressed human impulse: "In a sense, then, the new-woman movement marks a reversion to a more generic kind of human character, or a less differentiated expression of human nature."[21] As American life advanced both economically and industrially, far from the barbarian culture that dictated women held secondary status, as both consumers and producers women would be freed to pursue productive lives. However, despite his optimism about the positive influence of the New Woman movement, much of the chapter is given over to a negative assessment of female-dominated social welfare groups. Though the institutions they founded—such as nursery schools, libraries, and public health clinics—might appear to reject the "invidious purpose in life," he wrote, this was often secondary to their primary motivation to promote leisure-class taste and interests.

The groups associated with the local Arts and Crafts movement were a case in point. Although William Morris had strongly influenced him in his younger days, Veblen was no longer a disciple.

After meeting the great man on a visit to Great Britain in 1896, he had come away disillusioned.[22] Perhaps because of Veblen's humble rural upbringing, he did not share Morris's romanticized view of manual labor and disdain for modern machinery. *The Theory of the Leisure Class* mocks Ruskin and Morris for their reverence for handicraft, which Veblen labeled the "exaltation of the defective."[23] The sixth chapter of the book, entitled "Pecuniary Canons of Taste," presents a scathing critique of the Arts and Crafts movement, describing it as another way for the privileged members of the leisure class to demonstrate their exclusive tastes:

> Hand labor is a more wasteful method of production; hence the goods turned out by this method are more serviceable for the purpose of pecuniary reputability; hence the marks of hand labor come to be honorific, and the goods which exhibit these marks take rank as of higher grade than the corresponding machine product. Commonly, if not invariably, the honorific marks of hand labor are certain imperfections and irregularities in the lines of the hand-wrought article, showing where the workman has fallen short in the execution of the design. The ground of the superiority of hand-wrought goods, therefore, is a certain margin of crudeness.[24]

Just as participation in philanthropic activities like settlement house work served as an indicator of "pecuniary respectability," offering a clear contrast between the givers and receivers of charity, the production and purchase of costly handmade domestic goods was a sign of social status. Above all, Veblen pointed out the absurdity of valuing a product based on its all too obvious imperfections, observing that machine-made products are characterized by "greater perfection in workmanship and greater accuracy in the detail execution of design."[25] Laying the blame at the feet of Ruskin and Morris, he noted, "Their propaganda of crudity and wasted effort has been taken up and carried forward since their time."[26] Using the example of Morris's painstakingly handcrafted books, he wrote that the high cost of such books, the time necessary to make them, and the unlikelihood they would be read, rendered them expressions of conspicuous consumption.

Many of the activities of the CACS appear to legitimate Veblen's charge. Though it promoted the unification of art and labor, the society did little to engage with working people or those who managed industrial businesses. CACS hosted weekly meetings and lectures by international visitors including the English Arts and Crafts evangelist Charles R. Ashbee, the Russian anarcho-communist Prince Peter Kropotkin, and the Scottish sociologist Patrick Geddes.[27] While the group made some effort to establish subsidized craft workshops for the laboring class, including one at Hull House, the majority were interested in small-scale workshop production by members of their own class.[28] In local workshops such as Kalo and Krayle, CACS members produced Arts and Crafts objects in small quantities for leisure-class consumers.[29] Featured in early CACS exhibitions, these included enameling and metal-work by Florence D. Koehler, hammered copper by Madeline Yale-Wynne, and leatherwork by Louis Sanderson, all of which received critical praise in the popular press and in dedicated arts journals.[30] Together, these activities spurred a new canon of taste in Chicago, one forged in small workshops and promoted to the wider con-suming public through lectures, discussion groups, and exhibi-tions at numerous clubs and societies.

If there was a center of Arts and Crafts culture in Chicago, it was the Fine Arts Building on Michigan Avenue, a hive of studios, the-aters, and social clubs. Sandwiched between the Auditorium and the Chicago Club, this was one of three ornate buildings express-ing the city's cultural aspirations during the 1890s. A Romanesque building made up of rusticated gray limestone and red granite, it was designed by Solon S. Beman in 1885 as a showroom and assembly factory for the Studebaker carriage manufacturing company. After the business grew too big for the lakefront building, it decamped to larger premises, and in 1896 the building was converted into a cen-ter for the arts under the direction of manager Charles C. Curtiss. Even more so than the Woman's Temple, the Fine Arts Building was associated with artistic and civic reform. Besides artists' studios, it housed the Caxton Club (dedicated to making Arts and Crafts-style books), a lecture hall, the Chicago Woman's Club, and the offices of *The Dial* (a progressive literary journal) and the socialist-leaning Charles H. Kerr publishing company. From the eighth-floor rooms of Anna Morgan's drama studio, daringly fitted out by architect Irving K. Pond in black woodwork and grayish-purple burlap, to Browne's Bookstore and the cork-lined walls and oak-and-brass portfolio booths of the Thurber Art Gallery, both designed by Frank Lloyd Wright, the building exuded the artistic atmosphere that Curtiss worked hard to cultivate.[31] From 1898 until around 1920, life in the Fine Arts Building was a busy whirl of club meetings, afternoon teas, lectures, and exhibitions. A magnet for artists and socialites, these events disseminated the Arts and Crafts ethos through production, publishing, and merchandising. Here social and aesthetic reform found expression in genteel commercial enterprise, cementing interest in craft consumption in Chicago.

Veblen was not the only critic to point out that the activities on display at the Fine Arts Building and elsewhere operated within the system of pecuniary emulation that defined leisure-class culture. As the *American Architect and Building News* noted in 1899, the Chicago Arts and Crafts Society "educates many of the very class of people whose taste forms public taste."[32] Echoing Veblen's criticism, a description of the new South Park Workshop planned for Hyde Park in the *Chicago Tribune* was headlined, "Workshop for the Rich."[33] Adjacent to the new manual training school at the University of Chicago, this was to be a place where well-off Hyde Park residents could make their own pottery, furniture, and other household objects. Far from mechanisms of democracy, the Arts and Crafts movement offered the well-to-do a way to reverse their alienation from the material world by promoting handicraft work as a method of personal redemption while they remained isolated in their suburban enclaves.[34] Other critics were even less conciliatory when assessing the Arts and Crafts movement's aspirations against its achievements.

Reviewing the 1902 CACS exhibition for the *International Socialist Review*, a Charles H. Kerr publication, its editor, Algie M. Simons, noted that many of the exhibitors seemed completely divorced from the realities of working-class life. Though the show featured objects made by boys from the "Hull House quarter," working under its director, George M. R. Twose, engagement with working people was the exception to the rule. Most products on display were primarily decorative rather than functional. Some items,

Figure 5.4
Fine Arts Building between the Auditorium and the Chicago Club, Michigan Avenue, Chicago, c. 1895. Solon S. Beman, architect; J. W. Taylor, photographer.

Simons argued, including Deerfield rugs and baskets made in Massachusetts, were simply poorly made. In the hands of an industrial manufacturer, he wrote, such products might be more competently produced, at lower cost, with less waste of human energy. Acknowledging the origins of the Arts and Crafts movement in the socialism of Morris, Simons pointed out that the local group was removed from socialist politics in Chicago. Divorced from knowledge of the actual conditions of working people, they created objects that appeared simply "playthings for the wealthy," making them "reactionary rather than progressive."[35] He feared that the society, overly romantic and lacking awareness of the living circumstances of most urban dwellers, would soon become a parody of itself.

Unlike the ardent socialist Algie M. Simons, Veblen condemned the Arts and Crafts movement not because of the lack of value Arts and Crafts products held for working people but because of their utility as expressions of social difference for the well to do. There was, however, a branch of the Chicago Arts and Crafts movement with which Veblen had some sympathy. In 1902, he wrote a favorable review of a book entitled *Chapters in the History of the Arts and Crafts Movement* written by his university colleague Oscar Lovell Triggs.[36] Published in the *Journal of Political Economy*, Veblen's review is his most explicit statement about modern architecture and design. In economic terms, he wrote, the anti-machine doctrine of the Arts and Crafts movement was unfeasible. Because of the high cost of handmade goods, it could only operate where cost was not a factor, that is, in the luxury market. In contrast, "a democratic culture requires low cost and a large, thoroughly standardized output of goods."[37] Praising Triggs for educating the public about the potential of the industrial arts, Veblen ventured one his few explicit statements about modern aesthetics. Speaking of machine-made objects, he wrote: "The enduring characteristic is rather an insistence on sensuous beauty of line and color and on visible serviceability in all objects which it touches. And these results can be attained in fuller measure through the technological expedients of which the machine process disposes than by any means within the reach of the industry of the past age."[38] In other words, not only can machines make beautiful, serviceable things, they can achieve better results than any previous method of production.

In his review of Triggs's book, Veblen identified a schism within the local Arts and Crafts movement, between those who rejected machine production and those who accepted industrial methods as inevitable and desirable. Veblen's public support for his colleague Triggs links his theory of the leisure class to the program of progressive industrial reform active in Chicago at the turn of the twentieth century. This program took place not in the fashionable workshops and galleries of the Fine Arts Building, the Woman's Temple, or the South Park Workshop, but in a series of new kinds of social institutions located in the manufacturing districts that surrounded the central city.

New Industrialism in the Nineteenth Ward

Beyond the north-south spine of State Street, between the Loop and the prairie, a patchwork of neighborhoods housed Chicago's laboring class. These neighborhoods were connected to the city center by east-west corridors like Twelfth Street (now Roosevelt Road), one of many economic spines linking the busy downtown with the residential and manufacturing districts that supported it. Traveling by streetcar along Twelfth Street, heading away from the lake at the southern end of Grant Park, one left behind the tall buildings of Michigan Avenue and Dearborn and State streets, crossed Clark and the other sordid streets of the Levee, then the south branch of the Chicago River, before entering the lowly Nineteenth Ward. The center of the garment district, a ghetto of Italian and Jewish immigrants, this ward was one of the poorest parts of the city.

A district of humble commercial buildings and dilapidated wooden houses one mile west of the Loop, the Nineteenth Ward was dominated by hastily built wooden houses crammed with sweatshop laborers, particularly in the Jewish and Italian neighborhoods bordering Maxwell Street. In contrast with more familiar images of Chicago with its monumental commercial and institutional buildings and its romantic suburban homes, this was the back side of the industrial city, a debased and incomplete

Figure 5.5
Streetcar on Twelfth Street (now Roosevelt Road), looking east from Halsted Street, 1906. Charles R. Clark, photographer.

landscape where the process of urbanization met the agrarian frontier. Geographically and economically close but separated by an unbreachable social abyss, these two worlds, the Loop and its periphery, exemplify the deep divide between leisure and laboring classes that Veblen described.[39] As the economic boom of the 1880s gave way to the severe economic hardships of the 1890s, the quality of life on the Near West Side and in the southern neighborhoods became a growing concern. Academics, civic reformers, and labor leaders identified overcrowded housing and dangerous working conditions as a significant problem impacting not only workers but also the local and national economy.

In the Nineteenth Ward and elsewhere, industrial workers were agitating in favor of better pay and working conditions. While sympathetic to the cause, progressive-minded members of the leisure class cast these upheavals in terms of racial improvement rather than working-class activism. Inspired by the new discipline of sociology, early practitioners of social work undertook many surveys and

Figure 5.6
Hebrew Manual Training School, Chicago, 1889–1890. Adler & Sullivan, architects.

experiments in the ward, activities that inspired the more forward-thinking members of the Chicago Arts and Crafts Society to pursue a philosophy that would be called "new industrialism."

Where Twelfth Street intersected with Jefferson Street, travelers who stepped off the streetcar and walked one block south encountered a formidable-looking brick building, larger in scale than most buildings in the neighborhood. This was the Jewish Training School. Founded by the Sinai Temple, whose congregation included powerful and socially prominent German Jewish residents of Chicago such as Emil G. Hirsch, a respected rabbinical scholar, the school was established to educate the children of Russian and Polish Jewish immigrants newly arrived in the city, forced to flee their home countries following pogroms. Opened in 1890, the school was open to boys and girls of all ethnicities up to fourteen years old, provided they were in need. Classes, taught in English, followed the Illinois public school curriculum, supplemented by various sorts of "hand training." Sometimes known as the Hebrew Manual Training School, the building was designed by Dankmar Adler and Louis Sullivan in a variation of the stripped-down style they employed for loft buildings. Sitting on a rusticated base, its four symmetrical facades were pierced with grand arched windows. As Joseph Siry has described, the school was one of several architectural experiments dedicated to the expression of social betterment. While designed with the prominence of a synagogue, it was planned with the pragmatism of a manufacturing building.[40] Besides regular classrooms, the solid building incorporated three sewing rooms, carpentry and machine shops, and a kindergarten. Above the heavy decorative cornice, the flat roof allowed for a sunny exercise yard, maximizing the school's limited site in the middle of a crowded neighborhood.

Though nonsectarian, the Jewish Training School was directed primarily at the assimilation of the children of Jewish immigrants into American life and culture.[41] The rhetoric supporting the School reveals the theme of racial improvement that underpinned all Progressive Era social aid programs. At the turn of the twentieth century, ideas of race in America began to shift away from the idea of innate or genetic difference and toward the belief that the environment might influence racial progress.[42] But at the same time, the Italian and Russian Jewish people who emigrated to American industrial cities in large numbers were commonly described as members of distinctive, non-white, races. Highly segregated by ethnicity, inner-city neighborhoods tightly packed with working-class immigrants from southern and eastern Europe were regarded as "immigrant colonies" within the larger nation.

Social workers and sociologists described the inhabitants of these colonies as members of "backward" or less highly evolved races, "maladjusted" to their new environment.[43] This maladjustment was reported to result in poor health, insanity, high infant mortality, immorality, and broken families. These endemic problems led, in turn, to lowered productivity: a 1900 report described incapacitated workers as a form of "economic waste."[44] Seen as ill-adapted to life in the modern city, immigrants were easily exploited by both capitalist profiteers and radical labor organizers, who imported "un-American" ideas such as socialism and anarchism from Europe. The answer, for Progressive Era social reformers, was to assimilate the immigrant labor force as quickly as possible. This process, to be achieved primarily through education and public health reforms, was known as "Americanization."

In this rhetoric of assimilation and uplift, we see the obverse of Veblen's satirical employment of the language of race science in *The Theory of the Leisure Class*. Where Emil G. Hirsch recalled with repugnance the stereotype of the Jewish merchant as a leech, and others applied equally offensive labels such as the idle Irishman and the incompetent Italian, Veblen applied the same stigmatic label to the descendants of Germanic dolicho-blonds who controlled the city's largest and most profitable businesses.[45] With his identification of those who occupied the highest rung of the social ladder as a racially distinct group, one with an inherited aversion to work of any kind, he called out the hypocrisy of rhetoric that identified laziness and avarice with working-class immigrants.

Inspired in part by Veblen's attack on the American education system as a relic of feudalism, his friend Triggs took on education reform as a platform for the racial and cultural advancement of Americans of all backgrounds. In 1899, Triggs formed the Industrial Art League (IAL) and through this organization transformed himself from an academic of average achievements into an impresario of industrial arts education.[46] An instructor in English and committed socialist, Triggs had been a tireless publicist for aesthetic reform ever since he arrived in Chicago. Around the turn of the twentieth century, he lectured and published widely on the concept of "democratic art."[47] Inspired by his deep admiration for William Morris, his early writing promoted the idea that the machine could only produce ugliness and exploitation. But he soon reversed his position and accepted modern technology as an emancipatory force advancing American democracy. While the origins of his intellectual transformation are unclear, Triggs may have been influenced by Veblen, with whom he was well acquainted. For a time, the two men and their wives were neighbors at the Beatrice Hotel on Fifty-Seventh Street, a boarding house frequented by some of the more bohemian members of the University of Chicago faculty.

5 New Industrial Institutions

Triggs invested his hope for the future in the merger of two institutional typologies: the workshop and the school. This hybrid, he proclaimed, was the true democratic institution, a place to realize community consciousness of the importance of industrial production through education. Citing the examples of the Jewish Training School and Booker T. Washington's Tuskegee Institute in Alabama, he argued that diverse social and ethnic groups might be integrated into a national program of manual training schools, a model of democratic education serving all citizens.[48] The graduates of technical schools such as these would help establish a new type of culture, he argued, one that was active and inventive rather than passive and conservative.

Attempting to break with the capitalist model of wage labor, Triggs proposed a sort of nationalized guild system operating as a "series of workshops and studios under a single roof, owned and conducted by the craftsmen themselves," with the profits from sales returning directly to the workers. While each member would work individually, the enterprise would be managed collectively. "Cooperative individualism is the necessary working theory of the free workshop," Triggs proclaimed.[49] Such workshops would not be restricted to traditional crafts, but include the advanced methods of production: woodworkers, potters, and weavers would work alongside metal-workers, printers, etching specialists, chemists, and physicists, all dedicated to finding solutions to specialized industrial problems involving the crafts.[50] The result would be a form of industrial settlement—not a charitable enterprise, but a self-supporting business operating within the market economy.

For a brief period around the turn of the twentieth century, the Industrial Art League was an important organization, one that achieved powerful support in Chicago as well as national recognition. Capitalizing on the University of Chicago's interest in supporting industrial education, including its recent affiliation with the Chicago Manual Training School, it had the support of William Rainey Harper, the president of the university, and many members of the university's faculty including sociologists Charles Zueblin and George Vincent. It also attracted business leaders such as Stanley McCormick, heir to the agricultural machinery fortune, and real estate magnate Potter Palmer;

philanthropists like Marguerite (Mrs. Warren) Springer; educational reformers such as Emil G. Hirsch and Francis W. Parker; social workers like the Rev. Jenkin Lloyd Jones, Jane Addams, and Graham Taylor; writers including Hamlin Garland; and prominent architects such as Louis Sullivan and Frank Lloyd Wright.[51]

In 1899, the League made a start on its ambitious program, announcing plans to open the University Guild Workshop in a two-story brick structure on Lake Avenue near the university campus. This was to be a fully equipped workshop where craft workers produced goods for sale at the League's downtown salesroom on Michigan Avenue, with all profits returned to them, less costs. The project grew from there. At the League's annual meeting held at the Auditorium Hotel in November 1901, Triggs proposed a nationwide program of manual training schools.[52] In 1902, *Construction News* reported he was in discussions with the Rabbinical Association to erect thirty thousand buildings in connection with the Jewish Training School.[53] However, other aspects of the League's activities conformed to the older Arts and Crafts model. Triggs was involved in founding the South Park Workshop, where the residents of Hyde Park could make furniture or try their hand at bookbinding or pottery. This was far from the cooperative industrial settlement that Triggs had described with such enthusiasm.[54]

After a triumphant beginning, the Industrial Art League faded quickly. While the causes of failure were multiple, many stemmed from a mismatch between Triggs's rhetoric and his actions. Although he was an ardent socialist, Triggs depended on the support of business backers through traditional mechanisms of philanthropy. Beguiled by his convincing sales pitch, many wealthy and influential Chicagoans were persuaded to support his project. But in a few short years, the League's value fell sharply, like overinflated stock. Triggs failed to capitalize on the grand promises he had made and used up the goodwill he had accrued, embarrassing his socially prominent patrons, including his employer. By 1905, the League had folded, due in part to financial mismanagement. Triggs left the University of Chicago under a cloud to start his own school, the People's Industrial College, in the Michigan countryside, a venture that has left little trace.

Figure 5.7
Group of young men in the forge shop at Chicago Manual Training School, corner of
Michigan and Twelfth avenues, c. 1895.

Though Veblen was not involved in the Industrial Art League
or its failure, his professional fate was tied to that of his colleague.
According to Veblen's first biographer, Joseph Dorfman, it was
rumors of an affair with Triggs's wife Laura that led to Veblen being
asked to leave the university around the same time that Triggs was
exiled.[55] In recent years, scholars and biographers have cast doubt
on this version of events, arguing that university authorities, who
had wanted to get rid of Veblen for some time, used these rumors
as a pretext to dismiss him. Well-founded or not, the image of
Veblen as an unrepentant adulterer would dog him for the rest of
his career. Some have contended that this characterization helped
enhance his reputation as a rebel, an outsider, and a social iconoclast. Others have discussed his sympathy for the social position
of women as a praiseworthy trait. But at the same time, many commentators have ignored the centrality of gender relations to his
economic theory.[56] Searching for evidence of his support for wom-
en's rights leads to a curious fact. In 1902, Veblen gave a lecture
at the Hull House settlement in support of Jane Addams's Labor

Museum. In this venture, which was a hybrid of school, museum, and theater, his abstract ideas about the role of women in industrial society found their most concrete expression.

The Hull House Labor Museum and the New Woman

Three blocks north of the Jewish Training School, where Halsted Street intersected with Polk, a complex of red-brick institutional buildings stood, in stylized variations of the rustic English Gothic. One of the earliest American settlements, Hull House was founded by Jane Addams and Ellen Gates Starr in 1889, heavily influenced by the English settlement house Toynbee Hall, founded by Oxford academics in London's East End.[57] Such settlements, modeled after romanticized versions of the medieval village or colonial town hall, were meant to be places where citizens of different ethnic groups could come together and create a shared culture. In their Arts and Crafts aesthetic, they recalled an idealized medieval era of industrial production and social harmony. Begun in the parlor of a modest Victorian farmhouse, Hull House was extended in a series of additions designed by architects Allen and Irving Pond. Each new addition responded to a new function—a nursery, a school, a theater, and so on. Taking a pragmatic approach to the "social problem," Addams and Starr moved away from the traditional philanthropy practiced by educated and well-off women, toward a more liberal view of social reform. The goal of their settlement was social reunification: the assimilation of immigrants into American culture and the introduction of educated and well-off Chicagoans to the world of the immigrant working class. In concrete terms, the settlement was a new form of civic center incorporating meeting hall, school, health clinic, and citizens' advice bureau.

At Hull House, residents, philanthropists, business leaders, labor organizers, academics, architects, and designers met to discuss the creation of what Jennifer Gray has called "practical utopias."[58] These utopias were not just new forms of social organization; they also had their own pronounced aesthetic. Just as Charles Ashbee's School and Guild of Handicraft was an essential part of Toynbee Hall, Addams and Starr always intended that the arts and crafts would be part of the settlement's program of civic advancement, immigrant education, and industrial reorganization. In 1895, Addams wrote, "The attempt of Hull-House to make the aesthetic and artistic a vital influence in the lives of its neighbors, and a matter of permanent interest to them, inevitably took the form of a many-sided experiment."[59] This experiment involved overlapping groups, activities, and spaces, all supporting one another in various ways. Lectures and classes dominated the early education program, held in the Art Exhibit room of the Butler Building, the first addition the Pond brothers built in 1891.[60]

Established at Hull House six years later, the Chicago Arts and Crafts Society was part of this project.[61] In their effort to realign art with industry, its members understood the work of the society as the shared aesthetic expression of democracy. Addams put the mission in nationalistic terms: "Whatever its relation to larger movements [the settlement house movement] has never failed to recognize that its most immediate task is to aid in the Americanization of the immigrant colonies among which it is so intimately placed."[62] In these terms, the reform of craft production had a broader agenda, addressing not only the production of everyday objects but also the production of modern American subjects.

Though many of his colleagues at the university were regular visitors to Hull House, actively involved in the settlement's many activities, Veblen was not. The two or three years following the publication of *The Theory of the Leisure Class* represented the height of Veblen's professional reputation in Chicago, where his provocative ideas were discussed and cited with approval. While he might seem a natural ally to Addams and other Hull House residents, Veblen distanced himself from its mission, disparaging "the many efforts now in reputable vogue for the amelioration of the indigent population of large cities." While in some ways admirable, he wrote, the efforts of settlement house workers, many from the privileged class, were "in part directed to enhance the industrial efficiency of the poor and to teach them the more adequate utilization of the means at hand; but it is also no less consistently directed to the inculcation, by precept and example, of certain punctilios of upper-class propriety in manners and customs."[63] In other words, the settlement might be considered

Figure 5.8
Hull House, Halsted Street, c. 1900. Allen Pond and Irving Pond, architects; Charles R. Clark, photographer.

a leisure-class institution, designed to improve the productivity of industrial workers and indoctrinate them into the practice of conspicuous consumption.

Searching for traces of Veblen at Hull House turns up one suggestive event. On February 22, 1902, he gave a lecture entitled "The Day of the Craftsman and the Instinct of Workmanship" as part of a lecture series on "Industrial History" organized by Addams in support of her newly established Labor Museum. Held on Saturday evenings, these lectures were given in the Hull House auditorium. Other speakers included Emil G. Hirsch, who lectured on "Labor Conditions among the Jews," and Addams herself, who lectured on "The Development of the Factory Acts." Labor leaders Thomas J. Morgan, Thomas I. Kidd, and Abraham Bisno spoke, as did May Wood Simons, wife of Algie M. Simons, who was a student of economics at the University of Chicago and may have taken classes with Veblen.[64]

There is no trace of the text of Veblen's 1902 lecture at Hull House, but from its title we can assume he drew from an essay he had published in the *American Journal of Sociology* in 1898, "The Instinct of Workmanship and the Irksomeness of Labor." Central to Veblen's theory of the leisure class was its essential divorce from labor and the associated disparagement of manual work as lowly and abject. The answer to this rupture was to recover a psychological instinct to create, an instinct well-developed in primitive societies but repressed in the barbarian era. Veblen called this "the instinct of workmanship": "Under the canon of conduct imposed by the instinct of workmanship, efficiency, serviceability, commends itself, and inefficiency or futility is odious."[65] Though he noted it would be very difficult, if not impossible, to change the current social mindset in which labor was associated with lower social status, a return to this canon was central to Veblen's proposal to bridge the gap between the leisure and laboring classes.[66]

An innate human urge, the instinct to create had a biological and a social basis, he argued. Rooted in ancient practices of agricultural production, it was essential to the survival of communal tribes. With the rise of predatory culture over thousands of years of human evolution, however, productive labor became shunned in favor of looting and warfare. Although Veblen was vague about the mechanisms of change, he believed the instinct to create was in the process of revival, ushered in by modern technological advances. Inspired by the processes of industry, competitive culture would be overcome, the divide between the leisure and laboring classes narrowed, and society would return to a cooperative form of organization. Though there is no evidence of any ongoing association between Veblen and the Hull House settlement, some of his phrases, including the "instinct of workmanship," became part of Addams's lexicon.[67]

The Labor Museum is usually understood as an offshoot of the Chicago Arts and Crafts Society, but its original intent was somewhat different. In many ways, Veblen was a natural choice to speak in support of the enterprise. He shared several ideas central to the museum: the industrial arts as the driver of social evolution, the continuity of the industrial enterprise throughout human history and across races, and faith in modern processes of industrial manufacturing. Besides sharing these concepts, Addams had a particular reason to appreciate Veblen: his criticism of the debased position of women in a supposedly advanced society and his argument that the New Woman was the social leader of the future. *The Theory of the Leisure Class* reinforced the belief that the industrial arts were a natural sphere of activity for women because women had an equal share of the instinct of workmanship to men's.[68] Renewed attention to their historical roles as makers might serve as a model for cooperative industrial life.

A version of the "sociological museum" popular around the turn of the twentieth century, the Labor Museum began as an intellectual endeavor which Addams shared with her friends and acquaintances at the University of Chicago, including the sociologists Charles Zueblin and Albion Small, and the educational reformer John Dewey. A didactic institution, it was designed to demonstrate continuity between the centuries-long history of human industry and the present-day Chicago. The project was inspired by the Scottish biologist and town planner Patrick Geddes, who lectured to the CACS at Hull House in March 1899. His talk covered, among other topics, the Outlook Tower he had established in Edinburgh seven years earlier.[69] Built around a camera obscura, Geddes's Outlook Tower allowed visitors a privileged view of their position within the wider geographic and social context of the city and the world around them. To ascend the tower was to walk through a "cyclopedia" and a laboratory. As Zueblin noted admiringly, here the visitor could not "fail to be impressed with the relation of social conditions to topography."[70]

Inspired by this example, a number of University of Chicago academics held a meeting at their Hyde Park campus on February 17, 1900, to plan a similar sociological museum for Chicago. Geddes, who was in attendance, spoke in support of the proposal: "There are few people who know the real Chicago. Such a museum would present it and all its aspects in a nutshell. The action taken is one step toward establishing a museum of Chicago's life and environment."[71] Professor Small also supported the idea, describing the museum as a practical tool that would supplement the lectures at the university.[72] In Addams's absence, Zueblin proposed Hull House, closely connected to the Department of Sociology, as the ideal site.

Just as the Outlook Tower museum represented the surrounding city and region in miniature, Addams intended the Labor Museum to be a living survey of Chicago's material resources and related industries. In keeping with Geddes's model, she planned five departments: "(1) Metals with the copper of the Lake Superior region; (2) wood with the lumber region of Wisconsin and Michigan; (3) grain with the wheat and corn of Illinois and Indiana; (4 and 5) books and textiles which will be treated from the history of their own development, but connected so far as possible with the local conditions."[73] Each department would contain raw material specimens and demonstrations of their manufacturing processes. Using pictures, diagrams, and active human demonstrators, the museum would show that current industries, in their present debased form, might be reconciled positively with the long history of industrial labor. This knowledge would, in turn, be related to the tools and processes used in local factories, "i.e., copper in the Western Electric, wood in the Box Factory, bread in the Bremner Bakery, textiles in the sweatshops, etc."[74] (A severe structure, the Western Electric Building was a few blocks east of Hull House on Clinton Street, while the Bremner Bakery was on O'Brien Street, two blocks south of Twelfth.)[75]

Though the idea was to develop each of these departments to cover the range of industries on which Chicago's wealth was founded, the first department to be implemented when the Labor Museum opened, in November 1900, was the textile department. A 1902 report noted that the museum's cooking or "grain" department was the next to be developed, while the new Hull House shops would illustrate the wood and metal industries.[76] However, textiles remained the Labor Museum's primary focus until it was disestablished after Addams's death in 1935.

The museum's emphasis on the textile arts was appropriate to its location. The Nineteenth Ward was dominated by hastily built wooden houses crammed with sweatshop laborers, particularly the Jewish and Italian neighborhoods bordering Maxwell Street, as seen in figure 5.9. Along these streets, contractors carried piecework and finished garments back and forth between garment companies and nearby sweatshops, where immigrant workers stitched men's and boys' wear for the national market. In 1900, garment manufacturing was the second most productive industry in Chicago, after slaughtering and meatpacking. The basis of the garment industry was the sweating system, where fabric cut at central "shops" was sent out to contractors who arranged for the actual sewing, or "piece work," to be done by contract workers, sometimes in "outside shops" but more often in tenement house sweatshops, as seen in figure 5.10.[77] The system depended on the minute division of tasks and the ready supply of cheap labor, often that of women and children. The competitive nature of the business, in which contractors bid for work, led to low wages and poor working conditions for the immigrants who formed most of the workforce.

While Geddes's efforts in Old Town Edinburgh involved preserving historic buildings as part of a resistance to modern changes, Addams had no desire to preserve or romanticize the debased landscape of the Nineteenth Ward garment district. Recognizing the sweatshop as a critical example of a "belated" industry, she and her colleagues supported union efforts to reform the worst of its practices and undertook sociological studies to expose the scale of the problem. Led by resident Florence Kelley, Hull House was one of many organizations actively engaged in a battle

5 *New Industrial Institutions*

Figure 5.9
Rear of houses in the Maxwell Street area, 1907. Walter E. Lagerquist, photographer.

to make sweatshops illegal.[78] Considered in terms of social evolution, the garment industry was especially egregious, industrialization without the benefit of mechanization. Dependent on cheap human labor, it had failed to take advantage of technical innovation, tying those involved to a form of economic slavery in which wages and conditions were getting worse rather than better.

Where Addams was inspired by Geddes, Kelley was inspired by another observer of modern industrial life, Friedrich Engels, whose book *The Condition of the Working Class in England* she had translated for publication in the United States.[79] Upon moving to Chicago, Kelley began gathering data on the residents of the Nineteenth Ward as part of a federal Department of Labor study of slum conditions in the four largest American cities. Prompted by Kelley, the residents of Hull House undertook an ambitious social survey of a one-square-mile area to the southeast, gathering information about the ethnicity, income, and occupations of residents, which they represented graphically in the form of color-coded maps. Entitled *The Hull House Maps and Papers*, the results were published in 1895. While this collection of essays attempted to draw attention to the poverty and poor working conditions of the neighborhood via literary and graphic means, the Labor Museum approached the issue differently.

Addams was explicit about preferring the name "museum" instead of "school," with its childish connotations, seeing a museum as a more dynamic, engaging kind of institution, a place to engage the interest of female workers not interested in lectures and classes.[80] Addams had long been interested in the theater as an effective mode of education, and along with Hull House resident Jessie Luther, the curator of the museum, she emphasized the value of live performance.[81] Speaking to the *Chicago Record* in 1899, Addams claimed that, while commercial theaters were frequently "unwholesome," her institution had vast potential for social elevation.[82] Often using University of Chicago education professor John Dewey's description of education as a "continuing reconstruction of experience," she intended to show that, though contemporary industrial methods were new by historical standards, they were related to earlier practices of making. Comparing the work of the settlement to a painting or novel or song, she saw it as a form of artistic expression, not in a traditional artistic medium but, through actors or performers, in the medium of life itself. Although Addams, like Geddes, included visual displays, such as a wall chart illustrating the global history of textile manufacture, she placed special emphasis on human actors, local women who demonstrated the progress of the textile arts at different stages in their evolution.

A different kind of museum required a different kind of architecture, less reliant on Arts and Crafts models and more in keeping with the aesthetic of modernism emerging in Chicago at the turn of the twentieth century. In late 1901 or early 1902, the Labor Museum moved into a purpose-built space above the gymnasium, on the second floor of a new addition to Hull House on Polk Street, again designed by Allen and Irving Pond. The Pond brothers took a tactical approach with their Hull House additions: not monumental but at the scale of the city around them, each one had a different design to suit the multiple functions of the settlement and the needs of the moment.[83] In their several projects for Addams, the Ponds created a unique and underappreciated style of

5 *New Industrial Institutions*

Figure 5.10
Sweatshop at 132 Maxwell Street, 1905.

Chicago modernism, epitomized by the additions built along Polk Street, including the coffee house and auditorium building, with the gymnasium and workshops building across an alley behind. In contrast with the English Gothic style of their original Hull House extension on Halsted Street (a style employed in other Chicago settlements of the same era), these later buildings were as unusual architecturally as the Labor Museum was institutionally.

Rather than continuing to imitate rustic architectural types, the Ponds' later work at Hull House was more urbane, designed in a series as a coordinated street front, as seen in figure 5.11. Employing pressed brick, their ornament was inventive, mixing elements of the classical and the Gothic. Though the coffee house in the foreground is reminiscent of an agricultural building, the gymnasium building next to it has a flat roof. Reflecting local expressions of the Arts and Crafts and the emerging Prairie School style, the street facades are tied together by the same horizontal line. These buildings are wholly modern, not throwbacks to the medieval style, nor obviously reformist institutions with a dour aesthetic;

Figure 5.11
Hull House, coffee house and gymnasium, Chicago, 1889–1908. Pond and Pond, architects.

they are eclectic and decorative, in keeping with the commercial architecture of the surrounding neighborhood. This aesthetic aligned with Addams's goal to engage her audience on their own terms, offering the image of a museum as livelier and more interesting than a school. In this way, the Pond brothers recognized the need to appeal to the taste of the residents of the Nineteenth Ward, understanding them as not only subjects of reform but also discerning members of urban consumer culture.

Entering the gymnasium building from Polk Street and walking upstairs to the textile room, a large space illuminated by north-facing windows, visitors to the Labor Museum found the opposite of the sweatshop: an idealized vision of female production that was warm, welcoming, and clean. This was an active place equipped with "spinning wheels and looms, and exhibits of raw material and manufactured products in flax, wool, cotton occupy cases on the walls."[84] A living display of craft traditions from around the world, the museum had a permanent staff of four women of Irish, Danish, Italian, Syrian, and Russian heritage who demonstrated different textile-manufacturing processes. Visiting children were encouraged to weave blankets on a small Navajo loom provided, and a Navajo-style blanket may be seen hanging on the wall in many photographs. This room was not just an exhibition of crafts but a whole world, a living reproduction of the history of industrial evolution, enacted by women. Intended to illustrate the vital link between past, present, and future craft techniques, the museum was designed to help immigrant workers understand their importance in the evolving continuum of industrial history.

While the Labor Museum may be accused of the same romanticizing of "primitive" or "peasant" cultures endemic to the Arts and Crafts movement, Addams's intent was not simply nostalgic. She intended the presentation of the historical trajectory of the textile arts not only to revive interest in the past but also to show the future of mechanization. She later wrote: "It is not, of course, the design of the museum to keep to primitive methods, but so rapidly as possible to add the more complicated machinery and to illustrate by actual manufacturing."[85] By understanding the long history of the industrial arts, present-day industrial workers would understand the value their labor had for society. In addition to pride and the personal satisfaction of making something well, this knowledge would give them a sense of connection with others in their community and faith in the future. Educated in the principle of industrial evolution, which connected the crafts of the past and the industry of the present day, they would understand not only that the beautiful simplicity of traditional arts might be recovered but also that the social harmony of past cultures might again be achieved. Addams's comments about the women who performed the demonstrations underline the ethnographic basis of the project. Because some neighborhood women had not seen a spinning wheel before, they represented a form of craft revival. In demonstrating their craft at the Labor Museum, they were playing a dual role, both as themselves and as representatives of "primitive" cultures existing in the present day. Addams used them to illustrate the vital link between past, present, and future craft practices, all occurring along a continuum of industrial history.

The Labor Museum was a mechanism of progressive education aimed at female workers who lived in the neighborhood, as well as enlightened visitors. Its key message was that industries such as garment manufacturing could be bought up to date, with class and racial differences synthesized through a comprehensive view of global cultural and industrial progress.[86] Intended to solve the problem of the alienation of labor, the Labor Museum would increase awareness of industrial design's social and evolutionary character. Echoing Veblen's condemnation of barbarian warrior culture, Addams argued against teaching history with an emphasis on war and conquest. Instead, the focus should be on the collective social processes which "create and conserve civilization."[87] Like Veblen, she believed the rise of a modern industrial class and the decline of the leisure class would occur not through revolution but through evolution, an organic process in which the machine's logic fundamentally changed human thought and behavior.

Veblen's belief that women would be active agents in this evolutionary change made his theory especially attractive to the residents of Hull House. While outmoded social institutions were holding back progress, Veblen wrote, they could be reversed or brought up to date through attention to the rational logic of technology. The Labor Museum conformed to these ideals, offering the possibility of emancipation for women of both classes. Reconnected to the nobility of labor, educated women were freed from lives of vicarious futility, while uneducated women were released from lives of industrial drudgery. The question of women's role in the industrial economy was a vital issue in this period. Debated at many conferences, it was the subject of many scholarly publications, much political lobbying, and diverse forms of social activism, from the education of girls at the Jewish Training School, including exercises to strengthen the body as well as the mind, to legislation restricting the hours women could work in factories. The Labor Museum advanced that pragmatic work through theatrical demonstrations.

In much of her writing, Addams expressed support for the traditional division of labor. While she believed that women had a long and proud history as makers, she held the conservative position that women's work should take place in the home. Rather than banishing women from industrial work, Kelley and Veblen held a different view. Kelley lobbied for radical social reorganization to

5 New Industrial Institutions

Figure 5.12
Mrs. Molinaro demonstrating spinning, Labor Museum, Hull House, 1910.

benefit all workers. For example, she argued for the creation of
cooperatives in which women were equal participants in all areas
of life, including manufacturing.[88] Where Kelley was a committed
socialist, Veblen's political position was more closely aligned with
that of Beatrice and Sidney Webb than that of Marx and Engels.[89]
Sharing the agenda of Chicago progressives such as the journalist
and social reformer Henry D. Lloyd, he supported the argument
that the problem of industrialization was not that it exploited
workers, but that its emancipatory potential had yet to be realized.

The Workshop, the School, and the Museum   247

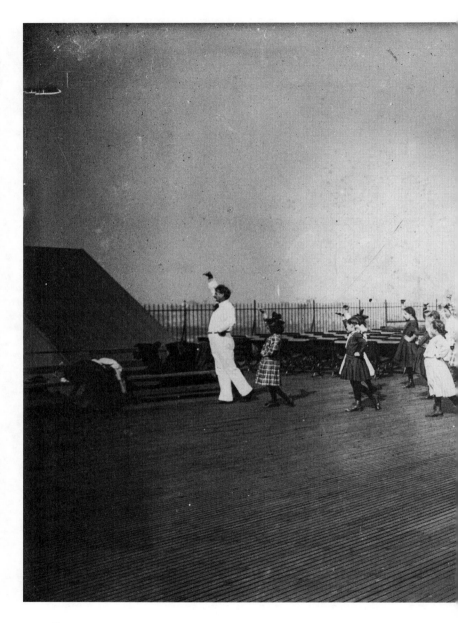

Figure 5.13
Schoolgirls doing exercises on the roof of the Jewish Training School, c. 1911.

In many ways, his lecture echoed the popular concept of a coming "industrial democracy."[90] Espoused by the Webbs, Lloyd, Zueblin, and many academics at the University of Chicago, along with members of the moderate labor movement, this term signified a range of meanings, but generally referred to some form of industrial collectivism where workers were no longer exploited but equal participants in the manufacturing process.[91] Understood as the ultimate stage in industrial evolution, this was a corporativist ideal of free labor, with shared management and no class or racial difference recognized.

To the extent that he was prepared to predict the future, Veblen believed the path of evolution was slowly bending away from barbarianism, and the power of the ruling leisure class diminishing. As an example of this transformation, he cited the changed social position of women that had occurred within the last generation. The patriarchal system of "ownership marriage" in which women had secondary status was already beginning to break down, he argued, because it was at variance with "the most ancient habits of thought of the race, as well as with the exigencies of a peaceful, industrial mode of life."[92] While Veblen gave few clues about the physical form of the future city, it is not difficult to see the Labor Museum as a materialization of its essential intellectual basis. As a room intended as an educational museum, it offered a corrective to the world of the department store. On State Street, the dictates of pecuniary culture reduced women to mute mannequins, exhibitors, through their dress, of the status of their husbands and fathers. In contrast, the Hull House Labor Museum presented a vision of a modern industrial community in which women were not objects of ownership but fully functioning members of society. In this sense, female emancipation marked progress for all, an overturning of the barbarian culture that dictated women held secondary status as both consumers and producers. For Veblen, this was both progress and a positive reversion to what he called a "peaceable or savage temperament."[93] This reversion would result in a society of equals and the decline of competition and warfare.

When predatory culture became obsolete, Veblen wrote, the social hierarchy in which women were equivalent to property

　　　　　　　　　5 New Industrial Institutions

would break down and disappear. Together with the engineer (educated not in the classical tradition, which reinforced ancient canons of taste and behavior, but in the applied sciences), the New Woman would bring about what he described as the natural decay of the all-powerful business enterprise. Emerging first among the daughters of leisure-class families, who chafed under the tedium of enforced idleness, this transformation would blossom when working-class women came to appreciate their long-repressed potential as creative makers. Released from confining practices of conspicuous consumption, these emancipated women were a sign of the evolution of society away from its barbaric patriarchal phase and a return to primitive communitarianism, a peaceful and industrious society operating at an advanced level. This hopeful scenario is the tentatively optimistic note on which *The Theory of the Leisure Class* ends.

Taming the "Monster Leviathan"

Despite the diversity of the activities it sponsored, the Chicago Arts and Crafts Society is best remembered for one event, the lecture Frank Lloyd Wright delivered there in March 1901. Rewritten and delivered many times, "The Art and Craft of the Machine" has become a key text in the history of modern architecture.[94] In his self-mythologizing *Autobiography*, Wright described the lecture as a pivotal moment, one that established his identity as a visionary iconoclast.[95] The lecture reveals his struggle to reconcile the romantic image of the architect as an artist possessing the unique capability to crystallize epistemic ideals into built form, with the emerging narrative of the architect as a technical specialist dedicated to advancing social causes.

As proof of the potential of industrial production methods, Wright offered examples from his professional experience, citing specific material technologies used in the Chicago building industry at the time. These included new processes applied to traditional materials, and new materials and fabrication techniques, such as decorative terra-cotta cladding, electro-plating, and metal casting processes. Wright placed these new materials and processes at the most advanced end of an evolutionary schema of human development, culminating in steel-framed construction with lightweight brick and terra-cotta tile cladding, the system local architects dubbed the "Chicago construction." Beyond what he called the "experimental station" of the Arts and Crafts workshop, the skyscrapers rising on downtown building sites offered the most instructive examples of the next stage of industrial progress.[96] Shaking off derivative historical eclecticism, they were the first realization of a truly original American architecture.

Inspired by the rhetoric of his mentor Louis Sullivan and by Oscar Lovell Triggs's call for a "new industrialism," Wright began by conjuring two antithetical images of the city with vividly contrasting qualities: the abject industrial city of the present, which he described as a "monster leviathan stretching acre upon acre into the far distance. High overhead hangs the stagnant pall of its fetid breath, reddened with the light from its myriad eyes endlessly everywhere blinking," and the perfected industrial city of the future.[97] In his condemnation of the degradation and ugliness of the American city, Wright echoed the lecture that Oscar Wilde had delivered nineteen years earlier. Chicago industry had advanced tremendously since 1882, but despite its industrial innovations and the rejection of explicit references to the Gothic, it continued to represent a barbaric race. Using both biological and technological metaphors, Wright described an alternative: the city as a living, breathing machine-organism, operating efficiently and coherently. Treated correctly, freed of false historicist references, the skyscraper might become a truly democratic art form. Potentially the greatest machine of all, the skyscraper city was waiting only for the architect-artist to bring it to life, to give it a soul, in Wright's words. Properly conjured, it would become a perfectly tuned mechanical organism, productive and efficient, with all parts working together in perfect harmony.

Casting himself as an outlier working against dominant professional and commercial interests, Wright later claimed his Hull House audience had denounced his lecture as "offensive heresy."[98] However, rather than being the isolated pronouncement of a lone genius, his was one of many lectures given on the sociological possibilities of industrialization offered at the Nineteenth Ward

Figure 5.14
Chicago River, looking west from the south bank toward the Rush Street Bridge, 1908.

settlement around 1900. Involved with the new industrialism movement, Wright's ideas were in keeping with those of many others involved in the Hull House group, not only Triggs but also Addams and Veblen himself. In fact, in 1939, Wright acknowledged the economist as one of his influences.[99] The two men share notable similarities. Both formed close relationships with emancipated New Women and later had cause to curse the social conservatism of Chicago which frowned on those relationships. Within a short span of time, both were tainted by personal scandal and forced to leave the city. Veblen left the University of Chicago for Stanford University in 1906; three years later, Frank Lloyd Wright closed his Oak Park studio before departing for Berlin and then Florence.[100] Beyond their personal trials, they shared a common belief in the evolutionary potential of industrialization.

Veblen and Wright praised the democratizing influence of machine production and cast the designer-engineer as the true "modern man" who would build the future. They both saw the future of human society in the perfection of industrial processes, believing that the universal adoption of machine logic, efficiency, and capacity would free workers from exploitative labor. But where Wright's rhetoric was grounded in the physical world, in the aesthetic and social potential of new materials and forms of construction (or "Machinery, Materials, and Men," as he later put it), Veblen focused on the psychological and anthropological context in which industrial production occurred.

Veblen had no personal agenda for the future of architecture and design: his interest lay in economic and social well-being. Unlike Sullivan and Wright, he was unconcerned with the aesthetic expression of democracy. For Veblen, the continued obsession with aesthetics as a cultural signifier was a sign of evolutionary inertia. He rejected architecture as the means through which the historical divide between leisure and labor might be healed (even the Pond brothers' more urbane design for the later Hull House additions, which borrowed the rhythm and varied ornament of a typical Chicago commercial street, might be seen as mimicking the culture of consumption, though it was reformist in spirit). As with urban design and planning, the profession remained a leisure-class institution beholden to its powerful business clients. Attempts by architects to discover a modern style by using industrial building systems and materials did little to erase the hierarchy in which the architect, a skilled interpreter of the national zeitgeist, was considered superior to the construction worker and the building site laborer. The only way to end the dominance of the leisure class and its defining desire for conspicuous consumption was to overcome belated or backward social institutions in which architecture, with its traditional dependence on patronage, was included. In this category, Veblen also included the institution of marriage, which restricted women to secondary roles, both as producers and consumers. Truly modern production would happen not in elite enclaves but at scale; it would appear not as a unique and identifiable style vulnerable to the caprices of fashion but invisibly and ubiquitously, through the social and economic transformations promised under the mantra of industrial democracy.

Turning away from small-scale philanthropic efforts such as Arts and Crafts workshops, Veblen and others, including Triggs and Jane Addams, conjured more ambitious visions. Veblen's writing supported their calls for the total reformulation of systems of production and consumption according to the logic of industry. Identifying initiatives aimed at realizing this transformation, he praised Triggs's Industrial Art League for recognizing the psychological potential of machine thinking, and (implicitly) Addams's Labor Museum for recognizing the role of women within industrial society. While Triggs was an avowed socialist, Veblen was not: he shared with Addams and many of his Progressive contemporaries a distrust of revolutionary politics and a belief in the advent of democratic socialism through the slow but inexorable process of evolution. And yet Veblen saw the future as very much hanging in the balance. Though he shared the progressive outlook of Triggs, Addams, Kelley, Lloyd, Wright, and others in the Hull House circle, he was also deeply skeptical of the ability of these reformers to achieve change. Industrial advancement and well-intentioned efforts at social reform might lead to female emancipation and a classless, raceless national collective. Or they could just as easily deepen the social divide.

Late in his career, Veblen named the engineer as the true leader of the modern era. Writing in 1919, soon after the Soviet revolution, he imaged a future state managed by a "Soviet of Technicians."[101] Published in the liberal *Dial* and later reprinted in his book *The Engineers and the Price System* (1921), this provocative essay is Veblen's most straightforward and accessible statement of the difference between industrial and business enterprises: a proposal for an advanced American republic governed by engineers and freed from the control of business cartels. Ever skeptical, Veblen emphasized there was no chance that such a revolutionary republic would ever be realized in the United States. Nevertheless, the argument was suggestive for members of what became known as the Technocracy movement.[102]

Veblen's call for a government of technocrats found popularity with architecture critics such as Lewis Mumford and the growing ranks of engineers and scientific management experts. The belief in social reconstruction via the collective management of industry and commerce became especially influential in architecture and planning circles during the Great Depression. Veblen was read avidly by housing reformers associated with the Regional Planning

Association of America, including Mumford and architect Frederick Ackerman, as well as the economist Rexford G. Tugwell, who founded the Resettlement Administration under President Franklin D. Roosevelt. Veblen's personal history, including his checkered academic career and his failure to make any impact in Washington, DC, during his brief time there during World War I did little to deter his followers, who believed the only way to tackle the entrenched problems of economic instability was at the level of the federal government. Shaped by the combined forces of big business and the New Deal government, the figure of the architect was transformed from a gifted artist into a specialist technician, not a form-giver but an organizer of resources. The manager of a team of professionals, the architect would solve not only the problems of building but also those of the city.

But Veblen's influence on New Deal architects and planners has perhaps been exaggerated. Even his most ardent admirers were frustrated that he did not propose concrete solutions to the problems he identified. And they paid little attention to his discussion of the essential role of women in the dual processes of industrial and social transformation. Ultimately, the value of Veblen's writing is not in the future it seemed to predict, but in the contradictions he identified in contemporary society and culture. Veblen recognized the complexity of consumption culture, and the difficulty of rejecting its multiple material manifestations in favor of asceticism. In terms of architecture, the idea of a universal and autonomous modern type developed from technology alone was all but impossible to achieve given that individual buildings exist in distinctly different social contexts, and that display is a primal function of cultural production.[103]

As provocative as his 1919 call for a "Soviet of Engineers" is, Veblen is less well-known for this seemingly revolutionary essay than he is for his concept of conspicuous consumption, published twenty years earlier. Based on the persistent influence of his first book, *The Theory of the Leisure Class*, he has joined a pantheon of fin-de-siècle cultural commentators who positioned the city as an expression of the crisis of modernity. Yet, while often described as a Progressive intellectual, Veblen was fervent in his criticism of programs of social amelioration. Crucially, in his indictment of the Arts and Crafts movement as merely another manifestation of leisure-class culture, he predicted the inner paradox of modern design just as it was beginning to appear. In the United States, those who desired an industrial democracy hoped that it would arise spontaneously, without the intervention of an elite. However, those in privileged social positions could not help but act as overzealous midwives to the new era, prodding and pulling it into existence. In their reverence for progress, they fetishized and aestheticized industrial processes, and thus industrial production remained subsumed within the pecuniary canon of taste. The modern city, Wright's "monster leviathan," could be tamed but not extinguished. This is the true prescience of Veblen's writing. Besides the early twentieth-century view of modernity that he shared with his European and American contemporaries—a modernity of advanced technology, efficiency, and functionalism—he identified the rise of a market-led consumer society, one in which the global marketplace was the ultimate machine.

Conclusion: Picturing Veblen's Chicago

The Theory of the Leisure Class is a book about an idea: conspicuous consumption. Published in 1899, when Thorstein Veblen was a political economist on the faculty of the University of Chicago, it was written as a contribution to scholarly debate, a volley in the assault on classical economics that had begun in American universities in the 1880s. The original subtitle—*An Economic Study in the Evolution of Institutions*—signals Veblen's intention to study the social institutions that form the basis of economic relationships using the lens of "evolutionary science."[1] Building on his breakthrough essay from 1894, "The Economic Theory of Woman's Dress," his first book challenged the belief that economic value was linked to pragmatic function. Overturning the assumptions of classical economics, Veblen sought "natural laws" to explain why conceptions of value changed over time. A supporter of the new "institutional" school of economics influenced by German academics, Veblen sought new theories based on the sciences of biology and anthropology to explain the growing divide between capital and labor, as well as the inequity all too visible on the streets of Chicago where he lived and worked, during the deep depression of 1893–1894. In this context, Veblen had little interest in aesthetics, and no intention to enter aesthetic debate. And yet the term "conspicuous consumption" has come to assume enormous influence not only in economics and sociology but also in architecture and design.

Veblen's theory of the leisure class is material: its origins lie in what he called the "doctrine of waste." Yet, while the phrase "conspicuous consumption" is now part of everyday language, its meaning commonly understood, it has no clearly defined image beyond a vague association with ornament and abundance. Like luxury, its historical predecessor, it cannot be identified with any particular style or material. Indeed, its chief characteristic is its variability. Conspicuous consumption is a practice, an effort to meet an ever-changing standard of reputability set by an urban elite deeply invested in sustaining the status quo while adhering to the vagaries of fashion. Borrowing a term already in widespread use, Veblen referred to this elite as the "leisure class." In earlier periods, this class had set itself apart from working people by its ostentatious idleness, which Veblen deemed "conspicuous leisure." But by the nineteenth century, this practice was overtaken by the ostentatious display of goods, especially in urban communities where people were increasingly strangers to one another. Although conspicuous consumption has no specific image, it is sited in a particular place and time: the American metropolis in the second half of the nineteenth century. Though he never mentions the city by name, Chicago, where Veblen wrote the book, features in *The Theory of the Leisure Class* on almost every page. Hiding in plain sight, Chicago is always present, though never clearly seen.

When Veblen described the city where he lived as a "representative city of the advanced pecuniary culture," he was referring not to the stockyards or the downtown skyscrapers but to the landscaped lawns and drives of Jackson Park, as seen in figure 6.1.[2] Ironically, Veblen chose as an exemplary illustration of his theory of the leisure class not an urban scene but an artificially pastoral one, a public park developed on the grounds of the former site of the World's Columbian Exposition. Naturalistic rather than natural, Jackson Park was the realization of a plan drawn up by Frederick Law Olmsted and Calvert Vaux for Chicago's South Park Commission in the early 1870s, part of a green ring planned to surround the city before much of the midwestern metropolis even existed.[3] The park was finally completed after a series of fires destroyed the exposition grounds during the turmoil of 1893–1894. As with Olmsted and Vaux's other metropolitan parks, this was an entirely urban artifice, a re-creation of nature tamed and civilized for the benefit of urban dwellers. Although much of the park was given over to picturesque lawns, lakes, and rambles, it also featured broad boulevards and carriage drives flanked by rows of trees designed for public promenading.

Organic, yet absolutely flat and formal, extending toward a distant and undefined vanishing point, these drives reflected both make-believe rusticity and the imperative of urban organization. For Veblen, who had observed the construction of Jackson Park from the University of Chicago next door, the popularity of this bucolic landscape might be explained by an incontestable love of nature borrowed from the leisure-class code of taste. This taste, which had spread from the leisure class proper to the middle and lower classes, dictated the planting of trees in treeless areas (such as the swampy western shore of Lake Michigan) and the deliberate replacement of native species with European varieties, such as maple, cottonwood, or willow, in other spaces.[4] In this sense, Jackson Park was an American simulacrum of a great man's expansive estate transposed onto the midwestern prairie. Describing the park in this way, Veblen foreshadowed one of the central themes of twentieth-century urban criticism, the idea that the capitalist city is defined by its illusory nature.

While Jackson Park was an unusual choice of subject to illustrate Veblen's scathing assessment of American urban culture, it exemplifies the breadth of his criticism. In 1899, he was one of many commentators to project his theory of modernity onto the great midwestern metropolis. *The Theory of the Leisure Class* may be considered part of a tradition of texts in which authors mapped out ideas of modernity onto Chicago. At the time of the World's Columbian Exposition, photographs of Chicago's crowded streets, elevated railroads, and tall buildings were published in newspapers, journals, and books and sent around the world to convey a sense of what the future might look like.[5] Yet, unlike other critics of the late nineteenth-century American city, Veblen did not limit himself to obvious markers of profit or exploitation, such as the splendid Board of Trade and the industrial-scale stockyards, or lowly factories and tenement buildings, for example. Instead, he claimed, an insidious pecuniary motivation lay behind almost every attempt at cultural uplift.

Veblen's description of advanced capitalist culture and the practice of conspicuous consumption has been stripped of its basis in nineteenth-century anthropology and expanded into a diagnosis applicable to all modern people. Since the early twentieth century, critics and historians have used *The Theory of the Leisure Class* to reinforce the dominant interpretation of modern architecture, first ideas of technocracy and functionalism and then theories of the spectacle and ornament. Published at the turn of the twentieth century, a moment perfectly poised on the brink of the modern period in architecture, the book is a perpetual reference

Figure 6.1
Trees along drive in Jackson Park, c. 1925.

in histories of architectural modernity. Despite the complexity of Veblen's writing, readers are captivated by its prescience: the endless anticipatory aspect of his famous book is a motor that drives his continual relevance and keeps this classic text in print. The variety and fleeting nature of the material references Veblen employed have led historians and critics to apply his ideas widely, including to types he did not discuss in detail, including the department store and the skyscraper. (Curiously, they have paid little attention to the one building type on which he wrote most extensively—the modern American university.) Yet, in extending Veblen's analysis of economic patterns of production and consumption to architecture, his writing is typically used to support accepted narratives about American architectural history and Chicago's place within it, rather than to open up new ones.

Beginning with Joseph Dorfman's 1934 biography, Veblen's perceptiveness has been ascribed to his position as a cultural outsider. During the early twentieth century, a scholarly narrative emerged in which Veblen's alienation from the ruling leisure class, with Yankees looking down at this son of humble Norwegian immigrant farmers, has been used to explain the perceptiveness of his critique.[6] Captured in Eva Watson-Schütze's evocative portrait of the economist in repose, the mythology of Veblen's productive alienation has never really been dispelled, despite recent revisionist scholarship. In this mythology, Veblen is part flâneur immersed in and amused by urban culture, and part disinterested scientist, a figure in the city but never really of it.

Often positioned as an American counterpart to Georg Simmel and Werner Sombart, Veblen is part of a cohort of turn-of-the-century intellectual figures whose writing was a bridge between nineteenth-century political economists and subsequent generations of writers who explored the material expression of capitalist culture and the ideological utility of taste, from Max Weber and Ferdinand Tönnies to Walter Benjamin, Siegfried Kracauer, Max Horkheimer, Theodor Adorno, Guy Debord, Jean Baudrillard, and Pierre Bourdieu.[7] Veblen's attention to the value placed on commodities as markers of status affiliation makes this genealogical construction reasonable. Beyond parallels with twentieth-century sociology and cultural criticism, Veblen has even been described as "the first theorist of the 'post-modern era,'" his work "premised on an uncanny premonition of many poststructuralist themes."[8] Overturning conventional hierarchies such as male and female, leisure and labor, savage and civilized, he held up a critical mirror to his peers.

In his explication of theoretical ideas through the example of everyday things, and his unplanned but decisive move from academia to journalism, Veblen's intellectual approach and life story have some similarities with Weimar-era cultural critics. In 1918, Veblen left mainstream academia for good, using his platform as an editor and writer for *The Dial* to attack the control of industry by "vested interests." The essays he wrote for the New York-based magazine primarily focused on politics and economics, leaving the cultural criticism of his Chicago days behind. But although his writing sharpened in response to the journalistic medium, he never returned to the fleeting imagery of leisure-class culture that captivated and entertained readers of *The Theory of the Leisure Class*, nor expanded on its potential.

With its theme of waste, *The Theory of the Leisure Class* is a theory not of surface effects but of matter. Where Benjamin and Kracauer focused on the imagery of transparency, Veblen was concerned less with the reflective surfaces of plate glass windows and mirrors and more with the constrictive boning of a woman's corset and the encumbrance of her serge skirt with its heavy folds. Beyond the example of women's clothing, his book deals with the spoils of recent wars and the ghostly presence of history, exemplified by the weight of stone and the intangible but vise-like grip of tradition. We might speculate that Veblen's vehement rejection of socially ingrained habits of wastefulness was grounded in an aspiration for the weightlessness, rationality, and freedom that advanced industrial production might bring. Indeed, that idea was embedded in utopian hopes for the frame system of construction to which he alluded, in an offhand comment, as the basis of modern building.[9] But while he may have aspired to the asceticism of modernity, Veblen's primary theme in his first and most influential book was not the sublimation of the quotidian but the material detritus that his contemporaries gathered around themselves. Still, beyond the persuasive example of women's clothing, *The Theory of the Leisure Class* paints few memorable images.

Inspired by Sigmund Freud's theories and by Eugène Atget's evocative photographs of the streets of Paris, Benjamin suggested the existence of an "optical unconscious," and called on the power of photography to "extend our grasp of the material world beyond the constraints of our sensory and cognitive apparatus."[10] In this spirit, one might construct an iconography for Veblen's classic book that explains his complex ideas and counters the accepted iconography of Chicago as the first city of American modernity. A catalog of Veblenesque imagery, such an iconography might include the reproduction of Battle Rock in southwest Colorado, the ancient home of a Pueblo Indian tribe known as the cliff dwellers, at the World's Columbian exposition; the heavily battlemented first University of Chicago building, Douglas Hall, its menacing Gothic towers overlooking the new Illinois Central Railway line; fashionably dressed women and men looking at displays of handkerchiefs and linens in the windows of the Marshall Field's department store on State Street; newly erected high-rise buildings, twelve and sixteen stories high, towering over decrepit two-story buildings covered with advertising signs in the streets of the south Loop; and a group of young girls exercising on the roof of the Jewish Training School, raising their arms and faces to the sun, away from the dirty streets of the Nineteenth Ward garment district in which the building sat.

This iconography counters the canonical images of Chicago created by European visitors such as Germans Ludwig Hilberseimer, Erich Mendelsohn, and Bruno Taut, and the Austrian Richard Neutra, who all visited the United States in the 1920s and '30s.[11] From grain silos to factories and tall office blocks, the industrial and commercial buildings springing up in the American cities of the Northeast and Midwest fascinated these avant-garde architects. Using photographs captured as they passed through, or clipped from books and magazines, they created iconic collaged images representing the city of the future. Setting these unprecedented, unadorned structures against historical forms, European architects interpreted them as the modern answer to the classical and the Gothic, an epistemic stylistic shift matching the tectonic global disruption of World War I.

In their books, and those of affiliated critics such as Walter Curt Behrendt, photographs of Chicago architecture featured as the realization of the *Neue Sachlichkeit*, the "new objectivity," sometimes translated as "functionalist" architecture.[12] For example, Mendelsohn's *Amerika, Bilderbuch eines Architekten* (1926), a book of expressionistic photographs of New York, Buffalo, Chicago, and Detroit, celebrated the imagery of the American industrial vernacular.[13] Apparently designed for practical purposes rather than the result of subjective design preferences and deference to fashion, this functional aesthetic became the model for the modern style developed in the early twentieth-century. Heavily cropped and partial, Mendelsohn's photographs showed Chicago not as it was but as it might become, an idea as much as a built reality.[14]

Throughout the twentieth century, the skyscraper dominated the narrative about the prototypical modernity of late nineteenth-century Chicago. Americans claimed it as their invention, the architectural type that made their cities definitively different from the industrial cities of Europe, a symbol of technical mastery removed from the weight of history.[15] Chicago, in particular, served up breathtaking examples of the unfamiliar new type. Like Mendelsohn, Behrendt admired Burnham and Root's 16-story Monadnock Building, decorated only by the smooth lines of its unusual purple-brown brick, for its "rigid functionalism," describing it as a triumph of social will over the individual caprice of the architect. In designing the Monadnock's massive masonry walls pierced by undifferentiated window openings and unrelieved by ornament, designer John W. Root had removed his subjective creativity in favor of the needs of the "actual social and economic world," Behrendt wrote.[16] In books such as Mendelsohn's, photographs of this brutal monument to pragmatism were heroic and hopeful propaganda for an idea of modernity not yet realized.

As critical text excoriating the urban environment and taste of the nineteenth century and preparing the way for the refined industrial aesthetic of the early twentieth, *The Theory of the Leisure Class* might be considered as aligned with these European publications. As Chicago's contribution to the rhetoric of modernist aesthetics, Veblen is sometimes assumed to have looked favorably on the emerging modern style. For example, the simple brick walls of the Monadnock appear to conform to his preference for "the dead walls of the sides and back of these structures, left untouched by the hands of the artist."[17] Yet, read more carefully, *The Theory of the Leisure Class* counters the assumptions behind modernist rhetoric, in particular the belief that the new style reflected the rise of a technocratic state and the decline of leisure-class culture.

Early twentieth century critics and architectural historians often presented Chicago's high-rise buildings as autonomous and authorless, examples of technology evolving spontaneously, outside the imperatives of class and culture. Veblen's theory, on the other hand, depends on the close and causal connection between human and technological evolution. While the rationality of industry might one day overcome barbaric habits of acquisition and display, that time had not yet come, he wrote. The industrial revolution had not produced the social revolution predicted by the avant-garde. Nor had it led to the rejection of conspicuous consumption. On the contrary, consumption itself was being industrialized. Veblen predicted the rise of a new phase of American capitalism, one in which businesses depended heavily on marketing and advertising to increase demand for mass-produced consumer goods. In this context, the structures associated with industrial production—the factories, lofts, and skyscrapers—are not separate from the rise of the global marketplace but part of it.

Modernist photographs of iconic buildings like the Monadnock obliterate their surrounding context through graphic editing. Famously, Mendelsohn pointed his camera upward; his collaged photographs captured heroic images of high-rise buildings such as the grain silo and the skyscraper, contrasting them against shadowy foregrounds, positioning them as the functionalist future. Veblen's view of the city, by contrast, is the horizontal perspective of the pedestrian. A 1908 photograph of Jackson Street (figure 6.2) reveals the shabby one- and two-story buildings directly beneath and adjacent to the Monadnock. Covered with advertising signs touting liquor, cigars, ketchup, men's suits, and steam vapor baths, they mark the boundary between the financial district and the Levee, the seamy South Side vice district. In Veblen's terms, these are the necessary context to Burnham and Root's iconic tower, graphic manifestations of the messy commercial world that gave rise to the skyscraper, among other modern forms.

*

Veblen's *The Theory of the Leisure Class* is structured by the defining principle of nineteenth-century political economics, the idea that societies evolve according to their environment and that technology is a crucial marker of evolutionary progress. The concept of progress that defined the World's Columbian Exposition, the nation-defining event that took place a year after Veblen arrived in Chicago, frames his theory. Yet his image of contemporary Americans is less aligned with the heroic pseudo-streets of the central boulevards of the fair, and more with the ethnographic displays that occupied the periphery. Offering a view different from the familiar photographs of the world's fair—photographs of parasol-wielding young women overlooking gleaming white neoclassical monuments—a more intimate image reveals the anthropological basis on which the world's fair was founded. A couple sits on a bench overlooking three modest birch-bark-covered tepees, replicas of a Penobscot Indian camp found in Maine. To the left, in the distance, two totem poles mark the entrance of a cedar-plank Kwakiutl house, reconstructed from an original the anthropologist Franz Boas had studied in the Pacific Northwest. Located on the edge of the fair, these reconstructions of Native American homes embody the academic argument that frames *The Theory of the Leisure Class*, the idea of differential human evolution, registered by different rates of industrial progress. This image illustrates the racial basis of claims about Chicago's progress. As shown at the World's Columbian Exposition, American progress was not equivalent to universal human progress. The idea of the industrial advances of "modern" men, embodied here by contemporary Americans, depended on material and visual contrast with "primitive" ones.

Veblen was far from the only critic to use the language of evolution and race science to distinguish "primitive" and "modern" psychological tendencies. His theory draws on a belief in technological determinism that makes his writing appear aligned with early twentieth-century criticism such as that of Austrian architect and critic Adolf Loos, in which ornament was characterized as backward, an expression of cultural devolution. For Veblen, however, the "primitives" were not only the descendants of far-off races but those Anglo-Americans who retained the psychological stamp of the barbarian. Veblen saw Americans, supposedly the most "advanced" race, as being accountable to their social institutions, institutions that inhibited rather than inspired progress. As the replica Pueblo cliff dwelling and tepees at the world's fair attest, for more skeptical social critics the past and present of human evolution might exist in the same place simultaneously.

The Theory of the Leisure Class is notable not only for its economic treatment of matters of style but also for its attention to a particular aesthetic, a local version of the Gothic Revival that the architecture critic Montgomery Schuyler called the "American eclectic Gothic."[18] Strangely, this aspect of Veblen's writing—his strong association between the contemporary pastiche of the Gothic and his theory of the leisure class, between predatory capitalism and feudal barbarism—has almost entirely escaped the attention of architectural historians. Although he touched on the structural frame as the image of modernity, Veblen's architectural paradigm differed from the rational, transparent steel-and-glass frame supposedly invented in Chicago. His focus was the persistence of the Gothic Revival, reproduced in a debased form on the far western frontier of European civilization. An example of the type was the heavily battlemented first University of Chicago building, Douglas Hall, built during the Civil War, overlooking the new Illinois Central Railway line on the Lake Michigan shore and the camp that housed thousands of Confederate prisoners. Veblen identified this style, the expression of cultural aspiration, as the product of dangerous barbarian psychology. For him, the university building exemplified the dual leisure-class standards of virtue: archaism and waste.[19]

In the common European characterization, Chicago was a tabula rasa, a city without history. Unformed and unrestrained by the habits of a particular culture, the frontier settlement had been transformed from a small colony of wooden cabins into a city of

Figure 6.2
South side of Jackson Street looking west from Plymouth Court, with Monadnock Building in the background, Chicago, 1908. Charles R. Clark, photographer.

steel and glass in less than one hundred years. Yet, for Veblen, the midwestern region of the United States did not stand apart from European culture; quite the opposite, it was the ominous result of eons of human evolution. Although Chicago is not named, the historical and environmental situation of what was then considered the American West is essential to Veblen's description of the formation of the leisure class. While the historical and geographic specificity of his writing is often overlooked, Veblen attributed the rise of this class to the generation that made its money following the Civil War.[20] Relying on rhetoric rather than images, Veblen described the American metropolis as the result of European history advancing in industrial terms while socially devolving. And he invented the term "conspicuous consumption" to describe the forms of cultural expression flowering in American industrial cities in the second half of the nineteenth century.

Inspired by an understanding of economics as an "evolutionary science," and influenced by sociologically minded German academics, Veblen framed the emergence of the American leisure class in explicitly racial terms. According to his version of the environmental theory of history, the transplantation of northern European races (which the economist William Z. Ripley referred to as the "dolicho-blond") to the untamed American frontier had resulted in a reversion to archaic tendencies. Explicitly dating the rise of the leisure class to the two decades following the Civil War, he posited barbarianism as an inversion of self-serving claims about the triumphant progress of American culture and society. Veblen used the term "barbarian" to make his argument that Gilded Age American society was regressing to a feudal state, evident in the greedy acquisitiveness and ostentatious display of the postbellum capitalist elite. To Veblen's frustration, in the face of industrial innovation, the wealthy and powerful Americans who controlled the city sought to recreate European-style feudal monuments and rituals. As monuments to their power, they converted old stylistic forms to promote the values of an emerging leisure class.

Veblen's economic perspective gave him the insight that industrial and technological advances were not inherently progressive; instead, such advances were more often created in the service of the "business enterprise," his term for capitalism. His 1904 book

The Theory of Business Enterprise, which may be read as a sequel to *The Theory of the Leisure Class*, advances the idea that capitalism was entering a new phase in the United States, one in which technology was more often diverted for nonproductive purposes. In this environment, new architectural forms (such as plate glass department store windows surrounded by ornamental ironwork) served as advertising, enticing an urban audience to new heights of consumption. However, his criticism extended beyond the decorative facade of the department store to include the construction of lofts, warehouses, and stores, all urban elements which served the growing market for fashionable goods. Rather than being ascetic responses to the culture of conspicuous consumption, the enormous loft buildings celebrated by modernist architects were yet another expression of the perversion of industrial progress under predatory capitalism.

In Veblen's historical framework, the turn of the twentieth century was a battleground between mutually contradictory evolutionary forces: technological development on the one hand and the persistence of leisure-class taste, expressed in ever more inventive ways, on the other. The battle between these forces—one progressive, the other regressive—were constantly in tension, resulting in an extended period of inertia, later described as cultural lag.[21] *The Theory of the Leisure Class* is about the social and material expressions of that lag. The desire to resolve this tension by speeding up history motivated diverse forms of avant-garde cultural production, from literature to drama to photography, film, and architecture. But although Veblen was fundamentally optimistic about the future, his position was far from radical, at least in the political sense. With its millennial overtones, the rhetoric of the turn of the twentieth-century avant-garde was predicated on the assumption that the historical process was accelerating, that the rapid and unprecedented growth of industrial cities such as Chicago and Berlin was reaching a stage of such forward momentum that it would lead to their destruction, and ultimately their renewal in idealized form.[22] To cite just one example of millennial urban projections, we might think of the crystal cities imagined by German writer Paul Scheerbart and expressionist architects such as Bruno Taut.[23] But while architects and architecture critics embraced the uncomfortable condition of perpetual change, a sense of the modern city, and the modern way of life coming into being, Veblen did not predict an imminent utopia. The tone of his writing was more cautious than euphoric.

Perhaps because he lived through the height of the labor and class unrest of the 1890s and the associated surge in popularity of radical politics in the United States, from polite middle-class dalliances with socialism to the overt embrace of anarchism, Veblen was anxious not to inflame revolutionary fervor. He actively suppressed such ideas, resisting any hint of a call to arms. Under the best possible circumstances, he argued, the organic process of evolution would nurture psychological development toward the recovery of the primitive "instinct of workmanship," leading to the gradual but inevitable decline in the power of the captain of industry.[24] Under the influence of progressive institutions like the manual training school, expanded to serve as a universal model of education for boys and girls of all classes, and city dwellers of all ethnicities, Veblen saw the first signs of this evolution in the growing influence of engineers and in the emancipated New Women who worked in Chicago's settlement houses.

And yet Veblen was also skeptical about the ability of professionals and other members of the leisure class, no matter how noble their professed motives, to effect change. As his 1919 essay "A Memorandum on a Practicable Soviet of Technicians" suggests, Veblen had little faith in the reformulation of architecture under the logic of advanced industrialism—the architectural profession was far too enmeshed in the imperatives of leisure-class culture for that.[25] In his 1902 criticism of the Arts and Crafts movement, Veblen implied the path to true industrial evolution lay not only in the modes of machine-making developed in local workshops and factories but also in methods of communal industrial management modeled by labor cooperatives working in concert with business.[26] Only once this cooperation expanded to displace the power of capitalistic business would the imperatives of production outweigh those of consumption.

This outcome—the transformation of society under the rational logic of advanced industry—was not inevitable. Where Marx's theory of class struggle depended on the struggle for subsistence living, in the United States, the battle was psychological rather than practical, Veblen claimed. Although a significant proportion of the urban population was experiencing economic hardship, the American standard of living was high enough to keep the instinct for conspicuous consumption alive. The critical issue, he believed, was not the risk of starvation but the temptations of pecuniary emulation, where the less well-off continued to ape the habits and dress of the very wealthy. Despite the prescience often attributed to him, Veblen never anticipated that fashion might emerge from anywhere but the social elite. While he rejected Marx's teleological view that human evolution was moving inevitably toward working-class revolution, Veblen was loyal to a similar literary construct. Where Marx saw communism haunting Europe, Veblen saw the cultural power of the European bourgeoisie haunting the United States.

Even though Veblen explicitly identified the rise of the leisure class with postbellum American frontier culture, the historical and geographic specificity of *The Theory of the Leisure Class* has been lost, aided, no doubt, by the opacity of his text. (This book is concerned with the Gothic not only as a style but as a mode of writing.) Glimpsed dimly through his heavy prose, Veblen's image of Chicago challenges the received idea of the gridded city filled with prototypical skyscrapers as a landscape of immanent modernity. Just as Mendelsohn's hazy photographic images of the American *Großstadt* (metropolis) came to represent an international global condition, Veblen's description of the semiotic role of goods in an advanced capitalist culture has been expanded into a diagnosis applicable to all modern people. Though it is never clear if he is being satirical or sincere, readers sense instinctively that he has something important to say. His has become an important voice in intellectual histories of the United States.

The Theory of the Leisure Class remains a classic literary work, one that is continually referenced, though far less often read. Veblen's contention that buildings and landscapes might be seen as the most overt form of conspicuous consumption explains his recurring role in architectural and urban history. But in the process, the city where he wrote his most famous book, and his specific commentary on the landscape that surrounded him, have largely been forgotten. In this sense, Veblen is a ghost haunting both Chicago and the received accounts of this city as the exemplar of modern American urbanity. Rereading *The Theory of the Leisure Class* alongside contemporary photographs helps us resituate his celebrated sociology of the American city. In modernist historiography, Chicago provided a raw urban image for Europeans to analyze, remake, and give new meaning in the service of anticapitalist goals. Looking at Chicago again through Veblen's eyes, *Barbarian Architecture* presents a new story of this iconic urban landscape. Challenging histories of the Chicago School that depend on hero figures and their masterworks, it recovers Chicago as an important site for the creation not only of modern object-buildings but also of a politically engaged theory of modern architecture, urbanism, and design.

Acknowledgments

Thorstein Veblen made a cameo appearance in my first book about Chicago and its architecture, published in 2009, and he has appeared fleetingly in other texts I have written since then. I must begin by thanking Thomas Weaver, my friend and now editor at the MIT Press, who convinced me that Veblen deserved a book of his own. Beyond being a brilliant editor, Tom has been endlessly supportive and patient through the process of writing and revising. I am also very grateful to the MIT Press's external readers for their detailed feedback, which improved the manuscript immensely. At the Press, my thanks are due to Gabriela Bueno Gibbs for managing the manuscript so professionally and to Paula Woolley and Matthew Abbate for their careful copyediting. I also want to acknowledge the expert contribution of Naomi Linzer, who compiled the index.

Many mentors, colleagues, friends, and students have helped me as research and writing on this manuscript progressed. Robert Bruegmann and David Van Zanten have been generous with their insight and advice for many years. Alexander Eisenschmidt gave me the opportunity to think about Veblen and architecture when he commissioned a book chapter on the Carson Pirie Scott building. Jonathan Mekinda and Bess Williamson hosted me at a symposium at the Art Institute of Chicago, where I first explored Veblen's connection to Hull House. I am indebted to Thomas Leslie, Carol Willis, and Don Friedman for their deep knowledge of the economics and material makeup of Chicago's built environment. My work on nineteenth-century American architecture in relation to questions of race, class, and labor owes much to Irene Cheng, Charles L. Davis, Kathryn Holliday, and Mabel O. Wilson. Thanks go to Lucia Allais for the opportunity to share some of this work at the Temple Hoyne Buell Center for the Study of American Architecture at Columbia University. At Victoria University of Wellington, I acknowledge the support of Andre Brown, Bruno Marques, Nan O'Sullivan, Robyn Phipps, and Marc Aurel Schnabel, as well as Hamish Clayton. My conversations with José Núñez Collado, Eva Forster-Garbutt, Laura Dunham, and other students continue to inspire my thinking about the connections between architecture, race, consumption, and visual culture.

Because the writing of this book coincided with the pandemic and its associated travel restrictions, it became necessary to alter my original work plan and to rely on digital texts rather than physical ones in many cases. I am grateful to librarians and archivists at the following institutions for their assistance accessing materials both in person and remotely: the Hanna Holborn Gray Special Collections Research Center of the University of Chicago Library; the Ryerson and Burnham Art and Architecture Archive at the Art Institute of Chicago; the Special Collections and University Archives, Daley Library, at the University of Illinois at Chicago; the Chicago History Museum; the Newberry Library; the Division of Rare and Manuscript Collections, Carl A. Koch Library, at Cornell University; and the George Eastman Museum.

I am deeply appreciative to the Graham Foundation for Advanced Studies in the Fine Arts for awarding me a research grant to support this project and their flexibility in extending the grant period more than once. I would also like to acknowledge assistance from the Victoria University of Wellington University Research Fund.

Early versions of this material have appeared elsewhere. Parts of the introduction and chapters 1 and 2 were published as "The Architecture of the Leisure Class: Thorstein Veblen and the University of Chicago," in the *Journal of the Society of Architectural Historians* 82, no. 1 (2023): 7–21. I am grateful to David Karmon, the journal's editor, for his guidance and permission to republish this material, and to the journal's reviewers for their helpful comments. A section of chapter 5 was previously published as "A Journey to the Experimental Nation: Henry Demarest Lloyd and the Search for Industrial Democracy in New Zealand" in *Fabrications: The Journal of the Society of Architectural Historians, Australia and New Zealand* 30, no. 3 (2020). Thanks to Cameron Logan, the editor of *Fabrications*, for allowing me to republish this material.

Finally, I am most grateful for the constant support of Mary Atwool, Brent Southgate, Laura Southgate, Ned Salisbury, and Calum Salisbury. Ned and Calum have lived in unusually close proximity to this book, and it could not have been written without them.

Image Credits

Figure 0.1 Eva Watson-Schütze, Thorstein Veblen c. 1902. Courtesy of the George Eastman Museum. Digital file 1981.1786.0012B.

Figure 1.1 Manufactures and Liberal Arts Building, World's Columbian Exposition, Chicago, 1891–1893. George B. Post, architect; Daniel H. Burnham, director of works. World's Columbian Exposition Collection, Ryerson and Burnham Art and Architecture Archives, Art Institute of Chicago. Digital file #000012 _ 110701-016.

Figure 1.2 Dedication Day, October 21, 1892, Manufactures and Liberal Arts Building, World's Columbian Exposition, Chicago, 1891–1893. George B. Post, architect; Daniel H. Burnham, director of works; C. D. Arnold, photographer. World's Columbian Exposition Collection, Ryerson and Burnham Art and Architecture Archives, Art Institute of Chicago. Digital file #M525828.

Figure 1.3 Cliff Dwellers exhibit, World's Columbian Exposition, Chicago, 1891–1893. Charles B. Atwood, architect; Daniel H. Burnham, director of works; C. D. Arnold, photographer. World's Columbian Exposition Collection, Ryerson and Burnham Art and Architecture Archives, Art Institute of Chicago. Digital file # M525857.

Figure 1.4 Anthropological Building, World's Columbian Exposition, Chicago, 1891–1893. Charles B. Atwood, architect; Daniel H. Burnham, director of works; C. D. Arnold, photographer. World's Columbian Exposition Collection, Ryerson and Burnham Art and Architecture Archives, Art Institute of Chicago. Digital file #M525856.

Figure 1.5 Penobscot Indian Camp, Ethnographic Exhibit, World's Columbian Exposition, Chicago, 1891–1893. Daniel H. Burnham, director of works; C. D. Arnold, photographer. World's Columbian Exposition photographs by C. D. Arnold, Ryerson and Burnham Art and Architecture Archives, Art Institute of Chicago. Digital file #198902_140619-E20981.

Figure 1.6 Massachusetts whaling boat next to Kwakiutl plank house, Ethnographic Exhibit, World's Columbian Exposition, Chicago, 1891–1893. Daniel H. Burnham, director of works. World's Columbian Exposition Collection, Ryerson and Burnham Art and Architecture Archives, Art Institute of Chicago. Digital file #000012_110701-029.

Figure 1.7 Hunter's Cabin, Boone and Crockett Club, World's Columbian Exposition, 1892–1893. Holabird & Roche, architects; Daniel H. Burnham, director of works; C. D. Arnold, photographer. Historic Architecture and Landscape Image Collection, Ryerson and Burnham Art and Architecture Archives, Art Institute of Chicago. Digital file #11796.

Figure 1.8 Hunter's Cabin, interior. World's Columbian Exposition, 1893. Hanna Holborn Gray Special Collections Research Center, University of Chicago Library. Digital file apf3-00050.

Figure 1.9 Exterior view of the Potter Palmer residence, 1350 North Lake Shore Drive, 1888. Cobb and Frost, architects; John W. Taylor, photographer. Chicago History Museum. Digital file ICHi-001256.

Figure 1.10 Potter Palmer residence, Chicago, 1885. Cobb and Frost, architects; Kaufmann & Fabry Co., photographer. Historic Architecture and Landscape Image Collection, Ryerson and Burnham Art and Architecture Archives, Art Institute of Chicago. Digital file #60418.

Figure 1.11 Potter Palmer residence, library, Chicago, 1885. Cobb and Frost, architects; Kaufmann & Fabry Co., photographer. Historic Architecture and Landscape Image Collection, Ryerson and Burnham Art and Architecture Archives, Art Institute of Chicago. Digital file #60417.

Figure 1.12 Residences on the 1400 block of North Lake Shore Drive, including homes of Franklin MacVeagh, S. E. Barrett, Mrs. F. E. Ogden, V. C. Turner, Mrs. Barbara Armour, and G. A. Armour, c. 1905. Charles R. Clark, photographer. Chicago History Museum. Digital file ICHi-071933.

Figure 1.13 Apartment building in Chicago, c. 1905. Charles R. Clark, photographer. Chicago History Museum. Digital file ICHi-070159.

Figure 2.1 Cobb Hall entrance, University of Chicago, c. 1891. Henry Ives Cobb, architect. Hanna Holborn Gray Special Collections Research Center, University of Chicago Library. Digital file apf2-01732.

Figure 2.2 Lakefront from Illinois Central Railway, Chicago, c. 1900. Library of Congress Prints and Photographs Division. Digital file LC-DIG-det-4a08060.

Figure 2.3 Armour Elevator A, Goose Island, Chicago, c. 1890. J. W. Taylor, photographer. J. W. Taylor Photograph Collection, Ryerson and Burnham Art and Architecture Archives, Art Institute of Chicago. Digital file #199303_120806_001.

Figure 2.4 The Pit of the Chicago Board of Trade, 1896. Chicago History Museum. Digital file ICHi-018146.

Figure 2.5 Jackson Street (now Jackson Boulevard), looking east at Fifth Avenue (now Wells Street), 1914. From right to left, Insurance Exchange Building and Board of Trade. Charles R. Clark, photographer. Chicago History Museum. Digital file ICHi-070820.

Figure 2.6 Two men foraging along shoreline, Chicago, 1894. Ray Stannard Baker, photographer. Library of Congress Prints and Photographs Division. Digital file LC-USZ62-110527.

Figure 2.7 Living conditions among the poor during the depression and Pullman strike, Chicago, 1894. Ray Stannard Baker, photographer. Library of Congress Prints and Photographs Division. Digital file LC-USZ62-24836.

Figure 2.8 Douglas Hall, Old University of Chicago, 34th Street and Cottage Grove Avenue, c. 1869. William W. Boyington, architect. Demolished in 1890. Hanna Holborn Gray Special Collections Research Center, University of Chicago Library. Digital file apf2-05358.

Figure 2.9 Group portrait of Confederate prisoners at Camp Douglas during the American Civil War, c. 1863. Chicago History Museum. Digital file ICHi-001800.

Figure 2.10 Aerial view, University of Chicago campus, c. 1901. E. W. Martyn, photographer. Hanna Holborn Gray Special Collections Research Center, University of Chicago Library. Digital file apf2-02563.

Figure 2.11 Ryerson Physical Laboratory, University of Chicago, 1894. Henry Ives Cobb, architect. Hanna Holborn Gray Special Collections Research Center, University of Chicago Library. Digital file 87959.

Figure 2.12 Hull Court, c. 1897. Henry Ives Cobb, architect. Hanna Holborn Gray Special Collections Research Center, University of Chicago Library. Digital file apf2-03723.

Figure 2.13 Old Gymnasium and Library, University of Chicago, 1893. Hanna Holborn Gray Special Collections Research Center, University of Chicago Library. Digital file apf2-03024.

Figure 2.14 University of Chicago football team, 1899. Hanna Holborn Gray Special Collections Research Center, University of Chicago Library. Digital file apf5-03217.

Figure 2.15 Cobb (Hull) Gate, University of Chicago, 1897. Henry Ives Cobb, architect. Hanna Holborn Gray Special Collections Research Center, University of Chicago Library. Digital file apf2-01699.

Figure 3.1 Marshall Field & Company, State Street, Chicago, c. 1910. J. W. Taylor, photographer. Historic Architecture and Landscape

Image Collection, Ryerson and Burnham Art and Architecture Archives, Art Institute of Chicago. Digital file #U525754.

Figure 3.2 Potenberg's Shoe Store, 872 North Lincoln Avenue (now 2959 North Lincoln Avenue), c. 1895. Chicago History Museum. Digital file ICHi-073616.

Figure 3.3 View of the Administration Building, looking south from Wooded Island bridge, World's Columbian Exposition, 1893. Chicago History Museum. Digital file ICHi-025087.

Figure 3.4 Jackson Street and Sherman Street, Chicago, c. 1910. J. W. Taylor, photographer. Historic Architecture and Landscape Image Collection, Ryerson and Burnham Art and Architecture Archives, Art Institute of Chicago. Digital file #16507.

Figure 3.5 Pedestrians looking in Marshall Field & Company windows, 1910. Chicago Daily News negatives collection, Chicago History Museum. Digital file DN-0008625.

Figure 3.6 Marshall Field & Company buildings, view from across the street intersection, c. 1902. Chicago Daily News negatives collection, Chicago History Museum. Digital file DN-0003251.

Figure 3.7 Interior view of Marshall Field & Company retail store, c. 1900. Chicago History Museum. Digital file ICHi-039800.

Figure 3.8 Christmas shoppers on State Street, c. 1905. Mandel Brothers department store, with a new facade by Jenney and Mundie, is on the right. Chicago Daily News negatives collection, Chicago History Museum. Digital file DN-0002539.

Figure 3.9 View of the intersection of State and Madison streets, including Mandel Brothers store on the left and the entrance to the Carson Pirie Scott & Co. building on the right, Chicago, c. 1905. Barnes-Crosby Company, photographer. Chicago History Museum. Digital file ICHi-019112.

Figure 3.10 Carson Pirie Scott & Co. store, Chicago, 1899. Louis H. Sullivan, architect. Sullivaniana Collection, Ryerson and Burnham Art and Architecture Archives, Art Institute of Chicago. Digital file #193101.081110-03.

Figure 3.11 Christmas shoppers in front of Marshall Field's department store, 1905. Chicago Daily News negatives collection, Chicago History Museum. Digital file DN-0002552.

Figure 3.12 Levi Z. Leiter (Second Leiter) Building, Chicago, 1891. Jenney & Mundie, architects; J. W. Taylor, photographer. Historic Architecture and Landscape Image Collection, Ryerson and Burnham Art and Architecture Archives, Art Institute of Chicago. Digital file #16451.

Figure 4.1 London Dime Museum and Theatre on State Street between Van Buren and Congress streets, c. 1912. Chicago History Museum. Digital file ICHi-004793.

Figure 4.2 Saloon interior, Chicago, c. 1905. Chicago Daily News collection, Chicago History Museum. Digital file DN-0003265.

Figure 4.3 Chinese-owned businesses on Clark Street between Van Buren and Harrison streets, c. 1900–1910. Chicago History Museum. Digital file ICHi-030835.

Figure 4.4 Marshall Field & Company department store, interior, Chicago, c. 1892–1914. Daniel H. Burnham, architect. Historic Architecture and Landscape Image Collection, Ryerson and Burnham Art and Architecture Archives, Art Institute of Chicago. Digital file #59982.

Figure 4.5 Mona B. Marshall, an alleged prostitute (called a "white slave"), Chicago, 1907. Chicago Daily News collection, Chicago History Museum. Digital file DN-0005021

Figure 4.6 Pedestrians walking in front of Auditorium Building at 430 South Michigan Avenue, c. 1909. Adler and Sullivan, architects. Fred M. Tuckerman, photographer. Chicago History Museum. Digital file ICHi-026942.

Figure 4.7 Auditorium Hotel Lobby. Andrew Dickson White Architectural Photograph Collection, Cornell University Library. Digital file #15-5-3090.

Figure 4.8 Harrison Street Police Station on the northeast corner of Harrison and LaSalle streets, c. 1900. Barnes-Crosby Company, photographer. Chicago History Museum. Digital file ICHi-019067.

Figure 4. 9 Plymouth Court, south of Jackson Street, c. 1908. Great Northern Hotel is visible at rear. Charles R. Clark, photographer. Chicago History Museum. Digital file ICHi-070897.

Figure 4.10 R. R. Donnelley and Sons Co. Lakeside Press Building, Chicago, 1897. Howard Van Doren Shaw, architect; Henry Fuermann, photographer. Historic Architecture and Landscape Image Collection, Ryerson and Burnham Art and Architecture Archives, Art Institute of Chicago. Digital file #2448.

Figure 4.11 Rand McNally building, Chicago, 1911–1912. Holabird & Roche, architects; J. W. Taylor, photographer. Historic Architecture and Landscape Image Collection, Ryerson and Burnham Art and Architecture Archives, Art Institute of Chicago. Digital file #16418.

Figure 5.1 View from the southwest corner of Dearborn Street and Monroe Street of the Honoré Block (foreground) and Grand

Pacific Hotel (background) following the Chicago fire of 1871. Jex Bardwell, photographer. Chicago History Museum. Digital file ICHi-177235.

Figure 5.2 Water Works, Chicago, 1869. William W. Boyington, architect. Historic Architecture and Landscape Image Collection, Ryerson and Burnham Art and Architecture Archives, Art Institute of Chicago. Digital file #50565.

Figure 5.3 Woman's Temple, Chicago, 1892. Burnham and Root, architects; Chicago Architectural Photography Co., photographer. Historic Architecture and Landscape Image Collection, Ryerson and Burnham Art and Architecture Archives, Art Institute of Chicago. Digital file# 60319.

Figure 5.4 Fine Arts Building between the Auditorium and the Chicago Club, Michigan Avenue, Chicago, c. 1895. Solon S. Beman, architect; J. W. Taylor, photographer. Chicago History Museum. Digital file ICHi-021992.

Figure 5.5 Streetcar on Twelfth Street (now Roosevelt Road), looking east from Halsted Street, 1906. Charles R. Clark, photographer. Chicago History Museum. Digital file ICHi-066025.

Figure 5.6 Hebrew Manual Training School, Chicago, 1889–1890. Adler & Sullivan, architects. Richard Nickel Archive, Ryerson and Burnham Art and Architecture Archives, Art Institute of Chicago. Digital file #201006_112A.3.

Figure 5.7 Group of young men in the forge shop at Chicago Manual Training School, corner of Michigan and Twelfth avenues, c. 1895. Chicago History Museum. Digital file ICHi-026549.

Figure 5.8 Hull House, Halsted Street, c. 1900. Allen Pond and Irving Pond, architects; Charles R. Clark, photographer. Chicago History Museum. Digital file ICHi-071955.

Figure 5.9 Rear of houses in the Maxwell Street area, 1907. Walter E. Lagerquist, photographer. Chicago History Museum. Digital file ICHi-035464.

Figure 5.10 Sweatshop at 132 Maxwell Street, 1905. Chicago Daily News collection, Chicago History Museum. Digital file DN-0002416.

Figure 5.11 Hull House, coffee house and gymnasium, Chicago, 1889–1908. Pond and Pond, architects. Pond and Pond Collection, Ryerson and Burnham Art and Architecture Archives, Art Institute of Chicago. Digital file #200101.080815-04.

Figure 5.12 Mrs. Molinaro demonstrating spinning, Labor Museum, Hull House, 1910. Hull House Archives, University of Illinois at Chicago Special Collections. Digital file JAMC_0000_0177_3015.

Figure 5.13 Schoolgirls doing exercises on the roof of the Jewish Training School, c. 1911. Chicago Daily News collection, Chicago History Museum. Digital file DN-0056693.

Figure 5.14 Chicago River, looking west from the south bank toward the Rush Street Bridge, 1908. Chicago History Museum. Digital file ICHi-093259.

Figure 6.1 Trees along drive in Jackson Park, c. 1925. Chicago History Museum. Digital file ICHi-029481.

Figure 6.2 South side of Jackson Street, looking west from Plymouth Court, with Monadnock Building in the background, Chicago, 1908. Charles R. Clark, photographer. Chicago History Museum. Digital file ICHi-071808.

Notes

Introduction

1. Colin Campbell, "The Sociology of Consumption," in *Acknowledging Consumption: A Review of New Studies*, ed. Daniel Miller (London: Routledge, 1995), 96–126; David A. Reisman, *The Social Economics of Thorstein Veblen* (Cheltenham, UK: Edward Elgar, 2012); and Colin Campbell, "Conspicuous Confusion? A Critique of Veblen's Theory of Conspicuous Consumption," in Campbell, *Consumption and Consumer Society: The Craft Consumer and Other Essays* (London: Palgrave Macmillan, 2021), 49–66.

2. Norbert Elias, *The Court Society*, trans. Edmund Jephcott (1969; repr., Dublin: University College Dublin Press, 2006), 70–80; Jonathan Massey, "New Necessities: Modernist Aesthetic Discipline," *Perspecta* 35 (2004): 125.

3. Donald J. Bush, "Thorstein Veblen's Economic Aesthetic," *Leonardo* 11, no. 4 (Autumn 1978): 281–285; Ákos Moravánszky, "'Truth to Material' vs 'The Principle of Cladding': The Language of Materials in Architecture," *AA Files* 31 (Summer 1996): 39–46; and Christopher Long, "The Origins and Context of Adolf Loos's 'Ornament and Crime,'" *Journal of the Society of Architectural Historians* 68, no. 2 (June 2009): 200–223.

4. Leon Ardzrooni, "Veblen and Technocracy," *Living Age* 344 (March 1933): 39–42; Edwin Layton, "Veblen and the Engineers," *American Quarterly* 14, no. 1 (Spring 1962): 64–72; Daniel Bell, "Veblen and the New Class," *American Scholar* 32, no. 4 (Autumn 1963): 616–638; William E. Aitken, *Technocracy and the American Dream: The Technocrat Movement, 1900–1941* (Berkeley: University of California Press, 1977), 1–26; Robert Wojtowicz, *Lewis Mumford and American Modernism: Eutopian Theories for Architecture and Urban Planning* (Cambridge: Cambridge University Press, 1996), 30–31.

5. Giorgio Ciucci, Francesco Dal Co, Mario Manieri-Elia, and Manfredo Tafuri, *The American City from the Civil War to the New Deal*, trans. Barbara Luigia La Penta (1973; Cambridge, MA: MIT Press, 1979); and David Gartman, *Culture, Class, and Critical Theory: Between Bourdieu and the Frankfurt School* (London: Routledge, 2012), 85.

6. Val K. Warke, "'In' Architecture: Observing the Mechanisms of Fashion," in *Architecture in Fashion*, ed. Deborah Fausch et al. (New York: Princeton Architectural Press, 1994), 124–147; Leila W. Kinney, "Fashion and Fabrication in Modern Architecture," *Journal of the Society of Architectural Historians* 58, no. 3 (September 1999): 472–481; Mark Wigley, *White Walls, Designer Dresses: The Fashioning of Modern Architecture* (Cambridge, MA: MIT Press, 1995); and Robin Schuldenfrei, *Luxury and Modernism: Architecture and the Object in Germany, 1900–1933* (Princeton, NJ: Princeton University Press, 2018).

7. Thorstein Veblen, *The Theory of the Leisure Class* (1899; repr., London: Penguin, 1979), 86. The book was originally subtitled *An Economic Study in the Evolution of Institutions*.

8. Veblen, *Theory of the Leisure Class*, 87.

9. Werner Sombart, "The Development of the American Proletariat," *American Journal of Sociology* 12, no. 1 (July 1906): 131.

10. Valuable recent titles include *Chicago Architecture: Histories, Revisions, Alternatives*, ed. Charles Waldheim and Katerina Ruedi Ray (Chicago: University of Chicago Press, 2005); and *Chicagoisms: The City as Catalyst for Architectural Speculation*, ed. Alexander Eisenschmidt and Jonathan Mekinda (Chicago: University of Chicago Press and Park Books, 2013).

11. Veblen, *Theory of the Leisure Class*, 138. An outline of Veblen's life is given in recent biographies, including Elizabeth Jorgensen and Henry Jorgensen, *Thorstein Veblen: Victorian Firebrand* (Armonk, NY: M. E. Sharpe, 1999), and Charles Camic, *Veblen: The Making of an Economist Who Unmade Economics* (Cambridge, MA: Harvard University Press, 2020). See also Martha Banta, *Taylored Lives: Narrative Productions in the Age of Taylor, Veblen, and Ford* (Chicago: University of Chicago Press, 1993); John P. Diggins, *Thorstein Veblen: Theorist of the Leisure Class* (Princeton, NJ: Princeton University Press, 1999); Stephen Edgell, *Veblen in Perspective: His Life and Thought* (Armonk, NY:

M. E. Sharpe, 2001); *Veblen's Century: A Collective Portrait*, ed. Irving Horowitz (New Brunswick, NJ: Transaction Publishers, 2002); *The Legacy of Thorstein Veblen*, ed. Rick Tilman (Northampton, MA: Edward Elgar, 2003); *Essential Writings of Thorstein Veblen*, ed. Charles Camic and Geoffrey Hodgson (London: Routledge, 2011); and Reisman, *The Social Economics of Thorstein Veblen*.

12. Russell H. Bartley and Sylvia E. Bartley, "In Search of Thorstein Veblen: Further Inquiries into His Life and Work," *International Journal of Politics, Culture, and Society* 11, no. 1 (Fall 1997): 129–173; Nils Gilman, "Thorstein Veblen's Neglected Feminism," *Journal of Economic Issues* 33, no. 3 (September 1999): 689–711; Tony Maynard, "A Shameless Lothario: Thorstein Veblen as Sexual Predator and Sexual Liberator," *Journal of Economic Issues* 34, no. 1 (March 2000): 194–199; and Camic, *Veblen*, 272–275.

13. Edgell, *Veblen in Perspective*, 25.

14. Thorstein Veblen, "A Memorandum on a Practicable Soviet of Technicians," *The Dial* 67 (November 1, 1919): 373–380.

15. Joseph Dorfman, *Thorstein Veblen and His America* (1934; repr., New York: Viking Press, 1940), 42.

16. Dorfman, *Thorstein Veblen and His America*, 249.

17. David Riesman, *Thorstein Veblen: A Critical Interpretation* (New York: Charles Scribner's Sons, 1953), 50. For a critique of the outsider narrative constructed

around Veblen, see John P. Diggins, *The Bard of Savagery: Thorstein Veblen and Modern Social Theory* (New York: Seabury Press, 1978), 222–223; and Ken McCormick, "Thorstein Veblen," in *The Wiley-Blackwell Companion to Major Social Theorists*, vol. 1: *Classical Social Theorists*, ed. George Ritzer and Jeffrey Stepnisky (Malden, MA: Wiley-Blackwell, 2011), 185–204.

18. Tom Wolf, *Eva Watson-Schütze, Photographer* (Albany, NY: Samuel Dorsky Museum of Art, SUNY, 2009), 21.

19. T. J. Jackson Lears, "Beyond Veblen: Rethinking Culture in America," in *Consuming Visions: Accumulation and Display of Goods in America, 1889–1925*, ed. Simon J. Bronner (New York: W. W. Norton, 1989), 73.

20. Jorgensen, *Thorstein Veblen*, 66.

21. Thorstein Veblen, "The Intellectual Pre-eminence of Jews in Modern Europe," *Political Science Quarterly* 34, no. 1 (March 1919): 33–42.

22. Veblen, "Intellectual Pre-eminence of Jews," 38.

23. Veblen, "Intellectual Pre-eminence of Jews," 39.

24. Sigmund Freud, "An Autobiographical Study" (1925), in *The Freud Reader*, ed. Peter Gay (New York: W. W. Norton, 1989), 4.

25. Bell, "Veblen and the New Class," 623. See also Wesley C. Mitchell, *What Veblen Taught: Selected Writings of Thorstein Veblen* (1936; repr., New York: Angus M. Kelley, 1964), xiv–xvi; Camic, *Veblen*, 357.

26. Camic, *Veblen*, 357–358.

27. Edgell, *Veblen in Perspective*, 32.

28. Veblen, *Theory of the Leisure Class*, 21.

29. For a discussion of this topic, see Veblen, *Theory of the Leisure Class*, chap. 2.

30. Veblen, *Theory of the Leisure Class*, xiv.

31. Alan Colquhoun, *Modern Architecture* (Oxford: Oxford University Press, 2002), 49.

32. Geoffrey Hodgson, "On the Evolution of Thorstein Veblen's Evolutionary Economics," *Cambridge Journal of Economics* 22 (1998): 417.

33. Shelton Stromquist, *Reinventing the People: The Progressive Movement, the Class Problem, and the Origins of Modern Liberalism* (Urbana: University of Illinois Press, 2006), 13–55.

34. Veblen, *Theory of the Leisure Class*, 345.

35. Dorfman, *Thorstein Veblen and His America*, 68; Jorgensen and Jorgensen, *Thorstein Veblen*, 28.

36. Veblen, *Theory of the Leisure Class*, xiv.

37. "Veblin [sic] Book on Higher Learning Is University of Chicago Puzzle: Dean Small Declares It Either Humor or Bolshevism," *Chicago Daily Tribune*, January 9, 1919, 10.

38. Elia W. Peattie, "Veblin [sic] on the Vested Interests," *Chicago Daily Tribune*, August 23, 1919, 9.

39. Campbell, "Conspicuous Confusion?," 49.

40. Veblen, *Theory of the Leisure Class*, xiv.

41. Walter Benjamin, *The Arcades Project*, ed. Rolf Tiedeman, trans. Howard

Eiland and Kevin McLaughlin (Cambridge, MA: Belknap Press of Harvard University Press, 1999).

42. Brian Ladd, *The Streets of Europe: The Sights, Sounds, and Smells That Shaped Its Great Cities* (Chicago: University of Chicago Press, 2020), 62–65.

43. William Dean Howells, "An Opportunity for American Fiction," *Literature: An International Gazette of Criticism* 16 (April 28, 1899): 362.

44. Howells, "An Opportunity for American Fiction," 386.

45. For example, David W. Noble, "Dreiser and Veblen and the Literature of Cultural Change," in *Studies in American Culture: Dominant Ideas and Images*, ed. Joseph J. Kwiat and Mary C. Turpie (Minneapolis: University of Minnesota Press, 1960), 139–152; and Clare Virginia Eby, *Dreiser and Veblen, Saboteurs of the Status Quo* (Columbia: University of Missouri Press, 1998).

46. The exceptions are Hugh Dalziel Duncan, "The Chicago School of Thought I: Veblen Clears the Ground for a Reconsideration of Art in a Democratic Society," in Duncan, *Culture and Democracy: The Struggle for Form in Society and Architecture in Chicago and the Middle West during the Life and Times of Louis H. Sullivan* (1965; repr., Bedminster Press, 1989), 209–218; Eileen Boris, *Art and Labor: Ruskin, Morris, and the Craftsman Ideal in America* (Philadelphia: Temple University Press, 1986); and Ellen Mazur Thomson, "Thorstein Veblen

at the University of Chicago and the Socialization of Aesthetics," *Design Issues* 15, no. 1 (Spring 1999): 3–15.

47. Marianne Weber, *Max Weber: Ein Lebensbild* (Tübingen: J. C. B. Mohr, 1926), 298; quoted in Edward Shils, "The University, the City and the World: Chicago and the University of Chicago," in *The University and the City: From Medieval Origins to the Present*, ed. Thomas Bender (New York: Oxford University Press, 1988), 219.

48. Thorstein Veblen, "On the Nature of Capital II. Investment, Intangible Goods, and the Pecuniary Magnate," *Quarterly Journal of Economics* 23, no. 4 (November 1908): 108.

Chapter 1

1. Charles Camic, *Veblen: The Making of an Economist Who Unmade Economics* (Cambridge, MA: Harvard University Press, 2020), 238.

2. Stuart C. Wade and Walter Scott Wrenn, *The Nut Shell: The Ideal Pocket Guide to the World's Fair and What to See There* (Chicago: The Merchants' World's Fair Bureau of Information Company, 1893), 61–63.

3. Rossiter Johnson, *A History of the World's Columbian Exposition Held in Chicago in 1893*, vol. 1 (New York: D. Appleton, 1898), 270. On the World's Columbian Exposition, see Neil Harris, *Grand Illusions: Chicago's World's Fair of 1893* (Chicago: Chicago Historical Society, 1993); and Donald L. Miller, *City of the Century: The Epic of Chicago and the Making of America*

(New York: Simon and Schuster, 1996), 488–532.

4. Johnson, *History of the World's Columbian Exposition*, 1:269.

5. John J. Flinn, *Official Guide to the World's Columbian Exposition in the City of Chicago* (Chicago: Columbian Guide Company, 1893), 57–58; James B. Campbell, *Campbell's Illustrated History of the World's Columbian Exposition*, vol. 1 (Chicago: N. Juul & Co., 1894), 434–435; and Ira Jacknis, "Refracting Images: Anthropological Display at the Chicago World's Fair, 1893," in *Coming of Age in Chicago—The 1893 World's Fair and the Coalescence of American Anthropology*, ed. Curtis M. Hinsley and David R. Wilcox (1991; repr., Lincoln: University of Nebraska Press, 2016), 261–336.

6. The design is credited to "Charles Kessel," probably referring to Chicago architect Charles A. Kessell, in Daniel Burnham, *The Final Official Report of the Director of Works of the World's Columbian Exposition* (New York: Garland, 1989), index.

7. W. H. Holmes, "The World's Fair Congress of Anthropology," *American Anthropologist* 6, no. 4 (October 1893): 423–434; "Document H. Cushing's Analysis of the Hazzard Cliff Dweller Collection, 1895," in Hinsley and Wilcox, *Coming of Age in Chicago*, 364–365.

8. Henry Blake Fuller, *The Cliff-Dwellers* (New York: Harper and Brothers, 1893). On Fuller's novel, see Ann Massa, "Henry Blake Fuller and the Cliff Dwellers:

Appropriations and Misappropriations," *Journal of American Studies* 36, no. 1 (2002): 69–84.

9. Letters from Thorstein Veblen to Sarah Hardy, December 15, 1895, and January 23, 1896, in Elizabeth Jorgensen and Henry Jorgensen, "Appendix—Letters between Veblen and Sarah Hardy, 1895–1920," in *Thorstein Veblen: Victorian Firebrand* (Armonk NY: M. E. Sharpe, 1999), 191, 194.

10. On the challenge to classical economics in American universities during the 1880s and '90s, see Camic, *Veblen*, 279–290.

11. Thorstein Veblen, "Why Is Economics Not an Evolutionary Science?," *Quarterly Journal of Economics* 12, no. 4 (July 1898): 387–388.

12. Thorstein Veblen, *The Theory of the Leisure Class* (1899; repr., London: Penguin, 1979), 196.

13. William Fielding Ogburn, *Social Change with Respect to Culture and Original Nature* (New York: Viking Press, 1922), 200.

14. Flinn, *Official Guide to the World's Columbian Exposition*, 52–53; Johnson, *History of the World's Columbian Exposition*, 1:309–311.

15. World's Columbian Exposition, *Plan and Classification, Department M: Ethnology, Archaeology, History, Cartography, Latin-American Bureau, Collective and Isolated Exhibits* (Chicago: The Exposition, 1892).

16. Frederick Starr, "Anthropology at the World's Fair," *Popular Science Monthly* 43, no. 5 (1893): 613.

17. Curtis M. Hinsley, "The World as Marketplace: Commodification of the Exotic at the World's Columbian Exposition, Chicago, 1893," in *Exhibiting Cultures: The Poetics and Politics of Museum Display*, ed. Ivan Karp (New York: Smithsonian, 2012), 345.

18. Irene Cheng, "Structural Racialism in Modern Architectural Theory," in *Race and Modern Architecture*, ed. Irene Cheng, Charles L. Davis, and Mabel O. Wilson (Pittsburgh: University of Pittsburgh Press, 2020), 135. On the racial frameworks underlying nineteenth-century American architectural theory, see Charles L. Davis, *Building Character: The Racial Politics of Modern Architectural Style* (Pittsburgh: University of Pittsburgh Press, 2019).

19. The *Inland Architect* served the so-called inland empire formed by the western states of Illinois, Indiana, Iowa, Michigan, Minnesota, Missouri, Ohio, and Wisconsin. Although the American frontier had reached California by the 1880s, the inhabitants of these inland states still called themselves "westerners." Editorial, *Inland Architect* 16, no. 5 (November 1890): 56.

20. Frederick W. Putnam, "Ethnology," in *The World's Columbian Exposition Chicago, 1893*, ed. Trumbull White and William Igleheart (Philadelphia: P. W. Ziegler & Co., 1893), 415. See also Franz Boas, "Ethnology at the Exposition" (1893), in Hinsley and Wilcox, *Coming of Age in Chicago*, 78–83.

21. Putnam, "Ethnology," 424.

22. Starr, "Anthropology at the World's Fair," 615. See also Flinn, *Official Guide to the World's Columbian Exposition*, 54–55; and Campbell, *Campbell's Illustrated History of the World's Columbian Exposition*, 434.

23. On the displays of Native American life at the World's Columbian Exposition, see Melissa Rinehart, "To Hell with the Wigs! Native American Representation and Resistance at the World's Columbian Exposition," *American Indian Quarterly* 36, no. 4 (2012): 403–442; Rosalyn R. LaPier and David R. M. Beck, "The World Comes to Chicago (The 1893 World's Columbian Exposition)," in *City Indian: Native American Activism in Chicago, 1893–1934* (Lincoln: University of Nebraska Press, 2015), 17–34; and David M. Beck, *Unfair Labor? American Indians and the 1893 World's Columbian Exposition in Chicago* (Lincoln: University of Nebraska Press, 2019), 3–48.

24. Rossiter Johnson, *A History of the World's Columbian Exposition Held in Chicago in 1893*, vol. 3 (New York: D. Appleton, 1898), 1.

25. Frederick Ward Putnam, draft of speech, September 21, 1891, quoted in Hinsley, "The World as Marketplace," 347.

26. Stuart Charles Wade, *Rand, McNally & Co.'s Handbook of the World's Columbian Exposition* (Chicago: Rand, McNally & Company, 1893), 142–143.

27. On the cultural significance of the Hunter's Cabin,
see Eric Kaufmann, "'Natu-
ralizing the Nation': The Rise
of Naturalistic Nationalism
in the United States and
Canada," *Comparative Studies
in Society and History* 40, no.
4 (October 1998): 666–695;
Shari M. Huhndorf, "Imag-
ining America: Race, Nation,
and Imperialism at the Turn
of the Century," in *Going
Native: Indians in the American
Cultural Imagination* (Ithaca,
NY: Cornell University Press,
2001), 19–78; Sarah Bonne-
maison and Christine Macy,
"Exhibiting Wilderness at the
Columbian Exposition, 1893,"
in *Architecture and Nature:
Creating the American Landscape* (London: Routledge,
2003), 13–70; and Alison K.
Hoagland, "Romancing the
Wilderness: The Log Cabin
as a Symbol of the Pioneer,"
in *The Log Cabin: An American
Icon* (Charlottesville: University of Virginia Press, 2018),
115–147.

28. Edmund Morris, *The
Rise of Theodore Roosevelt*
(New York: Modern Library,
2001); Douglas Brinkley, *The
Wilderness Warrior: Theodore
Roosevelt and the Crusade for
America* (New York: Harper
Collins, 2009).

29. "The Hunter's Cabin,"
in *The Dream City: A Portfolio
of Photographic Views of the
World's Columbian Exposi-
tion with an Introduction by
Prof. Halsey C. Ives* (St. Louis:
Thompson Publishing,
1893), unpaginated. See also
*Conkey's Complete Guide to the
World's Columbian Exposition,
May 1 to October 30, 1893* (Chi-
cago: W. B. Conkey Company,

1893), 41; and Johnson, *History of the World's Columbian
Exposition*, 1:168.

30. Frederick Jackson
Turner, "The Significance
of the Frontier in American
History," *Annual Report of the
American Historical Association
for the Year 1893* (Washing-
ton: Government Printing
Office, 1894), 201. This essay
was reprinted in Frederick
Jackson Turner, *The Frontier
in American History* (New York:
Henry Holt, 1920), 1–38.

31. David Roediger, "The
Pursuit of Whiteness: Prop-
erty, Terror, and National
Expansion, 1790–1860"
and "'Inbetween Peoples':
Race, Nationality, and the
'New Immigrant' Work-
ing Class," in *Colored White:
Transcending the Racial Past*
(Berkeley: University of Cal-
ifornia Press, 2003), 121–137,
138–168. See also Reginald
Horsman, *Race and Manifest
Destiny: The Origins of Amer-
ican Racial Anglo-Saxonism*
(Cambridge, MA: Harvard
University Press, 1981).

32. Montgomery Schuy-
ler, "American Domestic
Architecture: Old Types and
Modern Instances: I. The
Log-Cabin," *Art and Progress* 3,
no. 10 (August 1912): 673.

33. T. J. Jackson Lears, *No
Place of Grace: Antimodernism
and the Transformation of American Culture, 1880–1920* (Chicago: University of Chicago
Press, 1994), 28.

34. Thorstein Veblen, "The
Instinct of Workmanship and
the Irksomeness of Labor,"
American Journal of Sociology 4
(September 1898): 200.

35. Veblen, *Theory of the Leisure Class*, 197.

36. George W. Stocking Jr.,
"The Spaces of Cultural Representation: Reflections on
Museum Arrangement and
Anthropological Theory in
the Boasian and Evolutionary Traditions," in *The Architecture of Science*, ed. Peter
Galison and Emily Thomp-
son (Cambridge, MA: MIT
Press, 1999), 165–180.

37. Veblen, "Why Is Eco-
nomics Not an Evolutionary
Science?," 373; Carlos C. Closson, "The Real Opportunity
of the So-Called Anglo-Saxon
Race," *Journal of Political Economy* 9, no. 1 (December 1900):
76–97.

38. Veblen, *Theory of the Leisure Class*, 215.

39. Cheng, "Structural
Racialism in Modern Architectural Theory."

40. David A. Reisman,
*The Social Economics of Thor-
stein Veblen* (Cheltenham,
UK: Edward Elgar, 2012), 58;
Thomas C. Leonard, *Illiberal
Reformers: Race, Eugenics, and
American Economics in the Pro-
gressive Era* (Princeton, NJ:
Princeton University Press,
2016), 70–71.

41. Leonard, *Illiberal
Reformers*, 71.

42. Matthew Pratt Guterl,
*The Color of Race in America,
1900–1940* (Cambridge, MA:
Harvard University Press,
2001); David R. Roediger,
*Working Towards Whiteness:
How America's Immigrants
Became White; The Strange
Journey from Ellis Island to the
Suburbs* (New York: Basic
Books, 2005).

43. Veblen, *Theory of the
Leisure Class*, 197.

44. Veblen, *Theory of the
Leisure Class*, 153–154.

45. Lears, *No Place of Grace*, 28–37, 183–187.

46. *Rand, McNally & Co.'s Bird's-Eye Views and Guide to Chicago* (Chicago: Rand McNally, 1893), 183. On the Palmer mansion, also see John Drury, *Old Chicago Houses* (Chicago: University of Chicago Press, 1941), 128–131; Thomas Tallmadge, *Architecture in Old Chicago* (Chicago: University of Chicago Press, 1941), 184–185; David Garrard Lowe, *Lost Chicago* (New York: Watson-Guptill, 2000), 36–38; Susan Benjamin and Stuart Cohen, *Great Houses of Chicago: 1871–1921* (New York: Acanthus Press, 2008), 116–125; Sally Sexton Kalmbach, *The Jewel of the Gold Coast: Mrs. Potter Palmer's Chicago* (Port Townsend, WA: Ampersand, 2009); and Edward W. Wolner, *Henry Ives Cobb's Chicago: Architecture, Institutions, and the Making of a Modern Metropolis* (Chicago: University of Chicago Press, 2011), 40–52.

47. Veblen, *Theory of the Leisure Class*, 230.

48. On Palmer's development of State Street, see Joseph Siry, *Carson Pirie Scott: Louis Sullivan and the Chicago Department Store* (Chicago: University of Chicago Press, 1988), 15–20; and Miller, *City of the Century*, 137–141.

49. Benjamin and Cohen, *Great Houses of Chicago*, 120.

50. "Real Estate: Important Sales along the North Side Lake Shore Drive; Handsome Residences to Be Erected and Other Improvements Made," *Chicago Daily Tribune*, January 15, 1882, 12. On the development of the Gold Coast, see John W. Stamper, "Shaping Chicago's Shoreline," *Chicago History* 14 (Winter 1985–1986): 44–55; and Daniel Bluestone, "Charnleys by the Lake: Houses, Apartments, and Fashion on Chicago's Gold Coast," in *The Charnley House: Louis Sullivan, Frank Lloyd Wright, and the Making of Chicago's Gold Coast*, ed. Richard Longstreth (Chicago: University of Chicago Press, 2004), 37–58.

51. Bluestone, "Charnleys by the Lake," 40.

52. Harvey Warren Zorbaugh, *The Gold Coast and the Slum: A Sociological Study of Chicago's Near North Side* (Chicago: University of Chicago Press, 1929), 40.

53. "Potter Palmer: His Grand House on the North Side," *Chicago Daily Tribune*, February 22, 1882, 8. On the design and construction of the Palmer mansion, see Bluestone, "Charnleys by the Lake," 41; and Wolner, *Henry Ives Cobb's Chicago*, 40–52.

54. "Residence on the Lake-Shore Drive," *Chicago Daily Tribune*, April 9, 1882, 18.

55. "Potter Palmer: Rumors and Facts Concerning the North Side Residence," *Chicago Daily Tribune*, April 20, 1883, 8.

56. "A Chicago Palace," *Washington Post*, October 14, 1885, 6, reprinted from the *Chicago Inter-Ocean*.

57. Veblen, *Theory of the Leisure Class*, 154.

58. W. L. B. Jenney, "The Building Stones of Chicago," *Engineering News and American Contract Journal* (January 5, 1884): 1–3.

59. Thomas Leslie, "Traditional Materials: Stone, Brick, and Cast Iron," in *Chicago Skyscrapers, 1871–1934* (Urbana: University of Illinois Press, 2013), 3–4.

60. On the use of granite in the Board of Trade Building and the political meaning attached to it by Chicago's labor leaders, see Gretta Tritch Roman, "The Reach of the Pit: Negotiating the Multiple Spheres of the Chicago Board of Trade Building in the Late Nineteenth Century" (PhD diss., Pennsylvania State University, 2015), 280–282.

61. Veblen, *Theory of the Leisure Class*, 133–134.

62. Julian Ralph, *Our Great West* (1893), in *As Others See Chicago: Impressions of Visitors 1673–1933*, ed. Bessie Pierce (1933; repr., Chicago: University of Chicago Press, 2004), 303.

63. "On the Lake-Shore Drive," *Chicago Daily Tribune*, July 16, 1888, 8.

64. Veblen, *Theory of the Leisure Class*, 61.

65. Veblen, *Theory of the Leisure Class*, 57.

66. "Art Notes," *Chicago Daily Tribune*, October 10, 1885, 13; "Potter Palmer's Residence," *Chicago Daily Tribune*, January 13, 1884, 15.

67. "Bits of Architecture: Some Features of the New Chicagoesque School—Popularity of the Romanesque Style of Architecture in Chicago—Specimen Spots of Mr. Potter Palmer's Baronial Castle, Studebaker's Carriage Factory, the New Union League Club House, and Other Handsome Chicago

Buildings," *Chicago Daily Tribune*, November 7, 1886, 26.

68. "Four Residences for Potter Palmer at Elm Near State," *Building Budget* 3 (April 30, 1887): 65; "Group of Buildings Erected for Potter Palmer on Lake Shore Drive, Chicago," *American Architect and Building News* 27, no. 735 (January 25, 1890): 68.

69. Thomas C. Hubka has discussed H. H. Richardson's Glessner House as a response to the fear of socialist and anarchist uprising in Chicago during the 1880s. Thomas C. Hubka, "H. H. Richardson's Glessner House: A Garden in the Machine," *Winterthur Portfolio* 24, no. 4 (Winter 1989): 221.

70. Upton Sinclair, *The Jungle* (New York: Grosset and Dunlap, 1906), 282–283.

71. "Bits of Architecture," 26.

72. Richard Sennett, "Middle-Class Families and Urban Violence: The Experience of a Chicago Community in the Nineteenth Century," in *Nineteenth-Century Cities: Essays in the New Urban History*, ed. Stephan Thernstrom and Richard Sennett (New Haven: Yale University Press, 1969), 386–420.

73. John Wellborn Root, "The City House in the West," *Scribner's Magazine* 8, no. 4 (1890): 416.

74. Ralph, *Our Great West*, 302.

75. Veblen, *Theory of the Leisure Class*, 83.

76. On moral assessments of Victorian architectural aesthetics, see Timothy Hyde, *Ugliness and Judgment: On Architecture in the Public Eye* (Princeton, NJ: Princeton

University Press, 2019), 137–138.

77. Veblen, *Theory of the Leisure Class*, 154.

78. Leslie, *Chicago Skyscrapers*, 15. On the prevalence of brick party walls in Chicago in this period, see Daniel Bluestone, "Louis H. Sullivan's Chicago: From 'Shirt Front,' to Alley, to 'All Around Structures,'" *Winterthur Portfolio* 47, no. 1 (Spring 2013): 65–98.

79. "Razing of Potter Palmer Mansion to Remove Landmark of Famous Era," *Chicago Daily Tribune*, February 12, 1950, F1.

80. Al Chase, "Family Quits Potter Palmer Castle Forever," *Chicago Daily Tribune*, April 23, 1930, 1.

81. Bluestone, "Charnleys by the Lake," 56–58; Neil Harris and Teri J. Edelstein, *Chicago Apartments: A Century and Beyond of Lakefront Luxury* (2004; repr., Chicago: University of Chicago Press, 2020).

82. "Society People Desert Their Houses and Flock to Apartments and Hotels," *Chicago Tribune*, April 28, 1907, G5.

83. Thomas Tallmadge, *The Story of Architecture in America* (New York: W. W. Norton, 1927), 180.

84. On the origins of Mies's conception of modern metropolitan dwelling in prewar Berlin, see Robin Schuldenfrei, *Luxury and Modernism: Architecture and the Object in Germany, 1900–1933* (Princeton, NJ: Princeton University Press, 2018), 223–254.

85. Henry H. Reed, "Monumental Architecture: Or,

the Art of Pleasing in Civic Design," *Perspecta* 1 (Summer 1952): 50–54, 56; Wayne Andrews, *Architecture, Ambition, and Americans: A Social History of American Architecture, from the Beginning to the Present, Telling the Story of the Outstanding Buildings, the Men Who Designed Them, and the People for Whom They Were Built* (New York: Harper, 1955), 254–256, 262, 302; *Architecture in America: A Battle of Styles*, ed. William A. Coles and Henry Hope Reed Jr. (New York: Appleton-Century-Crofts, 1961), 41–42.

Chapter 2

1. David Allan, *The University of Chicago: An Official Guide* (Chicago: University of Chicago Press, 1916), 22.

2. Thomas Wakefield Goodspeed, *A History of the University of Chicago: The First Quarter Century* (1916; repr., Chicago: University of Chicago Press, 1972), 248.

3. On Veblen's fourteen years at the University of Chicago, see Joseph Dorfman, *Thorstein Veblen and His America* (1934; repr., New York: Viking Press, 1940), 90–270; Elizabeth Jorgensen and Henry Jorgensen, *Thorstein Veblen: Victorian Firebrand* (Armonk, NY: M. E. Sharpe, 1999), 32–92; and Charles Camic, *Veblen: The Making of an Economist Who Unmade Economics* (Cambridge, MA: Harvard University Press, 2020), 236–339.

4. Wesley C. Mitchell, *What Veblen Taught: Selected Writings of Thorstein Veblen* (1936; repr., Angus M. Kelley: New York, 1964), xii.

5. Edward Shils, "The University, the City, and the World: Chicago and the University of Chicago," in *The University and the City: From Medieval Origins to the Present*, ed. Thomas Bender (New York: Oxford University Press, 1988), 210–230; Robin F. Bachin, *Building the South Side: Urban Space and Civic Culture in Chicago, 1890–1919* (Chicago: University of Chicago Press, 2004), 23–104.

6. Camic, *Veblen*, 251–252.

7. James F. Short Jr., *The Social Fabric of the Metropolis: Contributions of the Chicago School of Urban Sociology* (Chicago: University of Chicago Press, 1971); Dorothy Ross, "Progressive Social Science, 1896–1914," in *The Origins of American Social Science* (Cambridge: Cambridge University Press, 1991), 143–302; and Craig Calhoun, *Sociology in America: A History* (Chicago: University of Chicago Press, 2007), 20–22.

8. J. Laurence Laughlin, "The Study of Political Economy in the United States," *Journal of Political Economy* 1, no. 1 (December 1892): 1–19.

9. Laughlin, "Study of Political Economy," 14.

10. Thorstein Veblen, "The Price of Wheat since 1867," *Journal of Political Economy* 1, no. 1 (December 1892): 68–103.

11. Thorstein Veblen, "The Food Supply and the Price of Wheat," *Journal of Political Economy* 1, no. 3 (June 1893): 365–379.

12. On the importance of the grain trade to Chicago and the grain elevator as a structure, see Bessie Louise Pierce, "The Economic Empire of Chicago: The Grain Trade, the Lumber Trade," in *A History of Chicago*, vol. 3: *The Rise of a Modern City, 1871–1893* (Chicago: University of Chicago Press, 1957), 64–107; William Cronon, "Pricing the Future: Grain," in *Nature's Metropolis: Chicago and the Great West* (New York: W. W. Norton, 1991), 97–147; and Thomas Leslie, "Chicago's Other Skyscrapers: Grain Elevators and the City, 1838–1957," *Journal of Urban History* 48, no. 1 (May 2022): 3–34.

13. Bessie Louise Pierce, "Storage Capacity for Chicago Grain Elevator Warehouses, 1893," in *A History of Chicago*, 3:530.

14. Armour bought out the business of George Armour (no relation), who had developed some of the earliest elevators in the city. Leslie, "Chicago's Other Skyscrapers," 19.

15. Veblen, "Price of Wheat since 1867," 89.

16. "Transportation of Grain in the United States," *Scientific American* 65, no. 17 (October 24, 1891): 258, 261.

17. On the fascination that American industrial architecture held for the architects of the European avant-garde, see Reyner Banham, *A Concrete Atlantis: U.S. Industrial Building and European Modern Architecture, 1900–1925* (Cambridge, MA: MIT Press, 1986); and Jean-Louis Cohen, *Scenes of the World to Come: European Architecture and the American Challenge, 1893–1960* (Paris and Montreal: Flammarion and Canadian Centre for Architecture, 1995).

18. Erich Mendelsohn, *Erich Mendelsohn's 'Amerika'* [*Amerika, Bilderbuch eines Architekten*] (1926; repr., New York: Dover, 1993), 47.

19. Cronon, *Nature's Metropolis*, 120.

20. Thorstein Veblen, "Industrial and Pecuniary Employments," *Publications of the American Economic Association* 2, no. 1 (February 1901): 202.

21. Thorstein Veblen, *Theory of Business Enterprise* (1904; repr., New York: Charles Scribner's Sons, 1919), 29.

22. On the architecture and operation of the Chicago Board of Trade, see Gretta Tritch Roman, "The Reach of the Pit: Negotiating the Multiple Spheres of the Chicago Board of Trade Building in the Late Nineteenth Century" (PhD diss., Pennsylvania State University, 2015).

23. *Biographical Sketches of the Leading Men of Chicago* (Chicago: Wilson & St. Clair, 1868), 215–222; *Industrial Chicago*, vol. 1: *The Building Interests* (Chicago: Goodspeed Publishing, 1896), 533.

24. Montgomery Schuyler, "Glimpses of Western Architecture I: Chicago," *American Architecture Studies* (New York: Harper & Brothers, 1892), 121.

25. Joseph Siry, "Anarchist Counterculture, the Board of Trade Building, and Haymarket, 1885–86," in *The Chicago Auditorium Building: Adler and Sullivan's Architecture and the City* (Chicago: University of Chicago Press, 2002), 114–121.

26. "Vicinity of the Board of Trade," *Rand, McNally & Co.'s Bird's-Eye Views and Guide*

to Chicago (Chicago: Rand, McNally & Company, 1893), 14. On the development of this area, see H. T. Sudduth, "LaSalle Street, Chicago," *Harper's Weekly* 34 (May 3, 1890): 346–347; and Homer Hoyt, *One Hundred Years of Land Values in Chicago: The Relationship of the Growth of Chicago to the Rise of Its Land Values, 1830–1933* (Chicago: University of Chicago Press, 1933), 152.

27. *Industrial Chicago*, 1:171.

28. *Rand, McNally & Co.'s Bird's-Eye Views*, 16.

29. Carol Willis, *Form Follows Finance: Skyscrapers and Skylines in New York and Chicago* (New York: Princeton Architectural Press, 1995).

30. See, for example, Carl W. Condit, *The Chicago School of Architecture: A History of Commercial and Public Buildings in the Chicago Area, 1875–1925* (Chicago: University of Chicago Press, 1964); Jane H. Clarke, Pauline Saliga, and John Zukowsky, *The Sky's the Limit: A Century of Chicago Skyscrapers* (New York: Rizzoli, 1990); Daniel Bluestone, "A City under One Roof: Skyscrapers, 1880–95," in *Constructing Chicago* (New Haven: Yale University Press, 1991), 104–151; Robert Bruegmann, *The Architects and the City: Holabird and Roche of Chicago, 1880–1918* (Chicago: University of Chicago Press, 1997); Joanna Merwood-Salisbury, *Chicago 1890: The Skyscraper and the Modern City* (Chicago: University of Chicago Press, 2009); and Thomas Leslie, *Chicago Skyscrapers, 1871–1934* (Urbana: University of Illinois Press, 2013).

31. Kenneth Turney Gibbs, *Business Architectural Imagery in America, 1870–1930* (Ann Arbor: University of Michigan Press, 1984), 17; Daniel J. Boorstin, "The Rise of the Skyscraper," in *The Creators: A History of Heroes of the Imagination* (1992; repr., New York: Random House, 2012), 550; Annette Condello, *The Architecture of Luxury* (London: Ashgate, 2014), 129–130.

32. Eric L. Hirsch, *Urban Revolt: Ethnic Politics in the Nineteenth-Century Chicago Labor Movement* (Berkeley: University of California Press, 1998); Richard Schneirov, *Labor and Urban Politics: Class Conflict and the Origins of Modern Liberalism in Chicago, 1864–97* (Urbana: University of Illinois Press, 1998); Shelton Stromquist, *Reinventing the People: The Progressive Movement, the Class Problem, and the Origins of Modern Liberalism* (Urbana: University of Illinois Press, 2006).

33. M. A. Lane, "The Distress in Chicago" and "Among the Unemployed of Chicago," *Harper's Weekly* 38 (January 13, 1894): 37–38.

34. "Some Tendencies of Socialism," *Chicago Daily Tribune*, January 8, 1895, 3.

35. Joseph Siry, "The Abraham Lincoln Center in Chicago," *Journal of the Society of Architectural Historians* 50, no. 3 (September 1991): 235–265.

36. Stromquist, *Reinventing the People*.

37. Forest G. Hill, "Veblen and Marx," in *Thorstein Veblen: A Critical Reappraisal; Lectures and Essays Commemorating the Hundredth Anniversary of Veblen's Birth*, ed. Douglas F.

Dowd (1958; repr., Westport, CT: Greenwood Press, 1977), 129–149; John P. Diggins, *The Bard of Savagery: Thorstein Veblen and Modern Social Theory* (New York: Seabury Press, 1978), 45–89.

38. Karl Marx, *A Contribution to the Critique of Political Economy* (Chicago: Charles Kerr Company, 1904), 299. This is an English translation by N. I. Stone of the second German edition published in 1897. The first edition, *Zur Kritik der Politischen Oekonomie*, was published in 1859.

39. Karl Marx and Frederick Engels, *The Civil War in the United States*, ed. Richard Enmale (New York: International Press, 1937).

40. Thorstein Veblen, "The Army of the Commonweal," *Journal of Political Economy* 2, no. 3 (June 1894): 456–461. See also Thorstein Veblen, "The Socialist Economics of Karl Marx and His Followers, I," *Quarterly Journal of Economics* 20, no. 4 (August 1906): 575–596.

41. Isador Lubin, "Recollections of Veblen," in *Thorstein Veblen: The Carleton College Seminar Essays*, ed. Carleton C. Qualey (New York: Columbia University Press, 1968), 138–139.

42. Ellen Mazur Thomson, "Thorstein Veblen at the University of Chicago and the Socialization of Aesthetics," *Design Issues* 15, no. 1 (Spring 1999): 3–15.

43. Thorstein Veblen, "The Economic Theory of Woman's Dress," *Popular Science Monthly* 46 (December 1894): 198–205; Thorstein Veblen,

"The Barbarian Status of Women," *American Journal of Sociology* 4, no. 4 (January 1899): 503–514.

44. Camic, *Veblen*, 283–290.

45. T. J. Jackson Lears, "Beyond Veblen: Rethinking Culture in America," in *Consuming Visions: Accumulation and Display of Goods in America, 1880–1925*, ed. Simon J. Bronner (New York: W. W. Norton, 1989), 73–74.

46. Thorstein Veblen, *The Theory of the Leisure Class* (1899; repr., London: Penguin, 1979), 120, 348.

47. On the first University of Chicago, see *First Annual Catalogue of the University of Chicago: Officers and Students for the Year 1859–60* (Chicago: Church, Goodman and Cushing, 1860); *Annual Catalogue of the University of Chicago: Officers and Students for the Year 1870–71* (Chicago: Globe Printing Company, 1871); and Edgar J. Goodspeed, "The Old University of Chicago in 1867," *Journal of the Illinois State Historical Society* 3, no. 2 (July 1910): 52–57.

48. Jack Wing, *The Great Chicago Lake Tunnel* (Chicago: Jack Wing, 1867), 56.

49. Frontispiece, *First Annual Catalogue of the University of Chicago*.

50. Veblen, *Theory of the Leisure Class*, 349.

51. Veblen, *Theory of the Leisure Class*, 373.

52. Alfred T. Andreas, *History of Chicago from the Earliest Period to the Present Time*, vol. 2: *From 1857 until the Fire of 1871* (Chicago: A. T. Andreas Publishers, 1885), 301–310; Joseph L. Eisendrath Jr., "Chicago's Camp Douglas,

1861–1865," *Journal of the Illinois State Historical Society* 53, no. 1 (Spring 1960): 37–63.

53. Theodore J. Karamanski, *Rally 'Round the Flag: Chicago and the Civil War* (Chicago: Nelson-Hall, 1993); Kurt A. Carlson, "Backing the Boys in the Civil War: Chicago's Home Front Supports the Troops—And Grows in the Process," *Journal of the Illinois State Historical Society* 104, nos. 1–2 (Spring/Summer 2011): 140–165.

54. On the rise of this class, see Frederic Cople Jaher, *The Urban Establishment: Upper Strata in Boston, New York, Charleston, Chicago, and Los Angeles* (Urbana: University of Illinois Press, 1982), 453–576.

55. Veblen, *Theory of the Leisure Class*, 373.

56. Veblen, *Theory of the Leisure Class*, 374.

57. Veblen, *Theory of the Leisure Class*, 364. On Veblen's opinion of academia, see Donald L. Miller, *City of the Century: The Epic of Chicago and the Making of America* (New York: Simon and Schuster, 1996), 396–402; John Diggins, "The Captains of Erudition," in Diggins, *Thorstein Veblen: Theorist of the Leisure Class* (Princeton, NJ: Princeton University Press, 1999), 172–181; and Stephen Edgell, "Personal Troubles and the Public Issue of Higher Education," in Edgell, *Veblen in Perspective: His Life and Thought* (Armonk, NY: M. E. Sharpe, 2001), 16–23.

58. Veblen, *Theory of the Leisure Class*, 368.

59. Veblen, *Theory of the Leisure Class*, 397.

60. Veblen, *Theory of the Leisure Class*, 392.

61. "Study for the University of Chicago," Henry Ives Cobb, architect, *Inland Architect* 22 (August 1893): plate. On Cobb's design and the construction of the university, see Jean Block, *The Uses of Gothic: Planning and Building the Campus of the University of Chicago, 1892–1932* (Chicago: University of Chicago Press, 1983); Bachin, *Building the South Side*, 43–51; Susan O'Connor Davis, *Chicago's Historic Hyde Park* (Chicago: University of Chicago Press, 2013), 104–119; and Edward W. Wolner, *Henry Ives Cobb's Chicago: Architecture, Institutions, and the Making of a Modern Metropolis* (Chicago: University of Chicago Press, 2011), 181–213.

62. Henry Ives Cobb was no relation to Silas X. Cobb, the donor after whom Cobb Hall was named.

63. Wolner, *Henry Ives Cobb's Chicago*, 189.

64. Edgell, *Veblen in Perspective*, 20.

65. Thorstein Veblen, *The Higher Learning in America: A Memorandum on the Conduct of Universities by Business Men* (New York: B. W. Huebsch, 1918), v–vi.

66. Veblen, *Higher Learning in America*, 137.

67. Paul Hardin Kapp, "The University Campus in the United States—As a Designed Work to Produce Knowledge; and as an Artefact of Cultural Heritage," *Built Heritage* 2 (2018): 49–65.

68. Hjalmar Hjorth Boyesen, "The University of Chicago," *The Cosmopolitan;*

A Monthly Illustrated Magazine 14, no. 6 (1893): 665.

69. Wolner, *Henry Ives Cobb's Chicago*, 185. On the urban growth machines of late nineteenth-century America, see John Logan and Harvey Molotch, *Urban Fortunes: The Political Economy of Place* (Berkeley: University of California Press, 1988), 50–98.

70. Goodspeed, *History of the University of Chicago*, 267–269.

71. Goodspeed, *History of the University of Chicago*, 13–23.

72. Frederick Starr, "Science at the University of Chicago," *Appleton's Popular Science Monthly* 51 (October 1897): 784–805; Goodspeed, *History of the University of Chicago*, 233–237; Wolner, *Henry Ives Cobb's Chicago*, 215–223.

73. Veblen, *Higher Learning in America*, 139–140.

74. Shils, "The University, the City, and the World," 216.

75. Charles E. Jenkins, "University of Chicago," *Architectural Record* 4, no. 4 (1894): 237.

76. Jenkins, "University of Chicago," 240.

77. Wolner, *Henry Ives Cobb's Chicago*, 193–194; Bachin, *Building the South Side*; Sharon Haar, "New Institutions for a New Environment: Pedagogical Space in the Progressive City," in Haar, *The City as Campus: Urbanism and Higher Education in Chicago* (Minneapolis: University of Minnesota Press, 2011), 23–27.

78. Michael W. Brooks, "Ruskin's Influence in America," in *John Ruskin and Victorian Architecture* (New Brunswick, NJ: Rutgers University Press, 1987), 277–297; and Lauren Weingarden, "Gothic Naturalism and the Ruskinian Critical Tradition in America" and "Ruskin's Reception in the Chicago School," in *Louis H. Sullivan and a Nineteenth-Century Poetics of Naturalized Architecture* (London: Ashgate, 2009), 71–96, 183–212.

79. Joanna Merwood-Salisbury, "The Gothic Revival and the Chicago School," in *Skyscraper Gothic: Medieval Style and Modernist Buildings*, ed. Kevin Murphy and Lisa Reilly (Charlottesville: University of Virginia Press, 2017), 88–111.

80. Veblen, *Higher Learning in America*, 143.

81. Wolner, *Henry Ives Cobb's Chicago*, 223–237.

82. Veblen, *Higher Learning in America*, 139.

83. Veblen, *Higher Learning in America*, 147.

84. Goodspeed, *History of the University of Chicago*, 227.

85. Dorfman, *Thorstein Veblen and His America*, 205.

86. Veblen, "Modern Survivals of Prowess," in *Theory of the Leisure Class*, 246–275.

87. Veblen, *Theory of the Leisure Class*, 261. The university's encouragement of athletic culture was aligned with a larger social movement to popularize athletic activities. Bachin, *Building the South Side*, 86–97.

88. Veblen, *Higher Learning in America*, 146.

89. Sigfried Giedion, *Space, Time and Architecture: The Growth of a New Tradition* (Cambridge, MA: Harvard University Press, 1941); Condit, *The Chicago School of Architecture*.

90. Veblen, *Higher Learning in America*, 145–146.

91. Veblen, *Higher Learning in America*, 144.

92. Veblen, *Higher Learning in America*, 146.

93. Joseph Schumpeter, *Capitalism, Socialism, and Democracy* (New York: Harper & Brothers, 1947), 84. Educated in Vienna at the beginning of the twentieth century, Schumpeter was a member of the school of political economists that was influential in the American academy.

94. Daniel M. Abramson, *Obsolescence: An Architectural History* (Chicago: University of Chicago Press, 2016).

95. In 1922, the Chicago-based National Association of Building Owners and Managers established that an office building had a "useful and profitable" lifespan of around thirty years. By the 1930s, this estimate was used to calculate the taxable value of office buildings. Abramson, *Obsolescence*, 21–29.

96. Wolner, *Henry Ives Cobb's Chicago*, 238–239.

97. Kevin Harrington, "Henry Ives Cobb's Chicago: Architecture, Institutions, and the Making of a Modern Metropolis," *Journal of the Society of Architectural Historians* 72, no. 1 (March 2013): 112. Cobb, one of the most important Chicago architects of the 1880s and '90s, is barely mentioned in Carl Condit's canonical *Chicago School of Architecture*.

98. Montgomery Schuyler, *A Critique (with Illustrations) of the Work of Adler & Sullivan, D. H. Burnham & Co., Henry Ives*

Cobb (New York: The Architectural Record, 1896), 103.

99. Peter B. Wight, "Modern Architecture in Chicago," *Pall Mall Magazine* 18 (July 1899): 299.

100. Jorgensen and Jorgensen, *Thorstein Veblen*, 93–98; Camic, *Veblen*, 345.

101. On the Fifty-Seventh Street Arts Colony, see Roy Kotynek and John Cohassey, *American Cultural Rebels: Avant-Garde and Bohemian Artists, Writers, and Musicians from the 1850s through the 1960s* (Jefferson, NC: McFarland, 2008), 63; Maggie Taft and Robert Cozzolino, eds., *Art in Chicago: A History from the Fire to Now* (Chicago: University of Chicago Press, 2018), 52–53, 65; and Michelle E. Moore, *Chicago and the Making of American Modernism: Cather, Hemingway, Faulkner, and Fitzgerald in Conflict* (London: Bloomsbury, 2019), 63.

102. Diggins, *Thorstein Veblen*, 176.

Chapter 3

1. Alfred T. Andreas, *History of Chicago from the Earliest Period to the Present Time*, vol. 2: *From 1857 until the Fire of 1871* (Chicago: A. T. Andreas Publishers, 1885), 695; *Rand, McNally & Co.'s Bird's-Eye Views and Guide to Chicago* (Chicago: Rand, McNally & Company, 1893), 124; *Industrial Chicago*, vol. 4: *The Commercial Interests* (Chicago: Goodspeed Publishing, 1894), 479–482; S. H. Ditchett, *Marshall Field and Company: The Life Story of a Great Concern* (New York: Dry Goods Economist, 1922); Robert W. Twyman, *History of Marshall*

Field & Co., 1852–1906 (Philadelphia: University of Pennsylvania Press, 1954).

2. Bessie Louise Pierce, "The Economic Empire of Chicago: Manufacturing and Merchandising," in *A History of Chicago*, vol. 3: *The Rise of a Modern City, 1871–1893* (Chicago: University of Chicago Press, 1957), 145–191.

3. On the architecture of nineteenth-century department stores in Chicago, see Carl W. Condit, *The Chicago School of Architecture: A History of Commercial and Public Buildings in the Chicago Area, 1875–1925* (Chicago: University of Chicago Press, 1964); Hugh Dalziel Duncan, "Setting the Stage for a New Urban Drama, the Drama of Shopping," in Duncan, *Culture and Democracy: The Struggle for Form in Society and Architecture in Chicago and the Middle West During the Life and Times of Louis H. Sullivan* (1965; repr., Bedminster Press, 1989), 123–131; Neil Harris, "Shopping—Chicago Style," in *Chicago Architecture, 1872–1922*, ed. John Zukowsky (Munich: Art Institute of Chicago and Prestel Verlag, 1987), 137–155; and Joseph Siry, *Carson Pirie Scott: Louis Sullivan and the Chicago Department Store* (Chicago: University of Chicago Press, 1988).

4. "Spring Beauties," *Chicago Daily Tribune*, May 18, 1900, 6. On "aesthetic nausea," see Thorstein Veblen, *The Theory of the Leisure Class* (1899; repr., London: Penguin, 1979), 178.

5. "The Enemies of Fashion," *Chicago Daily Tribune*, November 17, 1901, 12.

6. "New Simple Life Apostle," *Chicago Daily Tribune*, December 26, 1905, 1; Charles Wagner, *The Simple Life*, trans. Mary Louise Hendee (New York: McClure Phillips & Co., 1904).

7. Nevertheless, Veblen's writing is often discussed in this context. See, for example, Patricia A. Cunningham, *Reforming Women's Fashion, 1850–1920: Politics, Health, and Art* (Kent, OH: Kent State University Press, 2015), 11.

8. T. J. Jackson Lears, *No Place of Grace: Antimodernism and the Transformation of American Culture, 1880–1920* (Chicago: University of Chicago Press, 1994), 37.

9. Thorstein Veblen, *The Higher Learning in America: A Memorandum on the Conduct of the Universities by Businessmen* (New York: B. W. Huebsch, 1918), 145.

10. Thorstein Veblen, "The Economic Theory of Woman's Dress," *Popular Science Monthly* 46 (December 1894): 198–205.

11. Caroline A. Foley, "Fashion," *Economic Journal* (UK) 3, no. 11 (September 1893): 459.

12. Julian M. Sturtevant, *Economics, or the Science of Wealth* (New York: G. P. Putnam's Sons, 1879), 324.

13. Friedrich Kleinwächter, *Zur Philosophie der Mode* (Berlin: C. Habel, 1880); Friedrich Theodor Vischer, "Wieder einmal über die Mode," in *Mode und Zynismus* (Stuttgart, 1878). On German writing on fashion, economics, and design in this period, see Roman Meinhold and John Irons, *Fashion Myths: A*

Cultural Critique, trans. John Irons (Bielefeld: Transcript Verlag, 2013); Rebecca Houze, *Textiles, Fashion, and Design Reform in Austria-Hungary before the First World War: Principles of Dress* (London: Routledge, 2016); and Stefano Marino, "Philosophical Accounts of Fashion in the Nineteenth and Twentieth Century: A Historical Reconstruction," in *Philosophical Perspectives on Fashion*, ed. Giovanni Matteucci and Stefano Marino (London: Bloomsbury, 2017), 11–46.

14. J. Laurence Laughlin, "Economic Effects of Changes of Fashion," *Chautauquan* 19 (April 1894): 9–13.

15. As Charles Camic has explained, Veblen's analysis of elaborate and debilitating dress in terms of social utility allowed him to challenge economists from the "marginal utility school." Camic, *Veblen: The Making of an Economist Who Unmade Economics* (Cambridge, MA: Harvard University Press, 2020), 270.

16. Frederick Starr, "Dress and Adornment," *Popular Science* 39 (1891): 488–502, 787–801; Frederick Starr, "Dress and Adornment," *Popular Science* 40 (1891): 44–57, 194–206.

17. Ernst Grosse, *Anfänge der Kunst* (Freiburg: J. C. B. Mohr, 1894). Frederick Starr translated Grosse's book as *The Beginnings of Art* (New York: Appleton, 1897). On the possible influence of Grosse on Veblen, see Joseph Dorfman, *Thorstein Veblen and His America* (1934; repr., New York: Viking Press, 1940), 102; and Elizabeth Jorgensen and Henry Jorgensen, *Thorstein*

Veblen: Victorian Firebrand (Armonk NY: M. E. Sharpe, 1999), 37.

18. Veblen, "Economic Theory of Woman's Dress," 199.

19. Veblen, "Economic Theory of Woman's Dress," 200–201.

20. Veblen, *Theory of the Leisure Class*, 172.

21. Nils Gilman, "Thorstein Veblen's Neglected Feminism," *Journal of Economic Issues* 33, no. 3 (September 1999): 696. On feminism as a driver of Veblen's economic theory, see Barbara E. Ryan, "Thorstein Veblen: A New Perspective," *Mid-American Review of Sociology* 7, no. 2 (1982): 29–47; and Anne Jennings, "Veblen's Feminism in Historical Perspective," in *The Founding of Institutional Economics: The Leisure Class and Sovereignty*, ed. Warren Samuels (London: Routledge, 1998), 201–233.

22. Veblen, "Economic Theory of Woman's Dress," 205.

23. Colin Campbell, "The Sociology of Consumption," in *Acknowledging Consumption: A Review of New Studies*, ed. Daniel Miller (London: Routledge, 1995), 96–126.

24. On the discourse on fashion, luxury, and design in turn-of-the-century Germany, see Warren G. Breckman, "Disciplining Consumption: The Debate about Luxury in Wilhelmine Germany, 1890–1914," *Journal of Social History* 24, no. 3 (1991): 485–505; Sherwin Simmons, "Ernst Kirchner's Streetwalkers: Art, Luxury and Immorality in Berlin, 1913–16," *Art Bulletin* 82, no. 1

(March 2000): 117–148; and Robin Schuldenfrei, *Luxury and Modernism: Architecture and the Object in Germany, 1900–1933* (Princeton, NJ: Princeton University Press, 2018), 12–17.

25. Werner Sombart, *Luxus und Kapitalismus* (Leipzig: Duncker and Humblot, 1913). For the English translation, see Werner Sombart, *Luxury and Capitalism*, trans. W. R. Dittmar (Ann Arbor: University of Michigan Press, 1967).

26. Georg Simmel, "Fashion," *International Quarterly* 10 (October 1904): 130–155; reprinted in D. N. Levine, ed., *Georg Simmel on Individuality and Social Forms* (Chicago: University of Chicago Press, 1971), 294–323.

27. Adolf Loos, "Men's Fashion" (1898), "Ladies' Fashion" (1898/1902), and "Ornament and Crime" (1908), in Adolf Loos and Adolf Opel, *Ornament and Crime: Selected Essays* (Riverside, CA: Ariadne Press, 1998), 39–44, 106–111, 167–176.

28. George Hersey, "Reflections on Adolf Loos: Why Should Women but Not Buildings Be Ornamented?," *ANY* 4 (January/February 1994): 28–31; Ákos Moravánszky, "'Truth to Material' vs. 'The Principle of Cladding': The Language of Materials in Architecture," *AA Files* 31 (Summer 1996): 39–46; Jonathan Massey, "New Necessities: Modernist Aesthetic Discipline," *Perspecta* 35 (2004): 112–133; and Christopher Long, "The Origins and Context of Adolf Loos's 'Ornament and Crime,'" *Journal of the Society of Architectural*

Historians 68, no. 2 (June 2009): 200–223.

29. T. W. Adorno, "Veblen's Attack on Culture," *Studies in Philosophy and Social Science* 9 (1941): 389.

30. As Beatriz Colomina has discussed, Loos was one of many architects in this period who sought to free architecture from fashion even as they exploited the publicity mechanisms that advanced the economy of fashion, including popular magazines, exhibitions, and later, films. Beatriz Colomina, *Privacy and Publicity: Modern Architecture as Mass Media* (Cambridge, MA: MIT Press, 1994). See also Leila W. Kinney, "Fashion and Fabrication in Modern Architecture," *Journal of the Society of Architectural Historians* 58, no. 3 (September 1999): 472–481.

31. The superiority of Western culture was the basis for Loos's short-lived journal, *Das Andere* (1903), subtitled "A Journal for the Introduction of Western Culture into Austria." Adolf Loos, *Das Andere. Ein Blatt zur Einfuehrung abendlaendischer Kultur in Oesterreich* 1, nos. 1–2 (Vienna: Verlag Kunst, 1903).

32. Rukschcio Burkhardt and Roland Schachel, *Adolf Loos: Leben und Werk* (Salzburg: Residenz, 1982), 21–31; Benedetto Gravagnuolo, *Adolf Loos: Theory and Works*, trans. C. H. Evans (New York: Rizzoli, 1982), 42–52; Kurt Lustenberger, *Adolf Loos* (Zurich: Artemis, 1994), 9–10; and Janet Stewart, *Fashioning Vienna: Adolf Loos's Cultural Criticism* (London: Routledge, 2000), 42–51.

33. Burkhardt and Schachel, *Adolf Loos*, 30–31.

34. Sigfried Giedion, *Space, Time and Architecture: The Growth of a New Tradition* (Cambridge, MA: Harvard University Press, 1941); and Nikolaus Pevsner, *An Outline of European Architecture* (London: Penguin, 1951).

35. Richard Neutra gave this interpretation of Loos's admiration for the United States in Neutra, *Auftrag für Morgen* (Hamburg: Claassen, 1962).

36. Daniel Bell, "Veblen and the New Class," *American Scholar* 32, no. 4 (Autumn 1963): 617.

37. A. A. Hayes, "The Metropolis of the Prairies," *Harper's New Monthly Magazine* 61, no. 365 (October 1880): 711–732; Harold M. Mayer and Richard C. Wade, *Chicago: Growth of a Metropolis* (Chicago: University of Chicago Press, 1969), 54; Donald L. Miller, *City of the Century: The Epic of Chicago and the Making of America* (New York: Simon and Schuster, 1996), 137–141; Siry, *Carson Pirie Scott*, 15–20; Dominic Pacyga, *Chicago: A Biography* (Chicago: University of Chicago Press, 2009), 72–73.

38. Daniel Bluestone, "Louis H. Sullivan's Chicago: From 'Shirt Front,' to Alley, to 'All Around Structures,'" *Winterthur Portfolio* 47, no. 1 (Spring 2013): 65–98.

39. Veblen's use of this phrase comes in the context of his critique of the modern American university, as discussed in chapter 2. Thorstein Veblen, "Academic Prestige and the Material

Equipment," in *The Higher Learning in America*, 143.

40. Harris, "Shopping—Chicago Style," 145–146.

41. *Industrial Chicago*, vol. 1: *The Building Interests* (Chicago: Goodspeed Publishing, 1896), 171.

42. Marshall Field & Company, *The Store of Service: Marshall Field & Co.* (Chicago: Marshall Field & Company, 1920), 4; quoted in Emily M. Orr, *Designing the Department Store: Display and Retail at the Turn of the Twentieth Century* (London: Bloomsbury Visual Arts, 2020), 6.

43. Thorstein Veblen, *The Theory of Business Enterprise* (1904; repr., New York: Charles Scribner's Sons, 1919), 317.

44. Karl Marx, "The Fetishism of Commodities and the Secret Thereof," in *Capital: A Critique of Political Economy I: The Process of Capitalist Production*, ed. Fredrich Engels (1867; 1909 translation; repr., Chicago: Charles H Kerr Co., 1912), 81–95.

45. Veblen, *Theory of the Leisure Class*, 87–88.

46. Veblen, *Theory of Business Enterprise*, 15. Alan Trachtenberg, *The Incorporation of America: Culture and Society in the Gilded Age* (1982; repr., New York: Hill and Wang, 2007).

47. Veblen, *Theory of Business Enterprise*, 316.

48. Veblen, *Theory of Business Enterprise*, 50–59. For others who addressed advertising, see Stuart Ewen, *Captains of Consciousness: Advertising and the Social Roots of the Consumer Culture* (New York: McGraw Hill, 1976);

Richard Wightman Fox and T. J. Jackson Lears, *The Culture of Consumption: Critical Essays in American History, 1880–1980* (New York: Pantheon Books, 1983); Diane Barthel, *Putting on Appearances: Gender and Advertising* (Philadelphia: Temple University Press, 1988); Lori Anne Loeb, *Consuming Angels: Advertising and Victorian Women* (New York: Oxford University Press, 1994).

49. Veblen, "The Pecuniary Standard of Living," in *Theory of the Leisure Class*, 102–114.

50. Veblen, *Theory of the Leisure Class*, 113.

51. Veblen, *Theory of the Leisure Class*, 99.

52. Veblen, *Theory of Business Enterprise*, 50.

53. Pacyga, *Chicago*, 99–106.

54. "Modernizing Commercial Buildings," *Inland Architect and News Record* 31, no. 2 (September 1898): 18–19. On the Luxfer prism, see Dietrich Neumann, "The Century's Triumph in Lighting: The Luxfer Prism Companies and Their Contribution to Early Modern Architecture," *Journal of the Society of Architectural Historians* 54, no. 1 (March 1995): 24–53; and Thomas Leslie, "Glass and Light: The Influence of Interior Illumination on the Chicago School," *Journal of Architectural Education* 58, no. 1 (September 2004): 13–23.

55. On nineteenth-century strategies of store window display, see Siry, *Carson Pirie Scott*, 133–137; William Leach, "Strategists of Display and the Production of Desire," in

Consuming Visions: Accumulation and Display of Goods in America, 1889–1925, ed. Simon J. Bronner (New York: W. W. Norton, 1989); Anca Lasc, Patricia Lara-Betancourt, and Margaret Maile Petty, eds., *Architectures of Display: Department Stores and Modern Retail* (London: Routledge, 2017); and Orr, *Designing the Department Store*, 57–96.

56. "Modernizing Commercial Buildings," 18.

57. The first professional organization, the National Association of Window Trimmers, was founded in Chicago in 1898 by L. Frank Baum, a former employee of Seigel, Cooper & Co, better known as the author of *The Wonderful Wizard of Oz* (1900).

58. Orr is one of several scholars to make this claim. Discussing the retail display window as one of the primary publicity mechanisms for the German Werkbund in the 1910s and '20s, Robin Schuldenfrei claims that plate glass storefronts seen in Berlin in this period influenced Mies van der Rohe and other architects to adopt the veil-like curtain wall for other purposes. Orr, *Designing the Department Store*, 38–43; Schuldenfrei, *Luxury and Modernism*, 59–115.

59. Thorstein Veblen, "On the Nature of Capital II. Investment, Intangible Goods, and the Pecuniary Magnate," *Quarterly Journal of Economics* 23, no. 1 (November 1908): 104–136.

60. Veblen, "On the Nature of Capital II," 108.

61. Veblen, "On the Nature of Capital II," 118.

62. Veblen, *Theory of Business Enterprise*, 64.

63. In 1906, D. H. Burnham and Co. extended the building further, adding five new bays along State Street, following Sullivan's striking design.

64. Louis Sullivan, "The Tall Office Building Artistically Considered" (1896), in *Kindergarten Chats and Other Writings* (1924; repr., New York: Dover, 1979), 205.

65. Siry, *Carson Pirie Scott*, 133. On links between advertising and architecture, see Anne Hultzsch, *The Printed and the Built: Architecture, Print Culture, and Public Debate in the Nineteenth Century* (London: Bloomsbury, 2018).

66. Anca J. Lasc, "The Traveling Sidewalk: The Mobile Architecture of American Shop Windows at the Turn of the Twentieth Century," *Journal of Design History* 31, no. 1 (2018): 24–45. Karin Tehve discusses store window displays in relation to Veblen's theory of the leisure class in "Taste and Photography," in *Taste: Media and Interior Design* (London: Routledge, 2023), 46–68.

67. On Sullivan's use of ornament, see David Van Zanten, *Sullivan's City: The Meaning of Ornament for Louis Sullivan* (Chicago: University of Chicago, 2000); Wim de Wit, ed., *Louis Sullivan: The Function of Ornament* (New York: W. W. Norton, 1996); and Lauren Weingarden, *Louis H. Sullivan and a Nineteenth-Century Poetics of Naturalized Architecture* (London: Ashgate, 2009).

68. Siry, *Carson Pirie Scott*, 124.

69. Jane Addams, "The Subtle Problems of Charity," *Atlantic Monthly* 83, no. 496 (1899): 169.

70. Cunningham, *Reforming Women's Fashion*, 24.

71. Veblen, *Theory of the Leisure Class*, 345.

72. Veblen, *Theory of the Leisure Class*, 87–88.

73. Veblen, *Theory of Business Enterprise*, 326.

74. Veblen, *Theory of Business Enterprise*, 325.

75. Lears, *No Place of Grace*, 26–31.

76. T. J. Jackson Lears, "Beyond Veblen: Rethinking Culture in America," in *Consuming Visions: Accumulation and Display of Goods in America, 1889–1925*, ed. Simon J. Bronner (New York: W. W. Norton, 1989), 75.

77. Clare Virginia Eby, *Dreiser and Veblen, Saboteurs of the Status Quo* (Columbia: University of Missouri Press, 1998).

78. Loos, "Ladies Fashion," 106.

79. Loos, "Ladies Fashion," 107.

80. Charlotte Perkins Stetson [Gilman], *Women and Economics: A Study of the Economic Relation between Men and Women as a Factor in Social Evolution* (Boston: Small, Maynard, 1898). On Gilman and Veblen, see John P. Diggins, "Veblen and Charlotte Perkins Gilman," in *The Bard of Savagery: Thorstein Veblen and Modern Social Theory* (New York: Seabury Press, 1978), 158–161; and Martha Banta, introduction to Veblen, *The Theory of the Leisure Class* (New York: Oxford University Press, 2007), xviii–xxvi.

81. Adorno, "Veblen's Attack on Culture," 389–413.

82. Lears, "Beyond Veblen," 74. For a more expansive analysis of consumption through the lens of anthropology, Lears cites Mary Douglas and Baron Isherwood, *The World of Goods: Towards an Anthropology of Consumption* (New York: W. W. Norton, 1979), and Mihaly Csikszentmihalyi and Eugene Rochberg-Halton, *The Meaning of Things: Domestic Symbols and the Self* (New York: Cambridge University Press, 1981).

83. In partnership with William Otis, Jenney had designed an earlier building for Leiter in 1879 at Monroe and Wells streets, known as the First Leiter Building.

84. Homer Hoyt, *One Hundred Years of Land Values in Chicago: The Relationship of the Growth of Chicago to the Rise of Its Land Values, 1830–1933* (1933; repr., Washington: Beard Books, 2000), 458.

85. *Rand, McNally & Co.'s Bird's-Eye Views*, 152.

86. *Industrial Chicago*, 1:204.

87. Carl Condit has called this system "warehouse construction"; Condit, *The Chicago School of Architecture*, 89. See also Thomas Leslie, *Chicago Skyscrapers, 1871–1934* (Urbana: University of Illinois Press, 2013), 58–60.

88. Lewis Mumford, *Sticks and Stones: A Study of American Architecture and Civilization* (1924; repr., New York: Dover, 1955), 168.

89. Veblen, *Higher Learning in America*, 146.

Chapter 4

1. The first dime museum in Chicago was probably Kohl and Middleton's Westside Museum, founded in 1883 on Clark Street. In 1884, the company took over the Olympic Theater, transforming it into a vaudeville theater. Anthony Slide, *The Encyclopedia of Vaudeville* (Westport, CT: Greenwood Press, 1994), 96; Andrea Stulman Dennett, *Weird and Wonderful: The Dime Museum in America* (New York: New York University Press, 1997), 43; Konrad Schiecke, *Downtown Chicago's Historic Movie Theaters* (Jefferson, NC: McFarland, 2011), 7–12.

2. Miles D. Tillotson, *Tillotson's Pocket Map and Street Guide of Chicago* (Chicago: M. D. Tillotson, 1900), 151; Frank H. Richardson, *Richardson's Chicago Guide: A Complete Handbook to the City's Depots, Hotels ...* (Chicago: Monarch Book Company, 1905), 26.

3. Harold Richard Vynne, *Chicago by Day and Night: The Pleasure Seekers Guide to the Paris of America* (Chicago: Thomson and Zimmerman, 1892), 50.

4. Robert O. Harland, *The Vice Bondage of a Great City, or The Wickedest City in the World* (Chicago: Young People's Civic League, 1912), 72.

5. Louise de Koven Bowen and Juvenile Protective Association of Chicago, *The Road to Destruction Made Easy in Chicago* (Chicago: Hale-Crossley Printing Co., 1916), 7.

6. William Cronon, "Metropolitan Vice," in *Nature's Metropolis: Chicago and the Great West* (New York: W. W.

Norton, 1991), 350–356; Richard Junger, *Becoming the Second City: Chicago's Mass News Media, 1833–1898* (Chicago: University of Illinois Press, 2010), 156–193.

7. On the vital connection between local saloons and politics, see Donald L. Miller, *City of the Century: The Epic of Chicago and the Making of America* (New York: Simon and Schuster, 1996), 446–449.

8. On vice and vice reform in turn-of-the-century Chicago, see Walter C. Reckless, *Vice in Chicago* (Montclair, NJ: Patterson Smith, 1933); Richard Lindberg, *Chicago by Gaslight: A History of Chicago's Netherworld, 1880–1920* (Chicago: Academy Chicago, 1996); James L. Merriner, *Grafters and Goo Goos: Corruption and Reform in Chicago, 1833–2003* (Carbondale: Southern Illinois University Press, 2004); Dominic Pacyga, *Chicago: A Biography* (Chicago: University of Chicago Press, 2009), 106–109; and Chris M. Smith, "Chicago, Crime, and the Progressive Era," in Smith, *Syndicate Women: Gender and Networks in Chicago Organized Crime* (Berkeley: University of California Press, 2019), 42–64.

9. Homer Hoyt, *One Hundred Years of Land Values in Chicago: The Relationship of the Growth of Chicago to the Rise of Its Land Values, 1830–1933* (Chicago: University of Chicago Press, 1933), 97.

10. Charles Washburn, *Come into My Parlor: A Biography of the Aristocratic Everleigh Sisters of Chicago* (New York: Knickerbocker Press, 1934), 118.

11. Richardson, *Richardson's Chicago Guide*, 84; *Rand, McNally & Co.'s Bird's-Eye Views and Guide to Chicago* (Chicago: Rand, McNally & Company, 1893), 111.

12. Washburn, *Come into My Parlor*, 121.

13. Vynne, *Chicago by Day and Night*, 201–205.

14. Junger, *Becoming the Second City*, 165–166.

15. Junger, *Becoming the Second City*, 163.

16. Vynne, *Chicago by Day and Night*, 90.

17. Samuel Paynter Wilson, *Chicago and Its Cess-pools of Infamy* (Chicago: Samuel Paynter Wilson, 1910), 19–21.

18. W. T. Stead, "The Maiden Tribute of Modern Babylon," *Pall Mall Gazette* (July 1885), reprinted as *The Maiden Tribute of Modern Babylon: The Report of the Secret Commission*, by W. T. Stead, ed. Antony E. Simpson (Lambertville, NJ: True Bill Press, 2007); Stewart J. Brown, "The City of God and the Civic Church, 1888–94," in Brown, *W. T. Stead: Nonconformist and Newspaper Prophet* (Oxford: Oxford University Press, 2019), 91–134.

19. Although Stead did not attend the World's Columbian Exposition, a paper he wrote was read there at the World's Parliament of Religions, held in September 1893: see W. T. Stead, "The Civic Church," in *The World's Parliament of Religions II*, ed. J. H. Barrows (London, 1893), 1209–1215. On Stead's visit to Chicago, see Joseph O. Baylen, "A Victorian's 'Crusade' in Chicago, 1893–1894," *Journal of American History*

51 (1964): 418–434; D. B. Downey, "William Stead and Chicago: A Victorian Jeremiah in the Windy City," *Mid-America* 68 (1987): 153–166; Gary Scott Smith, "When Stead Came to Chicago: The 'Social Gospel Novel' and the Chicago Civic Federation," *American Presbyterians* 68, no. 3 (1990): 193–205; Miller, *City of the Century*, 533–541; and Brown, *W. T. Stead*, 119–122.

20. W. T. Stead, *Chicago Today: The Labor War in America* (London: Review of Reviews, 1894); W. T. Stead, *If Christ Came to Chicago! A Plea for the Union of All Who Love in the Service of All Who Suffer* (London: Review of Reviews, 1894).

21. Stead, *If Christ Came to Chicago*, 239–240.

22. Numerous accounts of the white slave trade were published around 1910, including Seth Cook Rees, *Miracles in the Slums or, Thrilling Stories of Those Rescued from the Cesspools of Iniquity* (Chicago: Shaw, 1905); Ernest F. Bell, *Fighting the Traffic in Young Girls* (Chicago: G. S. Ball, 1910); and Jean Turner-Zimmermann, *Chicago's Black Traffic in White Girls* (Chicago: Chicago Rescue Mission, 1911). On the phenomenon of the "white slave trade," see Mara L. Keire, "The Vice Trust: A Reinterpretation of the White Slavery Scare in the United States, 1907–17," *Journal of Social History* 35, no. 1 (2001): 5–41; Christopher Diffee, "Sex and the City: The White Slavery Scare and Social Governance in the Progressive Era," *American Quarterly* 57, no. 2 (2005): 411–437; Brian Donovan, *White*

Slave Crusades: Race, Gender, and Anti-Vice Activism, 1887–1917 (Urbana: University of Illinois Press, 2005); and Erika Jackson, *Scandinavians in Chicago: The Origins of White Privilege in Modern America* (Urbana: University of Illinois Press, 2019), 109–135.

23. "Dance Hall Is Doomed: Prima Will Be Closed, Following Story of Betrayal Told by 'White Slave,'" *Chicago Daily News*, May 27, 1907; "White Slave Inquiry On: Grand Jury Hears Story of Girl Rescued from Resort," *Chicago Tribune*, June 19, 1907, 3; Clifford G. Roe, *Panders and Their White Slaves* (Chicago: Fleming H. Revell, 1910), 37; Karen Abbott, "The Tragedy of Mona Marshall," in *Sin in the Second City: Madams, Ministers, Playboys, and the Battle for America's Soul* (New York: Random House, 2008), 119–127.

24. Vice Commission of Chicago, *The Social Evil in Chicago: A Study of Existing Conditions* (Chicago: Gunthrop-Warren, 1911). Mark Thomas Connelly, *The Response to Prostitution in the Progressive Era* (Chapel Hill: University of North Carolina Press, 1980).

25. Jane Addams, *A New Conscience and an Ancient Evil* (New York: Macmillan, 1912), 64–66. See also Louise de Koven Bowen, *The Department Store Girl* (Chicago: Juvenile Protective Association, 1911).

26. Harland, *The Vice Bondage of a Great City*, 63–67.

27. Thorstein Veblen, *The Higher Learning in America: A Memorandum on the Conduct of Universities by Business Men* (New York: B. W. Huebsch, 1918), 145.

28. Joseph M. Siry, *The Chicago Auditorium Building: Adler and Sullivan's Architecture and the City* (Chicago: University of Chicago Press, 2002), 271.

29. Louis Sullivan, *Kindergarten Chats and Other Writings* (1924; repr., New York: Dover, 1979).

30. Vynne, *Chicago by Day and Night*, 28.

31. The Leland Hotel opened in 1872 and the Hotel Richelieu in 1885. On the development of hotels in this area, see Siry, *The Chicago Auditorium Building*, 286–287.

32. *Rand, McNally & Co.'s Bird's-Eye Views*, 67.

33. Harland, *The Vice Bondage of a Great City*, 73.

34. Bettina Matthias, *The Hotel as Setting in Early Twentieth-Century German and Austrian Literature: Checking in to Tell a Story* (New York: Camden House, 2006), 10, 31–35. Annette Condello discusses the Auditorium Building and Palmer House hotels in terms of Veblenian luxury in *The Architecture of Luxury* (London: Ashgate, 2014), 120–127. On nineteenth-century hotels as centers of American social life, see A. K. Sandoval-Strausz, *Hotel: An American History* (New Haven, CT: Yale University Press, 2008); Molly W. Berger, *Hotel Dreams: Luxury, Technology, and Urban Ambition in America, 1829–1929* (Baltimore: Johns Hopkins University Press, 2011); and David Freeland, *American Hotel: The Waldorf-Astoria and the Making of a Century* (New Brunswick, NJ: Rutgers University Press, 2021).

35. Thorstein Veblen, *The Theory of the Leisure Class* (1899; repr., London: Penguin, 1979), 87.

36. Sigfried Kracauer, "Die Hotelhalle," in *Das Ornament der Masse* (Frankfurt/Main: Suhrkamp, 1963), 157–170. On Kracauer's essay, see Anthony Vidler, "Agoraphobia: Spatial Estrangement in Georg Simmel and Siegfried Kracauer," *New German Critique* 54, special issue on Siegfried Kracauer (Autumn 1991): 31–45; and Gertrud Koch, "The Early Phenomenology of Modernity and Mass Culture: Of Hotel Lobbies and Detective Novels," in *Siegfried Kracauer: An Introduction* (Princeton, NJ: Princeton University Press, 2000), 11–25.

37. On the public interiors of the Auditorium Building, see Lauren Weingarden, "Louis H. Sullivan's Ornament and the Poetics of Architecture," in *Chicago Architecture, 1872–1922: Birth of a Metropolis*, ed. John Zukowsky (New York: Prestel and the Art Institute of Chicago, 1987), 240–245; Siry, *The Chicago Auditorium Building*, 296–322.

38. Veblen, *Theory of the Leisure Class*, 253.

39. Jackson Lears, *Something for Nothing: Luck in America* (New York: Viking, 2003), 199–200.

40. Lears, *Something for Nothing*, 148–169.

41. Lears, *Something for Nothing*, 187.

42. John Cummings, "The Theory of the Leisure Class," *Journal of Political Economy* 7, no. 4 (September 1899): 425–455.

43. Charles R. Henderson, "Social Discussion and Reform," *The Dial* 28, no. 335 (June 1, 1900): 436.

44. Vynne, *Chicago by Day and Night*, 102.

45. Merrill A. Teague, "Bucket-Shop Sharks," *Everybody's Magazine* 14, no. 6 (June 1906): 723–735; Ann Fabian, *Card Sharps and Bucket Shops: Gambling in Nineteenth-Century America* (New York: Routledge, 1999); David Hochfelder, "'Where the Common People Could Speculate': The Ticker, Bucket Shops, and the Origins of Popular Participation in Financial Markets, 1880–1920," *Journal of American History* 93, no. 2 (2006): 335–358.

46. Veblen, *Theory of the Leisure Class*, 332–362.

47. Lears, *Something for Nothing*, 188; Merriner, *Grafters and Goo Goos*, 72–75.

48. Thorstein Veblen, "On the Nature of Capital II. Investment, Intangible Goods, and the Pecuniary Magnate," *Quarterly Journal of Economics* 23, no. 1 (November 1908): 109.

49. *Richardson's Chicago Guide*, 87; Richard C. Lindberg, *To Serve and Collect: Chicago Politics and Police Corruption from the Lager Beer Riot to the Summerdale Scandal, 1855–1960* (Carbondale: Southern Illinois University Press, 1998), 24.

50. Jonathan Matthew Finn, *Capturing the Criminal Image: From Mug Shot to Surveillance Society* (Minneapolis: University of Minnesota Press, 2009), 23–30; Josh Ellenbogen, *Reasoned and Unreasoned Images: The Photography of Bertillon, Galton, and Marey* (University Park: Pennsylvania State University Press, 2012).

51. Chicago Police Department, *Annual Report of the General Superintendent of Police* (Chicago, 1900), 58; Clifton R. Wooldridge, *Hands Up! In the World of Crime, or 12 Years a Detective* (Chicago: Stanton and Van Vlie, 1906), 357–360.

52. Chicago Police Department, *Annual Report of the General Superintendent of Police* (Chicago, 1906), 87.

53. Lindberg, *To Serve and Collect*, xiv.

54. Chicago Police Pensioners Protective Association, *Police History and Directory* (Chicago: The Association, 1916), 53.

55. On the intersection of politics and reform in this era, see Miller, *City of the Century*, 435–487; Andrew J. Diamond, "Capital Order," in *Chicago on the Make: Power and Inequality in a Modern City* (Berkeley: University of California Press, 2017), 15–58; Smith, *Syndicate Women*, 42–64.

56. To cite just a few examples, see Samuel Paynter Wilson, *Chicago by Gaslight* (Chicago: Samuel Paynter Wilson, 1910); William Gleeson, *Vice and Virtue: A Story of Our Times* (Chicago: W. F. Mecklenberg, 1913); Washburn, *Come into My Parlor*; Herbert Asbury, *Gem of the Prairie: An Informal History of the Chicago Underworld* (New York: Alfred A. Knopf, 1940); and Herman Kogan and Lloyd Wendt, *Lords of the Levee: The Story of Bathhouse John* and *Hinky Dink* (New York: Bobbs-Merrill, 1944).

57. Franklin Matthews, "'Wide Open' Chicago," *Harper's Weekly* 42 (January 22, 1898): 88–91.

58. Stead, *If Christ Came to Chicago*, 17–32.

59. Thorstein Veblen, *The Theory of Business Enterprise* (1904; New York: Charles Scribner's Sons, 1919), 269.

60. The 1893 Rand McNally & Co. guide to Chicago defined the original Printing House Row as "a double row of high buildings which lines Dearborn between Van Buren and Harrison Streets." *Rand, McNally & Co.'s Bird's-Eye Views*, 80. On the history of the district, see Ron Gordon and John Paulett, *Printers Row, Chicago* (Charleston, SC: Arcadia, 2003); and Robert Lewis, "Industrial Districts and Manufacturing Linkages: Chicago's Printing Industry, 1880–1950," *Economic History Review* 62, no. 2 (2009): 366–387.

61. Robert Bruegmann, "Theme and Variation: The Loft Building," in Bruegmann, *The Architects and the City: Holabird and Roche of Chicago, 1880–1918* (Chicago: University of Chicago Press, 1997), 207–232. See also Carl Condit, "Industrial Buildings and Warehouses," in *Chicago, 1910–1929: Building, Planning, and Urban Technology* (Chicago: University of Chicago Press, 1973), 136–144.

62. Frank A. Randall and John D. Randall, *History of the Development of Building Construction in Chicago* (Urbana: University of Illinois, 1999), 125.

63. Gordon and Paulett, *Printers Row, Chicago*, 15–28.

64. In 1899, the city of Chicago passed an ordinance granting the Illinois Telephone and Telegraph Company the right to construct a system of underground conduits in the Loop to support its telephone system. This ordinance was extended in 1903 to include the transportation of mail, packages, and merchandise. Beginning in 1912, the system was operated by the Chicago Tunnel Company. George W. Jackson, "Scope, Extent, and Construction of the Underground Conduits of the Illinois Telephone and Telegraph Co. in Chicago," *Journal of the Western Society of Engineers* 7, no. 5 (October 1902): 479–502.

65. "Harrison Street Station a Bar to Business Progress," *Chicago Tribune*, January 23, 1898, 38.

66. "Harrison Police Station Closes," *Chicago Tribune*, July 14, 1911, 20; "Old Harrison Is Gone," *Chicago Examiner*, July 14, 1911.

67. Wooldridge, *Hands Up!*, 364.

68. *Architectural Record* 31 (January–June 1912), 381–383; *Rand McNally & Company's Souvenir Guide to Chicago* (Chicago: Rand McNally & Co., 1912), 196.

Chapter 5

1. "Wilde," *Cleveland Leader*, February 20, 1882, 6; quoted in Roy Morris Jr., *Declaring His Genius: Oscar Wilde in North America* (Cambridge, MA: Belknap Press

of Harvard University Press, 2013), 109.

2. *Rand, McNally & Co.'s Bird's-Eye Views and Guide to Chicago* (Chicago: Rand, McNally & Company, 1893), 51–52.

3. A. A. Hayes, "The Metropolis of the Prairies," *Harper's New Monthly Magazine* 61, no. 365 (October 1880): 719. Ross Miller, *American Apocalypse: The Great Fire and the Myth of Chicago* (Chicago: University of Chicago Press, 1990).

4. "Oscar Wilde," *Chicago Tribune*, March 1, 1882, 7; quoted in *Oscar Wilde in America: The Interviews*, ed. Matthew Hofer and Gary Scharnhorst (Urbana: University of Illinois Press, 2010), 91.

5. "Truly Aesthetic," *Chicago Inter-Ocean*, February 13, 1882, 2; quoted in *Oscar Wilde in America*, 61.

6. Delivered on February 13, 1882, Wilde's first lecture was on "The English Renaissance." The second, which he gave on March 11, 1882, was entitled "Interior and Exterior House Decoration." They were published, respectively, in *Chicago Tribune*, February 13, 1882, 1; *Chicago Tribune*, March 11, 1882, 4.

7. Lilian Whiting, "They Will Show Him," *Chicago Inter-Ocean*, February 10, 1882, 2; quoted in *Oscar Wilde in America*, 53.

8. "A Man of Culture Rare," *Rochester Democrat and Chronicle*, February 8, 1882, 4; quoted in Morris, *Declaring His Genius*, 104.

9. Quoted in Morris, *Declaring His Genius*, 103.

10. "Philosophical Oscar," *Chicago Times*, March 1, 1882, 7.

11. "Oscar Wilde," *Chicago Tribune*, February 14, 1882, 7.

12. *Chicago Tribune*, February 15, 1882, 3.

13. Jack Wing, *The Great Chicago Lake Tunnel: The Causes which Led to Its Conception; The Great Undertaking; Obstacles Encountered; How the Work Was Performed; Launch of the Crib, Etc.* (Chicago: Jack Wing, 1867), 55–56.

14. Elizabeth Jorgensen and Henry Jorgensen, *Thorstein Veblen: Victorian Firebrand* (Armonk, NY: M. E. Sharpe, 1999), 72.

15. *Rand McNally & Co.'s Bird's-Eye Views*, 35.

16. Daniel Bluestone, "A City under One Roof: Skyscrapers, 1880–95," in *Constructing Chicago* (New Haven: Yale University Press, 1991), 104–151.

17. Matilda B. Carse, "The Temperance Temple," quoted in Donald Hoffman, *The Architecture of John Wellborn Root* (Chicago: University of Chicago Press, 1973), 193.

18. *Hull-House Bulletin* 6, no 2 (Autumn 1904): 15. On the founding of the Chicago Arts and Crafts Society, see Hull House, *The Chicago Arts and Crafts Society: Formed at Hull House, October 22, 1897*, issued as part of the eleventh annual exhibition of the Chicago Architectural Club, March 23–April 15, 1898, at Art Institute of Chicago (Chicago: Hull House, 1898).

19. On the Arts and Crafts movement in Chicago, see H. Allen Brooks, "Chicago Architecture: Its Debt to the

Arts and Crafts," *Journal of the Society of Architectural Historians* 30, no. 4 (December 1971): 312–317; Eileen Boris, *Art and Labor: Ruskin, Morris, and the Craftsman Ideal in America* (Philadelphia: Temple University Press, 1986), 45–48; Bruce Kahler, "Art and Life: The Arts and Crafts Movement in Chicago, 1897–1910 (Progressive Era, Intellectuals, Illinois)" (PhD diss., Purdue University, 1986); Richard Guy Wilson, "Chicago and the International Arts and Crafts Movement: Progressive and Conservative Tendencies," in *Chicago Architecture, 1872–1922: Birth of a Metropolis*, ed. John Zukowsky (Munich: Prestel Verlag/Art Institute of Chicago, 1987), 208–227; and Judith A. Barter and Monica Obniski, "Chicago, A Bridge to the Future," in *Apostles of Beauty: Arts and Crafts from Britain to Chicago*, ed. Judith A. Barter, Sarah E. Kelly, Ellen E. Roberts, Brandon K. Ruud, and Monica Obniski (Chicago: Art Institute of Chicago, 2009), 151–188.

20. Thorstein Veblen, *The Theory of the Leisure Class* (1899; repr., London: Penguin, 1979), 356, 359. On the idea of the "New Woman" around 1900, see Angelique Richardson and Chris Willis, eds., *The New Woman in Fiction and Fact: Fin-de-Siècle Feminisms* (London: Palgrave Macmillan, 2001); and Martha H. Patterson, ed., *The American New Woman Revisited: A Reader, 1894–1930* (New Brunswick, NJ: Rutgers University Press, 2008).

21. Veblen, *Theory of the Leisure Class*, 360–361.

22. Jorgensen, *Thorstein Veblen*, 65.

23. Veblen, *Theory of the Leisure Class*, 162.

24. Veblen, *Theory of the Leisure Class*, 159.

25. Veblen, *Theory of the Leisure Class*, 161.

26. Veblen, *Theory of the Leisure Class*, 162.

27. Ashbee and Kropotkin came to Chicago in April 1901; Geddes visited in 1899 and again in 1900. "Geddes at Hull House," *Chicago Daily Tribune*, April 1, 1899, 8; "World Improves, Says Kropotkin: Russian Socialist Takes an Optimistic View in His Lecture at Hull House," *Chicago Daily Tribune*, April 18, 1901, 5; "Briton Praises Chicago Spirit," *Chicago Daily Tribune*, April 22, 1901, 9.

28. Mabel Key, "Some Work of the Arts and Crafts Society: Chicago, Illinois," *Brush and Pencil* 3, no. 3 (December 1898): 148–152.

29. Polly Ullrich, "Arts and Crafts at the Kalo Shop in Chicago," *Metalsmith* 19, no. 5 (September 1999): 30–37. See also Judith A. Barter, "The Prairie School and Decorative Arts at the Art Institute of Chicago," *Art Institute of Chicago Museum Studies* 21, no. 2 (1995): 125–126.

30. Chicago Arts and Crafts Society, *A Catalogue of the Second Exhibition: April–May 1899* (Chicago: Hull House, 1899); "Arts and Crafts Exhibition," *Chicago Tribune*, May 7, 1899, 38; Gardner C. Teall, "Chicago Notes," *The Art Interchange* 42, no. 6 (June 1, 1899): 146; "Chicago," *American Architect and Building News* 65, no. 1228 (July 8, 1899): 12–14.

31. In 1908, Frank Lloyd Wright designed Browne's Bookstore for Francis Fisher Browne, editor of *The Dial*, which had its offices in the Fine Arts Building. The following year, W. Scott Thurber commissioned Wright to design rooms for his gallery, which occupied the entire fifth floor of the adjoining annex building on Michigan Avenue. Neither space survives. See *International Studio: An Illustrated Magazine of Fine and Applied Art* (February 1910): 95–96; Glen N. Wiche, ed., *Some Famous Early Tenants of the Fine Arts Building in Their Own Words* (Chicago: Caxton Club, 1995), 1; Adam Morgan, "When Frank Lloyd Wright Designed a Bookstore," *Paris Review* (March 22, 2018).

32. "Chicago" (*American Architect and Building News*), 12.

33. "Workshop for the Rich," *Chicago Daily Tribune*, May 17, 1903, 1.

34. Boris, *Art and Labor*, 45.

35. A. M. Simons, "Chicago Arts and Crafts Exhibition," *International Socialist Review* 2 (1902): 512.

36. Thorstein Veblen, "Arts and Crafts," *Journal of Political Economy* 11, no. 1 (December 1902): 108–111.

37. Veblen, "Arts and Crafts," 109.

38. Veblen, "Arts and Crafts," 110–111.

39. Susan E. Hirsch, "Economic Geography," in *Chicago Neighborhoods and Suburbs: A Historical Guide*, ed. Ann Durkin Keating (Chicago: University of Chicago Press, 2008), 64–75.

40. Joseph Siry, "The Abraham Lincoln Center in Chicago," *Journal of the Society of Architectural Historians* 50, no. 3 (September 1991): 241. Siry suggests that this project, designed while Frank Lloyd Wright was working for Adler and Sullivan, inspired Wright and Dwight Perkins's design for the Abraham Lincoln Center, an unbuilt project commissioned by Wright's uncle, the Rev. Jenkin Lloyd Jones.

41. "Jewish Manual Training School," *American Artisan* (Chicago) 19, no. 17 (October 25, 1890): 15; "Tis a Noble Work: Jewish Manual Training School; An Institution That Is Making Good Citizens for Chicago," *Chicago Tribune*, April 5, 1895, A2; Tobias Brinkman, *Sundays at Sinai: A Jewish Congregation in Chicago* (Chicago: University of Chicago Press, 2012), 162–169.

42. On anthropological theories of race in this period, see Regna Darnell, *Invisible Genealogies: A History of Americanist Anthropology* (Ann Arbor: University of Michigan Press, 2001); Thomas Carl Patterson, *A Social History of Anthropology in the United States* (New York: Oxford University Press, 2001); Richard W. Rees, *Shades of Difference: A History of Ethnicity in America* (Lanham, MD: Rowman & Littlefield, 2007).

43. Clare de Graffenried, "Some Social Economic Problems," *American Journal of Sociology* 2, no. 2 (September 1896): 190–201. On the Progressive movement and questions of race, see James

B. McKee, *Sociology and the Race Problem: The Failure of a Perspective* (Urbana: University of Illinois Press, 1993), 22–54; and Thomas C. Leonard, "Retrospectives: Eugenics and Economics in the Progressive Era," *Journal of Economic Perspectives* 19, no. 4 (Autumn 2005): 207–224.

44. Frances Buckley Embree, "The Housing of the Poor in Chicago," *Journal of Political Economy* 8, no. 3 (June 1900): 354–377.

45. See "Eloquence of Charity: The Anniversary of the Order of B'nai Brith Celebrated; Central Music-Hall Crowded by a Patriotic Gathering—A Large Sum Raised for the New Jewish Manual Training School," *Chicago Daily Tribune*, October 14, 1890, 3.

46. Christina Edith Ines Melk, "Oscar Lovell Triggs and the Industrial Art League of Chicago: A Chapter in the History of the Arts and Crafts Movement" (PhD diss., Tufts University, 1983); and Boris, *Art and Labor*, 48–49.

47. Oscar Lovell Triggs, "Arts and Crafts," *Brush and Pencil* 1, no. 3 (December 1897): 47–48; Oscar Lovell Triggs, "Democratic Art," *Forum* (September 1898): 66; Oscar Lovell Triggs, "Democratic Criticism," *The Sewanee Review* 6, no. 4 (October 1898): 413–432; Oscar Lovell Triggs, "The Workshop and School," *The Craftsman* 3, no. 1 (October 1, 1902): 20–33; Oscar Lovell Triggs, "The Industrial Art League," *House Beautiful* 12 (November 1902): 197–199; Oscar Lovell Triggs, "The Meaning of the Industrial Art

League," *House Beautiful* 15 (May 1904): 355–357.

48. "Triggs Attacks Modern Culture," *Chicago Tribune*, June 16, 1902, 3.

49. Oscar Lovell Triggs, "A Proposal for a Guild and School of Handicraft," in *Chapters in the History of the Arts and Crafts Movement* (Chicago: Bohemia Guild of the Industrial Art League, 1902), 192.

50. Triggs, "A Proposal for a Guild and School of Handicraft," 193.

51. "Industrial Art League to Open Its Workshop in Chicago," *Chicago Daily Tribune*, March 16, 1902, 60; "Notes from the Conference of The Industrial Art League," *The Craftsman*, November 1, 1902, 121; Boris, *Art and Labor*, 49.

52. Oscar Lovell Triggs, *Report of the Secretary of the Industrial Art League, Chicago, October 1, 1902* (Chicago: Art Institute of Chicago, 1902).

53. *The Construction News* 13, no. 8 (February 22, 1902): 123.

54. The *Chicago Tribune* included the South Park Workshop in a 1903 survey of local Arts and Crafts studios; see "Workshop for the Rich," 1.

55. Dorfman, *Thorstein Veblen and His America*, 253–254. See also Russell H. Bartley and Sylvia E. Bartley, "In Search of Thorstein Veblen: Further Inquiries into His Life and Work," *International Journal of Politics, Culture, and Society* 11, no. 1 (Fall 1997): 129–173; Tony Maynard, "A Shameless Lothario: Thorstein Veblen as Sexual Predator and Sexual Liberator," *Journal of Economic Issues* 34, no. 1 (March 2000): 194–199.

56. Barbara E. Ryan, "Thorstein Veblen: A New Perspective," *Mid-American Review of Sociology* 7, no. 2 (1982): 29–47; Anne Jennings, "Veblen's Feminism in Historical Perspective," in *The Founding of Institutional Economics: The Leisure Class and Sovereignty*, ed. Warren Samuels (London: Routledge, 1998), 201–233; and Nils Gilman, "Thorstein Veblen's Neglected Feminism," *Journal of Economic Issues* 33, no. 3 (September 1999): 689–711.

57. On the architecture of Hull House, see Allen B. Pond, "The Settlement House," *The Brickbuilder* 11 (1902): 184–185; Carl Condit, *The Chicago School of Architecture* (Chicago: University of Chicago Press, 1964), 206–207; Guy Szuberla, "Three Chicago Settlements: Their Architectural Form and Social Meaning," *Journal of the Illinois State Historical Society* 70, no. 2 (May 1977): 114–129; and Sharon Haar, *The City as Campus: Urbanism and Higher Education in Chicago* (Minneapolis: University of Minnesota Press, 2011), 16–23.

58. Jennifer Gray, "Social Practice and the Laissez-faire Metropolis: Dwight Perkins in Chicago, 1895–1915," *Architecture, Media, Politics, Society* 5, no. 1 (May 2014): 2. On Addams, see Louise W. Knight, *Citizen: Jane Addams and the Struggle for Democracy* (Chicago: University of Chicago Press, 2005); Daphne Spain, *How Women Saved the City* (Minneapolis: University of Minnesota Press, 2001); Maureen A. Flanagan, *Seeing with Their Hearts: Chicago*

Women and the Vision of the Good City, 1871–1933 (Princeton, NJ: Princeton University Press, 2002).

59. Jane Addams, "The Art-Work Done by Hull-House, Chicago," *Forum* 14, no. 5 (July 1895): 614.

60. Mary Ann Stankiewicz, "Art at Hull House, 1889–1901: Jane Addams and Ellen Gates Starr," *Woman's Art Journal* 10, no. 1 (Spring-Summer 1989): 35–39.

61. *Hull-House Bulletin* 2, no. 8 (December 1, 1897): 9; *The Chicago Arts and Crafts Society: Formed at Hull House, October 22, 1897*.

62. Jane Addams, *Hull House, 1889–1909* (Chicago: Hull House, 1909), 6.

63. Veblen, *Theory of the Leisure Class*, 344.

64. *Hull-House Bulletin* 5, no. 1 (1902): 1

65. Thorstein Veblen, "The Instinct of Workmanship and the Irksomeness of Labor," *American Journal of Sociology* 4, no. 2 (September 1898): 196. Five months before the essay's publication, on April 21, Veblen had delivered a lecture with a similar title, "The Irksomeness of Labor and the Instinct of Workmanship," to the University of Chicago's Philosophical Club at the Haskell Oriental Museum, as reported in *University Record* 3, no. 3 (April 25, 1898). Sixteen years later, Veblen published the book *The Instinct of Workmanship and the State of the Industrial Arts* (New York: Macmillan, 1914).

66. Veblen, "The Instinct of Workmanship," 201.

67. For example, Addams described the sad fate of a

Bohemian immigrant trained as a goldsmith. Unable to find skilled work, he became an alcoholic and later committed suicide. Addams called this the disastrous result of the "suppression of the instinct of workmanship." Jane Addams, *Twenty Years at Hull-House* (1910; repr., Urbana: University of Illinois Press, 1990), 246.

68. Veblen, *Theory of the Leisure Class*, 358.

69. *Hull-House Bulletin* 3, no. 12 (November-December 1899): 4.

70. Charles Zueblin, "The World's First Sociological Laboratory," *American Journal of Sociology* 4, no. 5 (March 1899): 588. On Geddes's museum, see Volker M. Welter, "The Return of the Muses: Edinburgh as a Museion," in *The Architecture of the Museum: Symbolic Structures, Urban Contents*, ed. Michaela Giebelhausen (Manchester, UK: Manchester University Press, 2003), 144–159.

71. "Plan a Social Museum," *Chicago Daily Tribune*, February 8, 1900, 5.

72. The Musée Social in Paris and the Wrania Museum in Berlin were also discussed as models, along with a similar project planned for New York. On the Musée Social, see Janet R. Horne, *A Social Laboratory for Modern France: The Musée Social and the Rise of the Welfare State* (Durham, NC: Duke University Press, 2002).

73. Jane Addams, "Labor Museum at Hull House," *Current Literature* 29, no. 4 (October 1900): 424.

74. Addams, "Labor Museum at Hull House," 424.

75. Bremner went on to become one of the founders of the grocery giant Nabisco. Lori Grove and Laura Kamedulski, *Chicago's Maxwell Street* (Mount Pleasant, SC: Arcadia, 2002), 15.

76. *Hull-House Bulletin* 5, no. 1 (Semi-Annual 1902): 12. Marion Foster Washburne, "A Labor Museum," *The Craftsman* 6, no. 6 (September 1, 1904): 570–581.

77. Florence Kelley, "The Sweating System," in *Hull House Maps and Papers: A Presentation of Nationalities and Wages in a Congested District of Chicago, Together with Comments and Essays on Problems Growing Out of the Social Conditions* (New York: Thomas Y. Crowell & Co., 1895), 27–45; Nellie Mason Auten, "Some Phases of the Sweating System in the Garment Trades of Chicago," *American Journal of Sociology* 6, no. 5 (March 1901): 602–645; Bessie Louise Pierce, "The Economic Empire of Chicago: Manufacturing and Merchandising," in *A History of Chicago*, vol. 3: *The Rise of a Modern City, 1871–1893* (Chicago: University of Chicago Press, 1957), 171–174; John B. Jentz and Richard Schneirov, *Chicago in the Age of Capital: Class, Politics, and Democracy during the Civil War and Reconstruction* (Urbana: University of Illinois Press, 2012), 122–124.

78. Sandra D. Harmon, "Florence Kelley in Illinois," *Journal of the Illinois State Historical Society* 74, no. 3 (Autumn 1981): 162–178; Joan Waugh, *Florence Kelley and the Anti-sweatshop Campaign of 1892–1893* (Berkeley: University of California Press, 1982); Cecelia Tichi, "Florence Kelley: The Wages of Work," in *Civic Passions: Seven Who Launched Progressive America (and What They Teach Us)* (Chapel Hill: University of North Carolina Press, 2009), 123–163.

79. Friedrich Engels, *The Condition of the Working-Class in England in 1844*, trans. Florence Kelley Wischnewetsky (New York: J. W. Lovell Co., 1887).

80. Addams, "Labor Museum at Hull House," 423; *Hull-House Bulletin* 4, no. 3 (Autumn 1900): 1; *First Report of the Labor Museum at Hull-House* (Chicago: Hull House, 1901–1902), 3; "For Those Who Work," *The Youth's Companion* 77, no. 8 (February 19, 1903): 90–91. On the Labor Museum, see Daniel T. Rodgers, "Mechanicalized Men," in *Work Ethic in Industrial America* (Chicago: University of Chicago Press, 1978), 82–86; Boris, *Art and Labor*, 132–133; Eileen Boris, "Crafts Shop or Sweatshop? The Uses and Abuses of Craftsmanship in Twentieth Century America," *Journal of Design History* 2, no. 2/3 (1989): 175–192; Marilyn Fischer, "Educating Immigrants," in *Jane Addams's Evolutionary Theorizing: Constructing "Democracy and Social Ethics"* (Chicago: University of Chicago Press, 2019), 124–146.

81. On theater and performance at Hull House, see Shannon Jackson, *Lines of Activity: Performance, Historiography, and Hull-House Domesticity* (Ann Arbor: University of Michigan Press, 2000).

82. "Influence of the Theater upon Life," *Chicago Record*, October 27, 1899.

83. "Fine New Addition to Hull House," *Chicago Times Herald*, July 9, 1899. Haar, *The City as Campus*, 17–18.

84. *Hull-House Bulletin* 5, no. 1 (Semi-Annual 1902): 12.

85. *First Report of the Labor Museum at Hull-House*, 12.

86. Jolie A. Sheffer discusses the Labor Museum in relation to the progressive mission of racial assimilation in "Bloods and Blankets: Americanizing European Immigrants through Cultural Miscegenation and Textile Reproduction," in Sheffer, *The Romance of Race: Incest, Miscegenation, and Multiculturalism in the United States, 1880–1930* (New Brunswick, NJ: Rutgers University Press, 2013), 149–170.

87. Addams, "Labor Museum at Hull House," 424.

88. Florence Kelley, "Married Women in Industry," *Proceedings of the Academy of Political Science in the City of New York* 1, no. 1 (October 1910): 90–96.

89. Veblen cited Beatrice and Sidney Webb's book *Industrial Democracy* (1897) in Veblen, *The Theory of Business Enterprise* (1904; repr., New York: Charles Scribner's Sons, 1919), 313, 333.

90. In addition to being the title of the 1897 book by the Webbs, the concept of industrial democracy was discussed in Charles Zueblin, "Industrial Democracy," *Journal of Political Economy* 7,

no. 2 (March 1899): 182–203.
See Milton Derber, *The American Idea of Industrial Democracy, 1865–1965* (Urbana: University of Illinois Press, 1970), 7–11.

91. Henry D. Lloyd, *Men, the Workers* (New York: Doubleday, 1909). According to Veblen's first biographer, Joseph Dorfman, "Liberal leaders, such as [Clarence] Darrow and Lloyd, admired Veblen, but when he talked with them, they had the impression that he considered them very foolish to occupy themselves with such matters as clean politics, municipal ownership, and other such reforms." Dorfman, *Thorstein Veblen and His America*, 247.

92. Thorstein Veblen, "The Barbarian Status of Women," *American Journal of Sociology* 4, no. 4 (January 1899): 514.

93. Veblen, *Theory of the Leisure Class*, 234

94. Frank Lloyd Wright, "The Art and Craft of the Machine," in *Catalogue of the Fourteenth Annual Exhibition of the Chicago Architectural Club* (Chicago: The Club, 1901), 12–31. On the professional and intellectual context of the lecture, see Robert C. Twombley, *Frank Lloyd Wright: His Life and His Architecture* (New York: Wiley, 1979), 32–94; *Frank Lloyd Wright: Collected Writings, I: 1894–1930*, ed. Bruce B. Pfeiffer (New York: Rizzoli, 1992), 58–69; Neil Levine, *The Architecture of Frank Lloyd Wright* (Princeton, NJ: Princeton University Press, 1996), 27; Joseph M. Siry, "Frank Lloyd Wright's

'The Art and Craft of the Machine': Text and Context," in *The Education of the Architect: Historiography, Urbanism, and the Growth of Architectural Knowledge*, ed. Martha Pollak (Cambridge, MA: MIT Press, 1997), 3–36; and Donald Leslie Johnson, *Frank Lloyd Wright, The Early Years: Progressivism, Aesthetics, Cities* (London: Routledge, 2016), 9–16.

95. Frank Lloyd Wright, *An Autobiography* (New York: Duell, Sloane and Pearce, 1943), 131–132.

96. Wright, "Art and Craft of the Machine," 27.

97. Wright, "Art and Craft of the Machine," 29.

98. Frank Lloyd Wright, "Machinery, Materials, and Men," in *The Future of Architecture* (New York: Horizon Press, 1953), 70.

99. In a 1939 address to the Association of Federal Architects, Wright acknowledged Veblen's influence, saying: "I have read Henry George, Kropotkin, Gesell, Prudhomme, Marx, Mazzini, Whitman, Thoreau, Veblen and many other advocates of freedom." Johnson, *Frank Lloyd Wright, The Early Years*, 15.

100. Jorgensen and Jorgensen, "Out of Chicago," in *Thorstein Veblen*, 85–92; Charles Camic, *Veblen: The Making of an Economist Who Unmade Economics* (Cambridge, MA: Harvard University Press, 2020), 341–342; Lisa D. Schrenk, "Closing the Studio (1909–1911): Escape and Retrospection," in *An Architectural Laboratory: The Oak Park Studio of Frank Lloyd*

Wright (Chicago: University of Chicago Press, 2020), 157–172.

101. Thorstein Veblen, "A Memorandum on a Practicable Soviet of Technicians," *The Dial* 67 (November 1, 1919): 373–380; later reprinted in Thorstein Veblen, *The Engineers and the Price System* (New York: B. W. Huebsch, 1921), 138–169. On Veblen's view of engineers, see Edwin Layton, "Veblen and the Engineers," *American Quarterly* 14, no. 1 (Spring 1962): 64–72; Daniel Bell, "Veblen and the New Class," *American Scholar* 32, no. 4 (Autumn 1963): 616–638.

102. Leon Ardzrooni, "Veblen and Technocracy," *Living Age*, no. 344 (March 1933): 39–42; Francesco Dal Co, "From Parks to the Region: Progressive Ideology and the Reform of the American City," in Giorgio Ciucci, Francesco Dal Co, Mario Manieri-Elia, and Manfredo Tafuri, *The American City from the Civil War to the New Deal*, trans. Barbara Luigia La Penta (1973; Cambridge, MA: MIT Press, 1979), 222–235; William E. Aitken, *Technocracy and the American Dream: The Technocrat Movement, 1900–1941* (Berkeley: University of California Press, 1977), 1–26; Guy Alchon, *The Invisible Hand of Planning: Capitalism, Social Science, and the State in the 1920s* (1984; repr., Princeton, NJ: Princeton University Press, 2016), 18–19; Robert Wojtowicz, *Lewis Mumford and American Modernism: Eutopian Theories for Architecture and Urban Planning* (London: Cambridge University Press, 1996), 30–31; Jess Gilbert,

Planning Democracy: Agrarian Intellectuals and the Intended New Deal (New Haven, CT: Yale University Press, 2015).

103. Dalibor Vesely, *Architecture in the Age of Divided Representation: The Question of Creativity in the Shadow of Production* (Cambridge, MA: MIT Press, 2004), 356n2.

Conclusion

1. Thorstein Veblen, "Why Is Economics Not an Evolutionary Science?," *Quarterly Journal of Economics* 12, no. 4 (July 1898): 373–397.

2. Thorstein Veblen, *The Theory of the Leisure Class* (1899; repr., London: Penguin, 1979), 138.

3. Daniel Bluestone, *Constructing Chicago* (New Haven: Yale University Press, 1991), 39–44.

4. Veblen, *Theory of the Leisure Class*, 139.

5. Arnold Lewis, *An Early Encounter with Tomorrow: Europeans, Chicago's Loop, and the World's Columbian Exposition* (Urbana: University of Illinois Press, 1997).

6. Ken McCormick, "Thorstein Veblen," in *The Wiley-Blackwell Companion to Major Social Theorists*, vol. 1: *Classical Social Theorists*, ed. George Ritzer and Jeffrey Stepnisky (Malden, MA: Wiley-Blackwell, 2011), 185–204.

7. This is the genealogy set out by Colin Campbell in "The Sociology of Consumption," in *Acknowledging Consumption: A Review of New Studies*, ed. Daniel Miller (London: Routledge, 1995), 96–126.

8. Graham Cassano, "Stylistic Sabotage and Thorstein Veblen's Scientific Irony," *Journal of Economic Issues* 39, no. 3 (September 2005): 741.

9. Thorstein Veblen, *The Higher Learning in America: A Memorandum on the Conduct of Universities by Business Men* (New York: B. W. Huebsch, 1918), 146.

10. See Walter Benjamin, "Little History of Photography" (1931), in *Walter Benjamin: Selected Writings*, vol. 2: *1931–1934*, ed. Michael W. Jennings, Howard Eiland, and Gary Smith (Cambridge, MA: Belknap Press of Harvard University Press, 1999), 507–530; Andrés Mario Zervigón, "Photography's Weimar-Era Proliferatino and Walter Benjamin's Optical Unconscious," in *Photography and the Optical Unconscious*, ed. Shawn Michelle Smith and Sharon Silwinski (Durham, NC: Duke University Press, 2017), 32–48.

11. For example, see Erich Mendelsohn, *Amerika, Bilderbuch eines Architekten* (Berlin: Rudolf Mosse, 1926); Walter C. Behrendt, *Städtebau und Wohnungswesen in den Vereinigten Staaten, Bericht über eine Studienreise* (Berlin: Guido Hackebeil AG, 1926); Ludwig Hilberseimer, *Groszstadtarchitektur* (Stuttgart: Julius Hoffman, 1927); Richard Neutra, *Wie baut Amerika? Gegenwartige bauarbeit Amerikanischer kreis* (Stuttgart: Hoffmann, 1927); Bruno Taut, *Die neue Baukunst in Europa und Amerika* (Stuttgart: Verlag Julius Hoffmann, 1929); and Richard Neutra, *Amerika. Die Stilbildung des neuen Bauens in der Vereinigten Staaten* (Vienna: Anton Schroll Verlag, 1930). For analysis of these German reactions to the architecture and urban landscape of the United States, see Reyner Banham, *A Concrete Atlantis: U.S. Industrial Building and European Modern Architecture, 1900–1925* (Cambridge, MA: MIT Press, 1986); and Jean-Louis Cohen, *Scenes of the World to Come: European Architecture and the American Challenge, 1893–1960* (Montreal: Canadian Centre for Architecture; Paris: Flammarion, 1995).

12. Walter Curt Behrendt, *The Victory of the New Building Style*, trans. Harry Francis Mallgrave (1927; repr., Santa Monica, CA: Getty Press, 2000).

13. On Mendelsohn's 1924 visit to the United States, see Cohen, *Scenes of the World to Come*, 86–92.

14. Alexander Eisenschmidt and Jonathan Mekinda, "Chicago as Idea," in *Chicagoisms: The City as Catalyst for Architectural Speculation*, ed. Alexander Eisenschmidt and Jonathan Mekinda (Chicago: Park Books/University of Chicago Press, 2014), 12–17.

15. Created by Chicago architects and historians like Thomas Tallmadge, this narrative was cemented in 1933 by an exhibition at the Museum of Modern Art in New York curated by Henry Russell Hitchcock and Philip Johnson. See Thomas Tallmadge, *The Origin of the Skyscraper* (Chicago: Alderbrink Press, 1931); Museum of Modern Art, *Early Modern Architecture in Chicago, 1870–1910: Catalogue of an Exhibition*

Held at the MoMA, New York 18 January to 23 February 1933, 2nd ed. (New York: Museum of Modern Art, 1940). On the Museum of Modern Art exhibition, see Joanna Merwood-Salisbury, "American Modern: The Chicago School and the International Style at the Museum of Modern Art," in Eisenschmidt and Mekinda, *Chicagoisms*, 116–129.

16. Walter C. Behrendt, *Modern Building: Its Nature, Problems, and Forms* (New York: Harcourt and Brace, 1937), 120. Mendelsohn included a photograph of the Monadnock, described as a "skyscraper of the second period," in *Erich Mendelsohn's 'Amerika'* [*Amerika, Bilderbuch eines Architekten*] (1926; repr., New York: Dover, 1993), 77.

17. Veblen, *Theory of the Leisure Class*, 154.

18. Specifically, Schuyler was referring to Boyington's Board of Trade building.

Montgomery Schuyler, "Glimpses of Western Architecture I: Chicago," in *American Architecture Studies* (New York: Harper & Brothers, 1892), 121.

19. Veblen, *Theory of the Leisure Class*, 397.

20. Veblen, *Theory of the Leisure Class*, 373.

21. William Fielding Ogburn, *Social Change with Respect to Culture and Original Nature* (New York: Viking Press, 1922), 200.

22. Alexander Eisenschmidt, "No Failure Too Great," in Eisenschmidt and Mekinda, *Chicagoisms*, 150–167.

23. Paul Scheerbart, "Glass Architecture" (1914), and Adolf Behne, "Review of Scheerbart's 'Glass Architecture'" (1918–1919), in *Architecture and Design, 1890–1939*, ed. Tim and Charlotte Benton (New York: Whitney Library of Design, 1975), 72–74, 76–78; Rosemarie Haag Bletter, "The

Interpretation of the Glass Dream—Expressionist Architecture and the History of the Crystal Metaphor," *Journal of the Society of Architectural Historians* 40, no. 1 (1981): 20–43; Iain Boyd Whyte, *Bruno Taut and the Architecture of Activism* (Cambridge: Cambridge University Press, 2010).

24. Thorstein Veblen, "The Instinct of Workmanship and the Irksomeness of Labor," *American Journal of Sociology* 4, no. 2 (September 1898): 187–201.

25. Thorstein Veblen, "A Memorandum on a Practicable Soviet of Technicians," *The Dial* 67 (November 1, 1919): 373–380. This essay is reprinted in Thorstein Veblen, *The Engineers and the Price System* (New York: B. W. Huebsch, 1921), 138–169.

26. Thorstein Veblen, "Arts and Crafts," *Journal of Political Economy* 11, no. 1 (December 1902): 108–111.

Index

Page numbers in italic indicate illustrations.

Index

Veblen; workers, and
neighborhoods
Laughlin, J. Laurence, 80–81,
84, 85, 136
Lears, T. J. Jackson, 9, 49, 98,
163, 194
Le Corbusier (Charles-
Édouard Jeanneret), 87
lectures, and Veblen
"The Day of the Craftsman
and the Instinct of
Workmanship," 237
at Hull House settlement, 6
"The Irksomeness of
Labor and the Instinct
of Workmanship,"
311n65
socialism, 95–96
"Tendencies of the
Socialistic Movement,"
95–96
Unitarian All Souls
Church, 6, 95
leisure class. See also
Chicagoesque style
advertisements and, 88,
153, 206
high-rise apartment
buildings, 24, 70–71
post-Civil War era and,
103–104
social unrest and
mansions of, 64, 295n69
leisure class, and conspicuous
consumption
department stores, 154,
157, 159–162, 166, 173,
188
luxury homes, 52, 59, 65,
70–71
leisure class, and Veblen,
259–260, 269, 272. See also
barbarianism
anthropology, 34–35, 57
architectural styles, 67,
68–69, 70, 189
critique of universities, 81–
82, 104–105, 115, 117, 121,
123, 302n39
cultural differences and
similarities, 34–35

dolichocephalic and, 14,
50, 57, 72, 230
economic
nonproductivity, 3, 4,
13, 58, 88
Jackson Park, 260–261, 262
post-Civil War era, 103–
104, 151–152, 272
racial progress narrative,
34, 143
social reform and, 16, 177,
195–196, 197, 215–216,
220
sports critique, 117
"theory of the leisure
class," 3
women's dress, 2–3, 133,
139–140
Leiter, Levi Z.
Field and Leiter store, 53,
132, 166
First Leiter Building
(1879), 304n83
Palmer and, 146
P. Palmer and Co.
acquisition, 53
Second Leiter Building
(1891), 165–166, 167, 173,
175, 304n87
Siegel, Cooper & Co. ("the
Big Store"), 166, 173.
See also Marshall Field
& Co.
Leonard, Thomas C., 51
Leslie, Thomas, 57
Levee, the. See South Side
Levee; vice, and the Levee
Lloyd, Henry Demarest, 2,
15–16, 247, 250, 255
lofts, 82, 177
architectural styles, 203,
204, 205, 206, 229
manufacturing and
merchandising, 168–
169, 203, 267, 268
predatory capitalism,
206–207, 273
urban infrastructure, 203,
204, 308n64
London Dime Museum and
Theater, 173, 174, 175

London, Great Exhibition of
1831, 29, 33, 41
Loop, the. See also Chicago
Board of Trade Building;
grain elevator buildings,
and the Loop
architectural styles, 90–
91, 92
buildings and leisure-class
consumers, 82, 189–
190, 190
conspicuous consumption
and, 145–146
demolition and
rebuilding, 120, 146–147
high-rise buildings, 70, 265
skyscrapers, 203
urban infrastructure, 203,
204, 308n64
vice and, 177, 195
Loos, Adolf
architectural styles critique,
143–144, 302nn30–31
industrial innovation,
143–144, 302n35
"Ladies Fashion," 163–164
ornament critique, 4, 142–
143, 163, 269
and women's dress, 141–
143, 163–164, 165
Luther, Jessie, 242
luxury, 3
capitalism, 141, 165
department store goods,
132, 159–160, 162–163
hotels, 53, 55, 192, 211
leisure class homes, 52, 59,
65, 70–71
luxury, and Veblen
architectural styles, 4–5,
269
Arts and Crafts movement
goods, 16, 225
conspicuous
consumption, 141
department stores and
goods, 22, 23–24, 147,
153
fashion, 4, 141
universities, 104, 302n39.
See also luxury

Veblen critique, 5, 19, 166, 168, 169
women's dress and, 135, 166, 168
Otis, William, 304n83
ownership marriage, and Veblen
women's dress, 140–141, 143, 163–164, 165, 188
women's role in industrial society, 250, 254

Palmer, Bertha Honoré, 53, 55, 57, 66, 70, 201. *See also* Palmer residence
Palmer, Potter, 53, 55, 66, 70, 231. *See also* Palmer residence
Field and, 53, 55, 132, 146, 166
Field and Leiter store/ Marshall Field's, 53, 132, 166
marriage, 53, 55, 57, 66, 70, 201
P. Palmer and Co., 53
real estate development, 53, 55, 62, 146
Palmer residence, 53–62
Chicagoesque style, 53, 59, 64
Cobb and Frost architects, 53, 55–56
conspicuous consumption, 58–59, 66, 71
dates for, 57, 70
exterior design, *54*, 56, *57*, *59*
interior design, 58–59, *60*–*61*
Norman Gothic style, 53, 55–56
pecuniary emulation, 53, 58, 64
Palmer House hotel, 53, 146, 190, 191
Paris, France, 132, 146, 181
expositions, 33, 41–42
Park, Robert, 192
Parker, Francis W., 232

Peattie, Elia W., 17, 18
Peck, Ferdinand W., 189
pecuniary emulation, 5, 13, 23, 99, 221, 261, 275
architectural styles, 52, 53, 58, 64, 65, 66
department stores, 150–151
workers and, 62, 81, 150–151
photographs of architectural styles, and Veblen, 22, 265–268, *270*–*271*, 275, 315n16
physical anthropology, 50, 51. *See also* anthropology, and Veblen
Plymouth Court, 179, 200–201, *201*, 203
police, and vice in the Levee, 175, 176, 199
bribes and protection, 178, 197, 198–199, 200
Harrison Street (Second Precinct) Police Station, 93, *196*, 197–198, 199, 203–204
journalists on, 199–200
politicians, 176, 178, 197, 198–200, 201. *See also* vice, and the Levee
political economics, and Veblen
academia, 1, 2, 6, 21, 80, 83, 215, 263
The Theory of the Leisure Class, 21, 268–269
politicians, and vice in the Levee, 176, 178, 197, 198–200
Pond, Allen, 222, 234, 235, 242–243, 244, 254
Pond, Irving K., 222–223, 234, 235, 242–243, 244, 254
Pontiac Building, 203
Post, George B., 30, *31*, *32*, 33, 35
post-Civil War era. *See also* Civil War
architectural styles, 22–23, 71, 80, 85, 275
barbarianism and leisure class, 103–104, 151–152, 272

economy during, 4, 102–103, 132, 176, 177–178, 272
social degeneration and, 49, 81, 94, 104, 105
vice and, 176, 177–178, 194
post-fire period, 154, *213*, 215
architectural styles, 211, 212, 214
buildings and rebuilding during, 154, 211–212, 214, 217
department stores and architectural styles, 147, 155, 166
grain elevators, 87
Grand Pacific Hotel reconstruction, 211–212, 217
saloons, 178–179, *179*
Powers, John, 200
Prairie School style, 72, 243
predatory capitalism
advertisements, 88, 153, 206
lofts, 206–207, 273
"On the Nature of Capital" (Veblen), 156
social reform, 202–203
The Theory of Business Enterprise (Veblen), 88–89
urban renewal, 196, 206–207, 273
vice and, 194–195, 197, 204, 206
predatory capitalism, and Veblen, 13–15, 124, 269. *See also* business enterprise, and Veblen; economics, and Veblen
buildings and, 101, 134
post-Civil War era, 103, 151–152, 273
urban renewal, 206–207
vice, 194–195, 197
Printing House Row, 177, *202*, 202–203, 206, 307n60
prostitution, 178
department store clerks, 183, *184*–*185*, 186–188, *187*
social reform, 201–202

Index

dismissal by administration, 7
graduate fellow, 6, 29, 30, 77, 84
instructor, 6, 78–81, 237
The Journal of Political Economy, 6, 84, 135, 225
lectures, 6
professional relationship with academia, 79–80
quantitative data reports, 83, 84, 85, 87
social institutions study, 93, 97–98
urban culture, 1, 12, 30, 34, 72
critique, 261
leisure class, 206
rural population versus, 5
urban renewal, 139. *See also* lofts
Harrison Street Police Station closure, 203–204
infrastructure, 203, 204, 308n64
predatory capitalism, 196, 206–207, 273
Printing House Row, 177, 202–203, *202*, 206, 307n60

Vacher de LaPouge, Georges, 50
Vaux, Calvert, 260
Veblen, Ellen Rolfe. *See* Rolfe, Ellen
Veblen, Thorstein. *See* academia, and Veblen; *Engineers and the Price System, The*; essays, and Veblen; *Higher Learning in America, The*; *Instinct of Workmanship and the State of the Industrial Arts, The*; lectures, and Veblen; *Theory of Business Enterprise, The*; *Theory of the Leisure Class, The*; University of Chicago, and Veblen
alienation narrative, 9–12, 216–217
birth, 6

characteristics, 8–9, 79–80
death, 8
iconoclasm, 2, 7–8, 9, 12, 13, 251
immigrant background, 6, 11, 12, 14, 48, 215
marriages, 7, 16, 124, 230
mythologizing of, 9, 263
"Oscar Wilde of economics," 215
outsider status, 8–12, 80, 233, 263
photograph of, 9, *11*, 124, 263
places lived, 6–8, 20, 77, 124, 253
rumors and personal scandals, 7, 233, 253
and the Triggs, 217, 225, 226, 230
Wright and economists' influences, 253, 313n99
vice, department stores and, 181, 183, *184–185*, 186–188, *187*
Veblen on, 176, 177, 192, 194, 197
vice, and the Levee, 176–178, 179, 190. *See also* police, and vice in the Levee; prostitution
dime museums, 173, *174*, 175, 304n1
guidebooks, 175, 176, 178, 179, 181, 190, 195
leisure class, 173, 177, 188
Plymouth Court, 179, 200–201, *201*
politicians, 176, 178, 197, 198–200
predatory capitalism, 194–195, 197, 204, 206
social reform, 177, 182, 195, 196, 197, 201–202, 206
sociological studies, 177, 181–183, 186, 188, 189, 196, 200
State Street, 173, *174*, 175, 176, 178, 181, 304n1
urban types ("bloods"), 175, 181, 192, 194

Vincent, George, 231
Viollet-le-Duc, Eugène-Emmanuel, 114, 120
Vischer, Friedrich Theodor, 135
Vynne, Harold, 181, 195

Wagner, Charles, 133
Washburne, Hempstead, 33
Water Tower (Water Works Tower), 101, 212, 214–215, *216*
Watson, Carrie, 183
Watson-Schütze, Eva, 9, *11*, 124, 263
Webb, Beatrice, 247, 250, 312n90
Webb, Sidney, 247, 250, 312n90
Weber, Max, 21, 263
"white slave trade." *See* prostitution
White-Slave Traffic Act (1890), 187
Whitman, Walt, 214, 313n99
Wight, Peter B., 114, 123
Wilde, Oscar, 211, 212, 214, 215, 217, 252, 308n6
Willis, Carol, 91
Wilson, Samuel Paynter, 181
Winslow Brothers and Co., 154, 157
Wolner, Edward, 121
Woman's Christian Temperance Union (WCTU), 217–218, 220
Woman's Temple, 217–218, *219*, 222, 226
women's dress. *See also* fashion
architectural styles as compared with, 141–143, 154
conspicuous consumption, *145*, 145–146, *155*, *164*
critique, 143, 163–164, 165
democracy and, 161, 165
dress reform, 133, 140, 143, 145, 168, 250, 300n7
leisure class, 129, *130–131*

women's dress (*continued*)
  ornament and, 135, 166,
    168. *See also* fashion
women's dress, and Veblen, 265
  architectural styles as
    compared with, 4–5,
    134, 141–143
  conspicuous
    consumption, 3, 97,
    132, 133, 135, 136–137,
    139, 140
  dress reform, 143, 300n7
  economics, 176, 188, 259,
    301n15
  leisure class, 3, 4, 133,
    139–140
  ownership marriage and
    sexual relations, 140–
    141, 143, 163–164, 165,
    188
  workers, 161–162, 165
women's role in industrial
    society
  Addams and, 238, 246, 255
  industrial education and,
    246–247
  Jewish Training School
    (Hebrew Manual
    Training School), 228–
    229, 246, 248–249, 265
  Veblen and Hull House
    settlement lecture,
    233–234
  Woman's Christian
    Temperance Union,
    217–218, 220
women's role in industrial
    society, and Veblen, 246,
    250–251, 256
  New Woman movement,
    19, 216, 220, 238, 251
  ownership marriage and
    sexual relations, 250,
    254
  social reform critique, 16,
    195–196, 220

Wooldridge, Clifton R., 204
workers, and neighborhoods
  conspicuous
    consumption, 161–
    162, 165
  immigrants, 226–227, 229,
    230, 240, 244
  industrial productivity
    and workers data
    reports, 84–85
  leisure class versus, 2, 3,
    62, 81
  neighborhoods described,
    226–227, 227, 228
  new industrialism
    movement, 225–226,
    227–228, 252–253
  pecuniary emulation, 2, 3,
    62, 81, 150–151
  post-Civil War era, 93–94,
    94, 103–104
  racial progress narrative,
    50, 227, 229–230
  sociological studies, 227–
    228, 229
  sweatshops, 226, 239, 240–
    241, 243
  Veblen on, 2, 3, 62, 81
workers' housing
  brick party wall, 67, 68–69,
    70, 82, 146
  tenements, 67, 68–69, 70
  wooden houses, 62, 82,
    226, 240, 241
World's Columbian
    Exposition (1893), 30, 78,
    268. *See also* buildings,
    and World's Columbian
    Exposition; early life in
    America, and World's
    Columbian Exposition;
    industrialization, and
    World's Columbian
    Exposition; race science,
    and World's Columbian
    Exposition

anthropology, 34–35, 36,
    39, 41
architectural styles and, 132
conspicuous
    consumption, 33–34
construction and location
    of, 29, 78
Dedication Ceremony, 30,
    32, 33
ethnography and dress,
    136–137, 139
guidebooks for visitors,
    35, 36, 179–180, 190,
    204, 206
Jackson Park and, 29, 144,
    260–261, 262
mass culture events, 33
mass production, 29
progress narrative, 49–50
visitors, 179–180
Wright, Frank Lloyd
  Adler and Sullivan
    architects, 310n40
  "The Art and Craft of
    the Machine" lecture,
    251–252
  Browne's Bookstore, 223,
    309n31
  industrial city as "monster
    leviathan," 252, 257
  industrial education, 232
  new industrialism
    movement, 252–254, 255
  personal scandals, 253
  Prairie School style, 72
  social reform, 251–252
  Thurber Art Gallery, 223,
    309n31
  Veblen and, 253, 313n99

Yale-Wynne, Madeline, 222
Yerkes, Charles, 114–115

Zorbaugh, Harvey Warren, 55
Zueblin, Charles, 231, 238,
    239, 312n90

© 2024 Massachusetts Institute of Technology

All rights reserved. No part of this book may be used to train artificial intelligence systems or reproduced in any form by any electronic or mechanical means (including photocopying, recording, or information storage and retrieval) without permission in writing from the publisher.

The MIT Press would like to thank the anonymous peer reviewers who provided comments on drafts of this book. The generous work of academic experts is essential for establishing the authority and quality of our publications. We acknowledge with gratitude the contributions of these otherwise uncredited readers.

This book was set in Haultin by the MIT Press. Printed and bound in Canada.

Library of Congress Cataloging-in-Publication Data

Names: Merwood-Salisbury, Joanna, author.
Title: Barbarian architecture : Thorstein Veblen's Chicago / Joanna Merwood-Salisbury.
Description: Cambridge, Massachusetts : The MIT Press, 2024. | Includes bibliographical references and index.
Identifiers: LCCN 2023015504 | ISBN 9780262547413 (paperback)
Subjects: LCSH: Architecture and society—Illinois—Chicago—History—19th century. | Veblen, Thorstein, 1857-1929. Theory of the leisure class. | Chicago (Ill.)—Social conditions—19th century.
Classification: LCC NA2543.S6 M495 2024 | DDC 720.1/030977311—dc23/eng/20230920
LC record available at https://lccn.loc.gov/2023015504

10   9   8   7   6   5   4   3   2   1